Little Lady
with a Big Drum

Little Lady with a Big Drum

Elayne Jones

ABOOKS
Alive Book Publishing

Little Lady with a Big Drum
Copyright © 2019 by Elayne Jones

For information, contact ALIVE Book Publishing at:
alivebookpublishing.com, or call (925) 837-7303.

Book Design by Alex Johnson

ISBN 13:
978-1-63132-066-8

ISBN 10:
1-63132-066-1

Library of Congress Control Number: 2019936753

Library of Congress Cataloging-in-Publication Data
is available upon request.

First Edition

Published in the United States of America by ALIVE Book Publishing
and ALIVE Publishing Group, imprints of Advanced Publishing LLC
3200 A Danville Blvd., Suite 204, Alamo, California 94507
alivebookpublishing.com

PRINTED IN THE UNITED STATES OF AMERICA

10 9 8 7 6 5 4 3 2 1

Prologue

I walked out of the offices of the San Francisco Symphony onto Franklin Street and took a deep breath of the cool afternoon air coming in off the Pacific Ocean. I smiled merrily at the first person I saw hurrying by, his coat wrapped tightly against the chill breeze and fog. The puzzled look on his face didn't bother me at all. I was on the threshold of being the happiest woman in the world. The date was May 14, 1974, and I had just completed an interview with a committee made up of members of the symphony who would vote on whether or not I received lifetime tenure with the orchestra.

As I headed for my car, I told myself this was the last step toward the ambitious goal I had set after graduating in 1949 from the Juilliard School in New York City. I wanted to become a tenured member of what would ultimately be the New York Philharmonic. That I would also be the first black woman principal player to achieve that goal was not incidental. Neither was the fact that I played the timpani, also called kettle drums, rather than the more traditional violin or flute.

Believe me, the last 26 years had been a struggle. To male dominated, European-derived symphony orchestras from coast to coast, I represented a triple threat. Bad enough that I was black and doubly disgusting that I was a woman. But for a black woman to have the audacity to play a "male" instrument, the timpani, well, that was just too much. Over and over again, I had to prove that I deserved a place among their ranks.

I had done it and now my efforts were about to pay off. What better place to hit the jackpot than San Francisco. If I couldn't live in New York, my home town, there was nothing wrong with the fabled "City by the Bay." With a reputation as the most liberal big city in America, it had great weather and was almost as cosmopolitan as the Big Apple.

After winning my job as timpanist during the audition two years earlier, I had been playing steadily with this highly-rated orchestra. I toured with them in Europe and the Soviet Union. My playing was praised everywhere. My appearance was unusual, according to audiences, and my performance was excellent, according to conductors and critics, I was mobbed by enthusiastic fans in London, Berlin and Moscow. There was little—in fact—no reason to believe I would not be granted tenure.

I was feeling so good about how my interview went that I impulsively decided to stop at my neighborhood Safeway store and buy a bottle of champagne. When I got in line to pay, I just had to share my good news with the check-out clerk.

"I'm going to have a big celebration on my way towards being a role model for other black musicians," I informed him mischievously. I wasn't surprised by his laconic response.

When I first moved to San Francisco, I was impressed with the friendliness of the grocery clerks. "How ya doin' today?" they always said, in that laid-back California accent. I was speechless. In New York, the clerks never even looked at you, never mind saying hello.

So, I'd smile and say, "I'm fine, how are you?"

Then, as they finished punching in the prices into the register and packing my items in bags and as I headed toward the exit, they would say, "Have a nice day."

"Hey, you too," I always responded.

At first I thought they really wanted to know how I was doing and hoped I would have a nice day. But over time, I noticed they never returned my responses. Usually, as I was calling back, "Hey, you too," they were already greeting the next customer in line. "How ya doin'?" It came out in the same robotic tone.

That afternoon I didn't care. "How'd you like to have some champagne with me to toast the fulfillment of my dreams?" I asked the clerk.

Without looking at me, he said, "No one's dreams are ever fulfilled."

"That's not true," I replied. "If you work hard you can realize your dreams."

"You believe that nonsense?" he asked, cynically, mechanically punching in the prices.

"I certainly do," I responded proudly.

"Well, good luck and have a good evening." And before I could react, he was asking the next customer in line. "How ya doin'?" I took my package thinking how unfortunate that this young man could be so bitter already. I dismissed him and got into my car and drove home.

My three teen-aged children, Stephen, Harriet and Cheryl, were anxious to drink the champagne right on the spot.

"No," I admonished. "Wait until it gets colder then we can have it after dinner."

"We could have it after the concert tonight," Stephen suggested.

"Good idea," I said. "We'll see if anyone from the orchestra wants to come home and celebrate with us."

The kids had been through thick and thin with me. I married their father, they were born, and later their father and I divorced. Then I moved them 3,000 miles from New York to San Francisco. Throughout their lives, I continued to work at my profession. When I was carrying Stephen, I played with the New York City Opera orchestra right up to the moment I went into labor and was back within eight weeks of his birth. I had no idea about a future other than being a teacher. My chosen path had been difficult from the moment I entered The High School of Music & Art in 1942 to the day 30 years later when I left New York for San Francisco to become the first black person in the world hired as a principal player with a symphony orchestra. Along the way, I had played under the batons of Leopold Stokowski, Leonard Bernstein and Arthur Fiedler, among others.

I wasn't satisfied with being a black star in a white world. Instead, I spoke to thousands of public school students, many of them black, demonstrating the timpani and percussion and telling the kids that they, too, could become classical musicians. I took part in union activities meant to open the door to that white world for black and other minority group people. My activism for equal opportunity, was considered subversive by the political conservatives. As a result, on Thursday, October 22, 1953, I was brought before a court chaired by the infamous Senator Joseph McCarthy and his frightening House Un-American Activities Committee.

That spring afternoon in 1974, as I stood at the stove preparing dinner, I reflected on the sacrifices and inconveniences my children had endured as I pursued my career. I thought about the housekeepers and babysitters I had to leave them with, some more qualified than others. And having a mom who rarely walked them home from school because she was at rehearsal. Doing their homework at night without Mom's oversight because she was performing downtown. It hadn't been easy for them. I quickly wiped away the tears that came to my eyes lest the salty fluid fall into the pot of rice and peas just coming to a boil. I looked at the clock. It was a quarter until five. In a couple of hours, they—and I—would reap our reward. At tonight's performance, or at least no later than tomorrow, I'd be notified that I'd been granted tenure and I'd be set for the rest of my career. It didn't happen that way.

On May 15, 1975, I was notified by telephone that my tenure

had been denied. My knees buckled and I grew weak with shock hearing the unbelievable news. How could this happen? This time, I couldn't stop the tears. I cried. I cried a river. I cried an ocean until no tears were left. Try as I might, I could not get over the deep hurt I felt.

Like a meteor, the news of the denial flared around the world. People began calling me not only in San Francisco but also from New York and Europe. "What happened?" they asked. I wanted to be brave and tell the story, but the pain was too great and I didn't want to cry. After all, I was the one everyone said was strong and capable of surmounting all obstacles. Strong people don't cry. How could anyone be weak and come as far as I had come in the clubby, closed classical music field?

Nevertheless, I hurt badly.

One other player had been denied tenure. Ryohe Nakagawa, a young bassoonist from Japan, had also been hired on probation along with me two years earlier and had also been critically acclaimed for his outstanding playing. When he, too, was rejected by the players' committee, he packed up his bassoon and returned to Japan. We were the only two non-whites in the orchestra. The other six players who were hired with us were more fortunate. All were given permanent positions with the orchestra; all were white.

After several days, I recovered my composure, but something did not seem right to me or to anyone I spoke to outside the players' committee. What about me was different from the others who had been granted tenure? It was definitely not the quality of my work. No conductor had ever stopped a rehearsal to instruct me. No critic had ever identified any flaws in my playing. It was not that I was female. There were, by then, several women playing in the orchestras. Could it be that no other black musician had cracked the shell that kept every American symphony orchestra totally white?

Granted, I probably should have turned around and returned

to New York, taking the children with me. But something deep inside me urged me to stay and fight the committee's decision. I decided to sue the symphony on grounds of racism. It was up to me to prove my case. I started with high hopes. As the months went by, however, and the suit slowly made its way through the preliminary hearings, I realized I had underestimated the depth of racism in San Francisco.

Chapter 1

EARLY DAYS
Growing Up in Harlem with West Indian Roots

I was born on January 30, 1928, in Harlem, New York City, where my parents had lived since emigrating from Barbados in the West Indies. My father, Cecil C. Jones, was sent to New York first, in 1925, with hopes of going into the printing business. He was a linotype operator in Barbados. My mother, Ometa, whose last name was also Jones, was sent to the United States in 1926, with ambitions of becoming a concert pianist. They met at a party where my mother was playing the piano. My father had heard her playing before at various functions, and loved her playing so much, he always went where he thought she would be performing. However, he was too shy to approach her. Finally, he asked his cousin and best friend, Lushington, to introduce them. After the introduction, he discovered Mum had studied piano with his father, an organist and piano teacher at St. David Parish Church, when she still lived in Barbados. Mom and Dad were married June 27, 1927.

By the time I came along, my parents had already bumped up against a society that refused to give African Americans a full chance to realize their ambitions. Their lives were rigidly proscribed by housing segregation, job discrimination and the prevailing prejudice throughout the United States. Black people, no matter where they came from, were blocked from taking advantage of the opportunities that white people, no matter where *they* came from, took for granted. By the late 1920s, blacks, including my parents, had reluctantly accommodated to the institutional racism that, although illegal in New York City, polluted the atmosphere. Dad worked as a porter and Mom as a domestic.

They brought me home from the hospital, a seven-pound, five-ounce bundle swaddled in soft pink blankets and a cap against the winter cold, to 2857 Eighth Avenue in Harlem. There in our two-bedroom apartment on the second floor of a five-story tenement, I began the long process of growing up with the children of other families transplanted from the West Indies to Harlem who struggled each day to make ends meet and have meaning to their lives.

My earliest memories are of the baleful influence of white society on our black community. I think of it as being born under the "aura" of the white woman. When my mother's friends dropped by on Saturdays or Sundays to visit, it was generally to chit-chat about their "lady." Like them, my mother worked to supplement my father's meager earnings by caring for white women's homes and children. Most of the women for whom Mom toiled did not work themselves. Their husbands put in many hours of hard labor to enable their wives to escape both an outside job and the drudgery of housework.

I would later learn that not every white woman employed servants, maids or housekeepers. Millions of poor women of all colors did their own housework. But the images I formed from those days, underscored by countless movies and television programs, were of black women working hard to make white women's lives easier.

By the time I was six, I also realized that most of my friends' parents who were not from the Caribbean, were from southern United States. Whether they acknowledged it or not, most had someone somewhere in their family history who was white. That generally came about because of rape or concubinage of black females during slavery. Despite that oppressive history, most blacks living in Harlem in 1934 who had the slightest hint of white admixture were considered special. Why? Because white was considered superior. If you had a drop of white blood, regardless of how you got it, you thought yourself better than other blacks. The evidence of your superiority was there for all to see: light skin and "good" hair.

My education began the year I entered first grade at PS 90 on 148th Street and Eighth Avenue. We six-year-olds were already conscious of our superficial physical differences. Starting school was traumatic enough, but coming from black homes in black neighborhoods and being confronted by a white teacher—one with long, blond hair at that—made it worse. On one hand, we were fearful and in awe of her, and on the other hand, we were full of secret admiration for her. We had been to the movies and seen the blond lady on the screen that everybody loved. Even at that young age, we wanted to be loved. To our childish perceptions, the only way to be loved was to look like those women in the films. So, we had already begun to believe that the way to be loved and successful was to be white—or the next best thing, beige.

During school days, we clustered in the girls' bathroom, combing our hair and basically socializing. Eyes would turn to one girl, Yvonne, whose locks were almost straight. Not only did her braids hang down to her shoulders, she could also twist them around her head. Those of us with shorter, kinkier hair stood in front of the mirror futilely pulling on our plaits to get them to fall below our necks. No such luck. Our hair would not follow our orders. Had it just been a question of not having long, straight hair, perhaps we who had "bad" hair could have lived with it. But the boys thought Yvonne was more appealing. Sneaking up behind her and pulling her braids formed part of the attraction. She also had another redeeming feature: her fair, almond-colored skin.

In those years, each school year was divided into two half grades beginning either in January or September. I turned six in January, so I started elementary school in January in class 1A-1.

The following September, I was promoted to 1B-1. I progressed through each grade, going from 1A-1 in January and so on up to 6B-1. Then I graduated to start junior high school. Because I had compensated for what I considered deficits in my appearance by getting good grades, I was skipped ahead to what were called the "Rapid Advance" grades. Throughout elementary school I met the scholastic challenge, even though it didn't always give me the desired result of attracting attention from the boys. Color still had more status than intellect. Fortunately, I didn't allow this form of exclusion to kill my spirit.

After being promoted from elementary school, my neighborhood cohorts and I moved on to junior High School 136 at 136th Street and St. Nicholas Avenue in Harlem, an all-black, all-girls' school with white teachers. Although I was surrounded by other black girls like me, I still felt uncomfortable about my skin color and self-conscious about my looks.

The challenging experiences I had in junior high with the other students were compounded by the attitudes and actions of the teachers. Yes, the students could be disruptive, but the way teachers handled these situations made for their lack of teaching us in the classroom. When the kids became unruly the teachers did nothing. Their only response was, "No use bothering or making you behave because you all will amount to nothing but maids, anyhow." That was the education these white teachers gave us young black girls. Little did I realize then that their negativity would eventually help me to get into an excellent high school. The other side of the coin, however, their disdain for us caused me to have a negative image of myself which would last almost my entire life.

When school let out for the summer, I had a little more luck with the boys, although of a different nature. During the summers, most of the kids in the neighborhood went down South to spend time with grandparents and other relatives or they went to a YMCA or church sponsored camp. The cost of camps, especially those run by churches and non-profit organizations, was minimal. Many of my buddies who didn't go south went to Camp Minisink. I longed to go with them, but my West Indian parents and their friends did not believe in sending children to camp because they didn't do that in the West Indian culture. My parents couldn't afford to ship me off to my grandparents, either, because they were far away in Barbados. In fact, because I had no brothers or sisters, they were not too anxious to have me out of their sight. My mother always joked that she had "all her eggs in one basket."

For most of my childhood summers, I wound up playing with some of the neighborhood boys who hadn't been sent off to other places. Under duress, they noticed me. For one thing, I was a "tomboy," I stood out in sports. Like a person possessed, I had learned to run faster, throw a ball farther or climb a fence or a tree quicker than anyone else. These exploits became the only way to get attention. Still, after the games were over, the boys ignored me in favor of the girls, a few who were still around especially with the "good" hair.

Being "one of the boys" really began to hurt when I got to the age of about 13 and wanted to have a guy "to go with," an expression we used to indicate having a boyfriend. I became acutely aware that I lacked the physical attributes they liked, starting with big "boobs."

To record their preferences, the boys put together a booklet which they called a *Slam Book*. Many a morning they would huddle on someone's stoop in the hot unpleasant summer air and leaf through the book, making notations with a stubby lead pencil. Their spiral-bound notebook with a red cover and lined paper included a separate page for every kid in the community with categories of breast size, ass size, general figure, penis size, height, weight and how many times a boy had "gotten into" a girl. The *Slam Book* was very important because in our youthful perception, the future of our lives was determined by what it said about you.

Needless to say, I didn't fare well. For the most part, my page was empty. Comments about being good in sports and being smart were not highly rated. As paltry as those ratings were, they made me continue to believe that if I excelled in my studies or in sports, perhaps a boy would eventually "go" with me. It never worked out that way. My full lips, flat nose, and kinky hair trumped all other attributes. I was sure my dark skin contributed to my being romantically ostracized by the boys whose attention I craved so badly.

Being of West Indian background didn't help either. My friends teasingly called me as well as all Barbadians, "monkey chaser" because my parents were from Barbados. I had no idea what the slur meant but it contributed to making me unhappy. There were days when I was sad because I didn't have light skin and didn't have straight hair, didn't look white, was a West Indian and wasn't from the South. There's a cruel saying among African Americans that reflected our experience in this country. "If you're white you're right, if you're brown, stick around, if you're black, get back." That ugly jingle seemed to fit me perfectly.

Mom was always playing the piano for people either in our apartment or when visiting friends. All of my parents' friends who were from the Caribbean had, if nothing else, a piano in their living room. Music permeated our lives, so it really didn't take much encouragement to get me to the piano. Having a good ear for music, I loved sitting at the piano and playing everything I heard on the radio—Duke Ellington, Count Basie and Billie Holiday. Then one day when I was six, my mother placed a sheet of music in front of me and began giving me piano lessons. From then on during the school year, when the other kids were outside playing and having fun, I had to go straight home from school to do my homework and practice the piano. Consequently, all this practicing along with my parents' strict rules prevented me from running on my own around the neighborhood.

The music for piano was created by composers whose music was not heard at the parties and dances I attended in our neighborhood. At first, I thought it was strange to have music that people didn't dance to, because we all loved dancing to swing music. However, I didn't reject this different kind of music and practiced it every day, growing to enjoy its irregularities.

Mother took me as far as she could with my piano lessons. I'm sure she was capable, but she thought I would do better if someone else taught me. I began taking lessons with such a woman named Wisdom St. Bishop, a plain, dull and lifeless woman. She did not press her hair. Was she a good pianist? Did she give concerts? I knew nothing about her musically or socially. All I knew was she didn't inspire me to play. I went dutifully to lessons once a week and practiced only because my mother made me. If my mother had not been a pianist, I would never have made any progress in music with a teacher like Wisdom St. Bishop. How could a person like her bring joy to music when she seemed so joyless? She also belonged to a strange religion headed by a man called "Father Divine."

Seeing that I needed another teacher, and making no progress, Mom began asking around. Someone told her about a teacher who was very strict and had a large number of students. The "very strict" part convinced Mom to send me to Catherine Stout who I would remain with for many years. For almost the first time, I was really challenged to play. I had been a free spirit when Mom taught me and I wasn't interested with Wisdom St. Bishop, but Mrs. Stout was different. She included theory and sight singing with my lessons. At first, all I played were scales and more scales. She took me through exercise books I never had before. After months of technical playing, she introduced me to classical music. We would learn, practice and memorize this music and then play it in a recital each year for our family and friends. At that time, I had no idea what I was playing, but the music glued itself to my memory, never to be forgotten.

In addition to taking piano lessons, I was allowed to join Girl Scout Troop No. 10. One of the activities the troop leader organized for us was a drum and bugle corps. I joined and wanted to play the bugle, but the leader said I was too skinny to blow a horn. She didn't think I had the strength, so she gave me a pair of drumsticks. Of course, she didn't realize that when you play snare drums in a parade or as part of a drum and bugle corps you have to also carry the drum. I managed not only to hold the lightweight drum sticks but to carry the drum, too.

For many of my childhood years, my mother's employers were Mr. and Mrs. Motz. She cared for their little son, Robin, and also cleaned their house. Mr. Motz was a college professor. In contrast to most white women who didn't work, Mrs. Motz was a high school teacher. They were "nice" as people go, but none the less my mother was very unhappy with her situation.

Domestic work was not what Mom was sent to the United States to seek. In Barbados, where she was born and raised, she had studied the piano and become quite proficient at it. Dreaming of becoming a concert pianist, she had migrated to New York to pursue her vision. Like millions of others, she had expectations of being successful in the "land of freedom and opportunity." Her mission, however, did not materialize as she had hoped. This detour in her life created the path I would eventually follow. Like a river that had changed course, Mom's ambition flowed from her innermost depths into me.

Although she preferred I go straight home from school to practice the piano, Mom also expected me to do well in my studies. Often, she said to me, "Come on up and meet me at my job so you can do your homework and perhaps Mrs. Motz could help you if you have any problems."

I hated going up to the Bronx to meet her. I took the Independent Subway in Manhattan "D" train from 135th Street, from the stop where my junior high school was located, rode up to Fordham Road and got out in the Bronx, a predominantly Jewish community. Black women walking down the street in these areas were assumed to be housemaids. When Mom and I left the Motz house and walked to the subway we were accosted by Jewish matrons.

"Hey, you girls looking for work?" they called out. Our background didn't matter to them. As far as they were concerned, we were black, we all looked alike, and we were only good enough to clean houses.

Mom had to take this abuse because my father was relegated to the kind of demeaning work at low salaries reserved for black men in New York. He had also immigrated from Barbados to pursue his goal of getting into printing, but sadly, like Mother, he would never realize his full artistic talents. Facing limited opportunities, he also completely submerged his talents in order to survive in his adopted but racist country. Dad was elated, however, when he got a job as a porter in the garment district on the Lower East Side for $15 a week. No matter how low level the job, he always tried to do it as well as or better than anyone else. He made being a porter a work of art, and his diligence would pay off.

With intelligence and perseverance, Dad took the Civil Service Exam and landed a job as a conductor with the New York City subway system. He was proud to get this job because the subways had just broken the race barrier and was hiring black men. Certainly, this was a step up from being a porter and it was a union job with a decent salary for a black man.

Mike Quill became the head of the MTA, Metropolitan Transportation Association at that time. During the course of his reign as president, the job in the subway offered a contract with a good salary and many benefits like medical and a pension. Dad never missed a day's work and often worked overtime. Eventually through his efforts he rose to the top to being among the first black man to reach the position of dispatcher with the

New York City Transit System. This determined attitude prevailed in both my parents. My mother developed the reputation among women who hired domestics, as the best house cleaner and the warmest person around to care for their children.

Whether I met Mom at her job or went home to do my homework and practice the piano, she always stopped to shop for food in the Jewish neighborhood where she worked. She never shopped in Harlem grocery stores because the meats and produce there weren't fresh or of the best quality. The prices, however, were always higher than in the white communities.

Soon after getting home, Mom had a Caribbean-style dinner on the table. I didn't always like the meals of yellow split peas and rice or coo-coo. Sometimes I sneaked out and went next door to eat some greens and what Mom called, soft white rice cooked by our neighbor Mrs. Foye for her family from the South. After my last bite of food, Mom gave me the "time to get to the piano" look. It was interesting to compare my life with those of my friends. They invariably complained about having to do the dishes after dinner. I complained about having to practice the piano, and then do my homework. My parents did the dishes and when they finished cleaning up the kitchen, Dad sat down in the living room with the newspaper and Mom walked into the living room where the upright piano held an honored spot. She sat next to me knitting wool into scarves for Dad and me to wear around our necks in the winter. She may have been knitting, but Mom was keenly aware of every note I played. If I struck an errant chord, she would gently rap me on the knuckles with the knitting needles. Mom had absolute pitch, sometimes called perfect pitch. She knew exactly what note I was playing without looking. At the time, I didn't realize how special that was, something I would later learn.

Sixty minutes was the designated time for my piano practice. That looked like a long time to me, but once I started playing, time went out the window. I got great satisfaction from conquering a piece of music, no matter how long it took to play. Sometimes, I ended up willingly practicing for hours.

Besides occasionally riding the subway to the Bronx, the other regular break in my routine occurred on Monday evenings when Mom and I went to the movies. We patronized the Odeon movie house in Harlem on 145th Street and Eighth Avenue for MGM movies or the Roosevelt movie house on Seventh Avenue at 145th Street for RCA movies. Each feature started on Tuesday and ran until Monday, the following week. If a film generated a really large attendance, it would run for two weeks but that didn't happen very often. Monday became our movie day for two reasons. First, it was generally the last day a film ran before a new one began the following day. Second, it was the day Mom didn't have to cook. It wasn't until I was a teenager that I got to go to a movie without my mother.

Going to the movies stirred up reactions about race that sat in the pit of my stomach. Although the section of Harlem we lived in was not the typical run down tenement, it still didn't compare with the houses where my mother worked or the ones we saw in movies.

Sunday was Mom's major cooking day. She always prepared a big Bajan dinner and served it after we returned from church. A typical Sunday dinner included chicken fricassee with lots of gravy, rice and peas cooked up together. She boiled a sweet potato or yam for my dad but no vegetable. For a side dish, she fried a plantain but there was no vegetable. My dad loved his rice and peas piled high to the brim of the plate. Then he asked for his hot pepper sauce. He put his food in his mouth using his knife and fork and leaned into it with the most infectious look of contentment on his face. He loved my mother's cooking, and my mother loved to cook.

Like most Barbadians, Mom always cooked enough food on Sunday to last for two days or to have on hand should a friend or neighbor drop by after church services. After our Monday movie, when we came home, Mum didn't have to cook as we had Sunday leftovers for dinner. Then I headed straight for my school books or the piano, and Mom went to a place where she could oversee my homework or practicing.

Many days I came home from school and hated my mother for making me go inside to practice. She had two reasons for insisting on such diligence. First, she wanted me to be the pianist she never got a chance to be. Second, she didn't like the neighborhood youngsters.

"I don't want you running around with those no-account children," she said in the West Indian accent which I found lovely on her, but undesirable for myself. "You come home to do your homework and practice the piano!"

This strictness coupled with my being an only child meant I learned to keep my own company. As a tomboy in a town with three professional sports teams, I grew to love major league baseball. I listened to all the games on the radio streaming out from the taxis waiting in front of our buildings for the fans leaving the games and Harlem. I visualized what was happening on the baseball field. The thought of actually seeing a game in person excited me, but not any of the girls I knew. I couldn't or wouldn't ask any of the boys to go with me for fear they'd reject me by saying they weren't interested. Listening to the radio one day I heard the announcer say that there was a day set aside called "Ladies Day" when ladies could get into the game for ten cents. I *had* to go. With fear and trepidation, I asked my mother if I could go to a game.

"Who you goin' with?" she said.

"No one, Mom, because no one wants to go with me," I was so afraid she'd say something like, "You crazy girl to go there by yourself."

"Yes, pleez," I pleaded. "I only have to walk up the block to the polo grounds and today is 'Ladies Day' and I only have to pay ten cents."

My mother finally consented! Off to the games I went, all by myself, sat by myself, talked to myself and came back home by myself. I didn't let the fact that I had to go alone deter me from doing what I wanted. And that would be my pattern all my life. Although I didn't go as far as Brooklyn to see the Dodgers, I went across the Harlem River Bridge to see the Yankees play. I continued attending games by myself until I became aware no black players were on either the Giants and Yankees teams. I stopped going to any games until 1948 when Jackie Robinson, the black player, broke the color line with the Dodgers. The other New York team, the Giants, gradually began to employ African-American players as well. The Yankees were the last.

Only on Friday and occasionally Saturday nights I was allowed to "run wild" in the streets. Friday night was especially fun for everybody young and old. Before any other activity, however, there was choir rehearsal at St. Luke's Episcopal Church at 140th Street and Convent Avenue. I never missed choir rehearsal because I loved music and whenever I loved anything or committed myself to it, I gave it all my energy. Most Barbadians of African descent who had moved from the Islands to Harlem had inherited the Episcopal faith, the American version of the Church of England also called the Anglican Church, from the British colonizers. Our membership at St. Luke's Episcopal Church played an integral role in my life. Choir practice was a happy time for me. I always wanted to sing the alto part because I could harmonize which I loved. That was far more exciting than singing the melody line. No matter what hymn was played, I never had trouble singing the inner voices of the chords. The choir director loved me and I loved him.

With or without relatives in tow, my parents and the other Barbadians living in Harlem enjoyed getting together either at one another's homes or the church party on Friday and Saturday nights to eat, dance and otherwise let their hair down. Suddenly the grind of daily living and the necessity to conform to the way of the white people who controlled New York, gave way to music and clapping, toe tapping and finger snapping, outbursts of laughter as jokes were exchanged and high-pitched chatter among all generations. Everybody brought a West Indian dish to share at these relaxed potluck dinners. The evening's hosts put Duke Ellington, Count Basie and other swing and jazz band records on the phonograph as well as Calypso music. Everybody from toddlers to seniors bounced and jounced around the room. I always felt comfortable and cozy at these events. I was part of the fold and I knew I had a secure place in this hybrid Carib-American culture. Here my dark brown skin and black coiled hair were the norm. Everyone, or nearly everyone, looked like me. It was the rare West Indian with a pale complexion and straight hair who had to assert his or her identity in the group.

Only years later would I realize the significance of this socializing. Where I lived, no one went to the theater or to concerts. Those events were downtown and you never knew how you would be received there. When we dressed up, it was primarily to go to church or to these neighborhood affairs uptown where we knew we were welcome. As I lived that sheltered uptown life I didn't know that one day I would suddenly find myself attending school below 125th Street and mixing with future forerunners and leaders of the artistic world.

Chapter 2

BARBADOS
Embracing My Family, History and Culture

During the spring of 1939, something happened that made me feel better about being black and West Indian in a city where neither seemed highly valued. I overheard my parents discussing the possibility of Mum and me going to Barbados for the summer. The costs for passage by ship for all of us would be prohibitive, so Dad decided to stay behind in New York. Because I had done well in school, this trip was a reward from my parents. Also, the fact that I was 11 made my fare half price. If they waited another year until I was 12, my ticket would cost full fare. I was breathless at the mere possibility taking such an adventure.

"Hey Mom," I finally said one day. "Is it true we're going away for the summer?"

"Yes, dear," she replied. "As soon as you get out of school." I was giddy with happiness. Here was my chance to be like the other kids. I couldn't wait to go out and tell everybody.

"Hey," I said to the first pals I saw. "I'm going to Barbados this summer!"

I was surprised and a bit puzzled when they acted like they were jealous, considering they always got to go away. But they were going to familiar locations in the United States. I was headed overseas to some distant and mysterious place.

Being so anxious to be on my way to Barbados made the last month of school go by with agonizing slowness. As the time to leave approached, Mom explained more about the trip to me as she cooked dinner one evening. When she said that we would take a train to Boston and get on a ship there to Barbados, I remembered driving down the West Side of Manhattan with her often in the past and seeing ocean-going vessels docked at the piers.

"But, why are we going all the way to Boston when there were perfectly good ships right there in New York Harbor?" I said.

"That's where we will board a British ship," she said, standing over the stove stirring a pot. She told me that because Barbados had been an English colony since the 1620s, it was easier and cheaper to book passage for Barbados on a British ship even with the cost of traveling from New York to Boston was factored into the fare. Second, she said, on an American ship, black people were restricted to third class. On British ships, we could go second class. First class was, of course, out of the question. Mom tried to ease her humiliation at having to explain those facts of life to me.

"Even if we were allowed to go first class," she said, "we couldn't afford it anyway." She quickly looked away and continued preparing dinner.

Learning about the harsh realities of Anglo-American segregation did little to dampen my enthusiasm. On July 1, my eleven-year-old-self left New York City for the first time in my life. Mom and I boarded a train at Grand Central Station. Arriving in Boston, we climbed on a bus right at the train station that took us across town to Boston Harbor.

When we boarded the *Lady Nelson*, a man in a beautiful white uniform directed us to our stateroom, a very small inside compartment with no porthole. Undeterred, we stowed our luggage and went back up on deck. It was dizzying watching the people scurrying around, packing boxes on and off the ship. Then in amazement, I watched and felt the motion as the huge ship slowly eased away from the pier and glided out into the Atlantic Ocean. It was thrilling. We were on our way at last.

After our first three days at sea, seeing no land, we found ourselves sighting and approaching land at last—Bermuda. From the height of the ship's deck, it looked as though we were on top of a hill and the island sat in the valley. After a lifetime in Harlem where all the buildings were brown and dirty, what a sight it was to see every building in a pastel hue. Even more astounding, each town was painted in one color, such as pink, blue or yellow. We only spent one day in Bermuda, and it was a lovely and delightful experience for me. It was startling, however, for me to be on the island where everyone was black!

During the next six days, we stopped at the islands of Montserrat, Nevis, and St. Lucia, spending two days on each. And then, after ten days at sea, we arrived in Barbados, the home of our family, my ancestors. In the following days, I would meet my mother's brothers and sisters—my uncles and aunts.

My mom, Ometa, or "Meta," as she was called, came from a family of achievers. She was the first of five sisters and three brothers born in Barbados to William and Viola Jones. Her sisters Daisy, Ima and Sybil were highly respected school teachers recognized for their outstanding contributions to the teaching profession. Barbadian schools were under the domain of the Church of England whose policies prohibited teachers from marrying, supposedly the better to concentrate on their students. Although all were attractive bright women, Mom's sisters did not marry during their teaching days.

Aunt Daisy, who passed away soon after retiring, never married. Aunt Sybil met Girwood "Bud" Springer, a man with two daughters and one son. After his wife had died giving birth to a second son, Sybil married Bud. He became the United Nations representative from Barbados and Aunt Sybil raised the youngest son as her own. The son grew up to become the first black native man to manage a hotel in Barbados. Unhappily, the stress and overwork triggered his untimely death from a brain hemorrhage, leaving a wife, Sue Springer, and two daughters

Naomi and Natalie bereft.

After receiving several awards for outstanding dedication to teaching, Aunt Ima married late in life but had no children. She had said in retrospect that the rule against teachers getting married had more to do with the paltry wages they were paid than with the requirement for dedication. Teachers just couldn't earn enough money to live independently, which is why Aunts Daisy, Sybil and Ima lived at home with Ma-Ma until she passed.

Another one of Mom's sisters, Violet, owned a green grocer shop known for fresh varieties of reasonably-priced fruits and vegetables. Mom's brother, Oswald, the Reverend O.E. Jones was an Anglican priest at St. Philips Parish Church and a professor of Latin at Codrington College in St. Philips. Her brother Frank, loved to sing. If he had been living anywhere else, he probably would have taken lessons and become a professional singer.

They all lived and worked in Barbados except for Mom's brother, Dan. Uncle Dan, also a teacher, thought Barbados was not big enough for him. Being a small island 14 miles wide by 21 miles long, Barbados had little contact with the culture of the other islands and countries beyond the ocean. The only way to reach it was by boat which took 10 days. So, when my parents and others traveled to the United States there was no coming back and forth. Once there, you remained there. Like his siblings, Dan had taught school in Barbados, but he believed there was much more in the world for him to explore so he took off for New York and eventually sold real estate in his own business.

Although Barbados was colonized by the British, the people never lost their African cultural roots or their love of music and dance. There was always a party with dancing Friday and Saturday with Sunday being the day of rest and preparation for going to work Monday morning. What brought the men and

women together? Music! My mom attracted Dad with music and
I would attract my husband with music.

Every country has its hangouts for the men and Barbados
was no exception. The women would stay home and cook, while
the men gather at the local watering hole to relax, talk, argue and
drink the rum and play dominoes. My grandfather William
Jones or "The Major," as he was affectionately called, had a rum
shop on the corner of Eagle Hall and Black Rock. Men came
there on Saturday nights to talk politics, work, and family, as
they enjoyed their rum and the Barbadian tradition of eating
"pudding and souse." They loved coming to grandfather's place
because of my mum playing the piano with music coming from
the rear of the shop.

Although the men frequented the Rum Shop regularly, talk
of drunkenness was minimal and hush-hush. They didn't
consider drinking rum to be detrimental to health and life. If
anything, it was just the opposite. Rum was considered
medicinal. You drank it if you had a cold, a headache, arthritis,
anything that ails you. The only competition to this remedy was
a swim in the beautiful, healing Caribbean Sea.

The concept of the rum shop did not travel overseas. People
traveled to the United States, leaving the Rum Shop behind, but
not the drinking of rum. The Bajans brought gallons of rum to
the United States due to no restrictions at that time on the
amount of rum you could bring into the country. Even though
they left Barbados, the rum industry did not suffer.

Music brought my mother into the Rum Shop which had a
piano in the rear room. Definitely not a common sight. However,
my grandfather loved music, and he installed the piano there so
his daughter, Meta, could practice. Women were not encouraged
to come into the rum shops, but no one could or would deny
The Major his delight of listening to his daughter on the piano.
Mum played and the men began not only to accept her, but
asked for her if she wasn't there. Eventually she got the

reputation as "the rum shop lady."

The central location of the Rum Shop and the alluring music coming from it brought people to the attention of Mom's playing. Word got around on the small island about the young girl who played the piano. In no time, she was invited to play all the important events and with other outstanding musicians. Mom's talent didn't go unnoticed. She accompanied Barbadian violinist, James Millington. The church was the foundation of Barbadian life. The powers that be within the church gathered together and agreed it would be good for Ometa Jones and Barbados if she could further her music development in the United States. In no time at all, she was sent off to that "promise land" for just that purpose.

Visiting Barbados and all the other islands introduced me to places in the world where the people were black like me. Not just neighborhoods, like in Harlem, but whole countries. For the first time, I felt good about being a Negro and not just about being a Negro whose parents were "Bajans" from Barbados. It really wasn't enough, though, to make me want to undo my efforts back in Harlem to get rid of my accent. My parents and their friends spoke differently than those blacks from the South and I loved listening to the lilting, undulating West Indian speech patterns. I returned home with a heightened respect for everything West Indian. Never again would I be ashamed of my heritage.

Chapter 3

THE HIGH SCHOOL OF MUSIC & ART
Stepping into a Whole New World

There was a distinct difference between the schools in the valley on Eighth Avenue where we lived and the schools on the hill. After attending and graduating from JHS 136 for girls or JHS 139 for boys, our neighborhood children were required to attend Wadleigh High School known as the worst school in Harlem. It was notorious for fights among students after school. That's what I hated about JHS 136, but at Wadleigh, the girls were older, making me even more apprehensive to go there. In junior high, I managed to avoid scuffles by showing that I didn't want to fight and by focusing on getting good grades, earning me the title, "stuck-up." I didn't think that strategy would work at Wadleigh.

It was a different story for the schools on the hill on Convent and St. Nicholas Avenues where the more affluent black and Jewish people lived. They had the prestigious George Washington High School in their district. Many parents where I lived were reticent about sending their children to Wadleigh, so they found ways to get their children into George Washington. A common practice was to submit a false address belonging to someone they knew in the district with the good schools.

My mother was sad when I heard her talking to my dad about the school preferences. "I really wish we could find someone who lives on Convent or St. Nicholas Avenue that wouldn't mind letting us use their address."

With resignation Dad added, "I've even asked some of the men in my lodge but none of them live on the hill. All live down here on Seventh Avenue or Lenox Avenue in the bowels of Harlem and in the districts of JHS 136 and 139." Mom wasn't ready to give up hope.

While talking to our next-door neighbor Mrs. Campbell, Mom learned of The High School of Music & Art where Mrs. Campbell's son, Hughie, and daughter, Jean, had eventually attended. Hughie had been in the first graduating class of the school.

Mayor Fiorello LaGuardia created "Music & Art" in 1936 to provide a unique education for outstanding students in the arts. It was an experiment that would make its way into New York history. At the time, I was too young to know anything about this special high school, and I had paid no attention to Hughie's joy when he was accepted there. I had no idea that years later, I would feel that same joy.

Everything Mum heard about Music & Art impressed her, especially because she loved music herself. She found out as much as she could about the school and encouraged me to submit an application. When I heard about Music & Art, it appealed to me, too, but I was afraid I couldn't pass the required exam to get in, especially when I heard who was accepted there. They were piano students primarily from white neighborhoods in New York City.

Mom persevered, though, and continued to encourage me. She told my piano teacher, Catherine Stout, of the possibility of me going to Music & Art. Mrs. Stout was also enthusiastic and encouraging. "I'll have Elayne come in for extra lessons," she said thoughtfully. "Fortunately, our final recital will take place just before she has to take the examination and that will give her a chance to play before an audience, which will be good for her." We all agreed and Mrs. Stout gave me the extra piano lessons.

Mum also learned that not only music ability was required, but academic achievement was mandatory as well to get into Music & Art. Knowing how little we were taught at JHS 136, she realized I would have to work hard to meet the academic requirements. Mum's employer and his wife were school teachers. During the years, Mr. and Mrs. Motz sometimes helped me with my homework. In her infinite wisdom, Mum approached Mrs. Motz and told her about the impending opportunity I had to get into Music & Art. She asked Mrs. Motz if she could give me some extra help with my studies.

"You take care of our son with such love that there was nothing I won't do to show my appreciation," Mrs. Motz said. Mum was surprised and thrilled with her warm response. With that kind of support all around me, I could not let them down. I *had* to do well.

After playing in my year-end piano recital, everyone told me how lovely I played and said I should have no problems with the Music & Art exam. That was good to hear, but I still had doubts. By then, I wanted with all my heart to pass that exam. Jean and Hughie Campbell had been fanning the fires of my desires, making me practice more and more diligently. As I practiced, I was also keenly aware that my grades were an integral part in being accepted at Music & Art. So, in addition to practicing more, I studied even harder.

Mum and Dad especially made me study and complete the little homework we were given at JHS 136. As a result, I graduated with an 86 percent average. Then came the next challenge: the application and audition for Music & Art.

On June 30, 1942, a letter from Music & Art arrived. My hands trembled as I opened the envelope. I couldn't believe what I was reading. "Elayne Jones has passed the necessary requirement for entrance into the ninth grade in The High School of Music & Art." My parents and I were ecstatic. My mother was especially joyful, grateful and relieved. Her wishes and efforts to get me into the school on the hill had materialized even better than anything we could ever have imagined. I did it! We did it! Our joy spread throughout the neighborhood. I,

Elayne Jones, was the third person in our Harlem apartment building to attend Music & Art, a school even more prestigious than George Washington High School. How ironic that in the five boroughs of New York City, three black students from Harlem who lived in the same apartment building were admitted to such a celebrated school.

My three years at Music & Art would give me ammunition to survive in the racist world, socially, musically and politically. Initially, though, I was catapulted into a formidable realm that scared me into feeling numb and dumb. When I auditioned, I had spoken through my piano because I was ashamed of my accent. Even in Harlem, people looked down on my West Indian accent. To fit in with my peers at school, I did everything I could to change my voice to sound like an "American."

My fellow classmates came from affluent families in the Bronx, Queens, Brooklyn or Manhattan. Many were Jewish, meaning less than one percent of the student body would be present during Jewish holidays. As a skinny black girl from Harlem, I was in awe of all my classmates. Regardless of ethnicity or religion, they were all different from me. I felt as if I knew nothing and they knew everything. I was a faded flower amongst a field of blooming lilies.

I was the least aware of any cultural activity below 125th Street. My exposure to the arts had consisted of going to the movies every Monday with my mother, listening to music at our Episcopal church every Sunday and of course, my piano lessons. I had lived in a small, limited circle and then at Music & Art, I suddenly found myself with students who were not only smart, but were forerunners and future leaders of the artistic world. During those first days at the school, I saw a door opening that would eventually lead me to becoming the first black musician to play with a symphony orchestra.

Once accepted at Music & Art, all piano students were required to choose to play an orchestral instrument. Lessons were given on that instrument. I was excited about the prospect of playing a violin. I don't know why I felt compelled to pursue this instrument. Living in Harlem and going to parties and dances there, I had hardly any experience with the violin. The live bands I heard and saw were made up of brass and wind instruments. But, there I was in Music & Art, with the group of students who had chosen the stringed instruments—violin, cello and bass. There were no violas to choose in those days because everyone was taught initially on the violin. Then later as students grew, if they desired, they would switch to viola which was bigger than the violin.

As we stood in line for our instrument, everyone in front of me was given a violin to fit their measured size. Then came my turn. Instead of measuring me and handing me a violin, the teacher, Mr. Isadore Russ, said, "I see you requested the violin, but looking at you, I say you're too skinny to play a violin." I knew I was skinny, but it never occurred to me that my weight would stand in the way of playing a violin.

"Just a minute," said Mr. Russ as he walked out of the room. He returned shortly with the brass and percussion teacher, Mr. Bernard Weiss.

"Mr. Weiss has a suggestion for you Miss Jones," Mr. Russ continued.

But before he could tell me the suggestion I said, "How about substituting the trombone?"

"Well, that won't work either," Mr. Weiss intervened. "I recommend that you study the drums." He handed me a pair of drumsticks. "We all know that Negroes have rhythm."

Being too young and intimidated at the time to put up a protest, I took the drumsticks. Afterwards, I reasoned that I had fallen in love with the drums in Barbados and loved playing on the drums in the drum and bugle corps in my neighborhood. Studying drums at Music & Art would simply be a natural progression for me as if it was meant to be. Right? Much later, however, I would realize that the teachers had manipulated me into taking the drums. The idea and action were racist because they were not aware of my past involvements with drums. Instead, they just saw me as a Negro girl who, by tradition, would graduate high school and most likely NOT go to college but perhaps marry then have babies. Playing a stringed instrument was for students with expectations of a musical future. Why spend money and time on a Negro female with no hopes for the future in this career? After all, were there any Negro males or females playing the violin anywhere in the world that we knew of at that time? The irony of this flawed logic was that less than half of the Music & Art graduates would pursue music as a career. They were attending the school because it was an academically outstanding for college bound students.

The teachers didn't sit down and think things out. This is what institutionalizing racism was all about. That's just the way it was then. So, when Mr. Weiss gave me a pair of drumsticks and said, "We all know that Negroes have rhythm," no questions were asked.

I went with Mr. Weiss into the brass and percussion room with the boys. No other girls were in the brass or percussion section. Surprisingly, that racist action would make me happy because I really did enjoy playing the drums!

We didn't waste any time getting assignments. The percussion room was filled with a myriad of instruments I had not seen or heard before. My only contact with the drums was with the drum set in the bands, which included the snare drum, a bass drum (played with the right foot pedal) and the high-hat cymbals (two cymbals which struck together all played with a left pedal). In the percussion room, I saw all sizes of Tom-Toms and various cymbals of different timbres. We were required to play all the instruments in that room. When I had watched the drummers in Barbados and later started learning to play in the neighborhood drum corps, I didn't know how little I knew. I was made aware of this fact, however, on my very first day at Music & Art. I would soon learn that the classical symphony drummer had to study just like a pianist.

Mr. Weiss, entered the room with our music books. Until then, I had never seen any drummer, swing or otherwise, with music. Why did we need music books? We didn't have to wait long before Mr. Weiss said we would be learning to play rudiments and drum exercises.

As a pianist, I was raised on scales and exercises which I hated. There were exercises to strengthen my fingers, develop my facility, train my eyes to read music, all with books for each discipline. I was accustomed to exercises for the piano, but for drums? I thought all you had to do was pick up the sticks and play a la the neighborhood drum corps.

I politely asked Mr. Weiss, "Why do we need exercises to play the drums?"

He patiently demonstrated what was required of a classical drummer. I was flabbergasted. All the beats I had played previously had names with specific ways of executing them. I couldn't compare what I started learning at Music & Art with the drum corps or any band, big or jazz.

Being a college-bound high school, we were expected to excel in academics as well as music. We had a full academic program making a long daily schedule followed by music classes that included theory, harmony and music appreciation. This schedule would slowly pull me away from my neighborhood friends. I had entered into a new community of white people and symphonic classical music.

English class was one of the most frightening experiences for me. The teacher, Mr. Mannheim, was a large, imposing man with a voice and personality that filled every corner of the room. His speech was like that of a British stage actor. My lack of exposure to the arts, outside of music, came to the forefront right away when we got our first assignment. Pacing up and down the room like the "king of the beasts" stalking his prey, Mr. Mannheim announced, "Tomorrow, you will bring in playbills to decorate the classroom."

Easy assignment? For the other students, yes. But for me, devastating! I looked around the room, and saw that everyone looked content with the task. What is a playbill? I thought. I was too embarrassed to ask. This was one of many times I pretended to know something everyone else seemed to know so that my teachers and classmates wouldn't see me as ignorant.

The following day, I watched to see what the other students brought to class. When Mr. Mannheim asked everyone to turn in their playbills, I just said I had forgotten and asked for more time to bring it in. Meanwhile, I was stunned to discover an actual playbill. All my peers presented their playbills and commented on the play or musical they had seen. Even their pronunciation of the word "theatre" was strange to me, since I had only heard it pronounced a few times as "the-a'-ta" instead of "thea-ter."

The orchestra program at Music & Art was unusual. I entered with instrumentalists who were mostly violinists. They had the opportunity to play in one of the orchestras. There was an orchestra each year at the third term progressing to the coveted eighth term or senior orchestra, the goal of most of the students.

Orchestra? Band? I confronted these two concepts. I always heard people speak of bands: Duke Ellington and his band, Count Basie and his band, the Calypso band, but orchestra? No mention. I had never gone anywhere to see or hear an orchestra. Again, I faced a foreign concept, but was too shy to ask and too fearful of looking ignorant. And again, I just waited until all was revealed to me.

During the initial weeks of the first term, we were all engaged in getting to know each other, the school, the schedules and the teachers. It was a tall order for me with so many new ideas to absorb. I felt like a fledgling bird learning to fly among the high-soaring eagles. Everything was new and everything was a challenge. Using my inner antennae, I feigned knowing everything as I listened carefully and absorbed all I could to understand.

After being settled with all our necessary academic classes and responsibilities, we were introduced to the music routines. Mr. Weiss gave us our assignments and our exercises to practice, saying that we wouldn't always meet in our practice room. All the freshmen students were required to gather and go up to the huge orchestra room on the top floor of the school. We had entered the class of the Third Term Orchestra because we came in to the school in ninth grade rather than eighth grade like students from other schools.

We were instructed to go and stand by the member of the orchestra playing our particular instrument. After looking around for our sections, we made our way through the mass of students and their instruments. Some of the new students were in the violin section, the cello section, the flute section and two of us were in the percussion section. We percussion students had to walk past all the musicians to the back of the orchestra where the other percussion players stood. Hmmm, this is the orchestra, I noted to myself. All these players and instruments are unfamiliar to me.

It didn't take long for me to see the difference between an orchestra and a band. The swing band generally had a drummer, a string bass player, four wind players, four brass players and a pianist, about eleven people. When I looked around Music & Art orchestra room with all the instruments, I saw at least sixty players with their instruments set so differently from a band. The majority were string players: violins, violas, cellos and basses. I looked and saw what I later learned were oboes, flutes and bassoons. I had never seen them. Strangely though, the orchestra had no saxophones. I recognized the trumpets and trombones, but I also saw strange instruments beside the percussion called French horns and another huge instrument called the tuba.

There was a cacophony of sounds around us as we walked through the room toward our instruments' place. All the players were busy practicing their individual parts. I had never heard such a noise. After I reached the percussion section, I introduced myself. Then I saw something truly unique and most amazing: the big kettle drums. Such an instrument didn't exist in the swing band. I was fascinated immediately without even hearing their sound. One student, a girl also named Elaine, was playing a snare drum, and a young male student was standing behind those kettle drums.

We heard a tapping sound which was the signal for tuning and practicing to cease. I looked up and saw a man standing on a box in front of the orchestra holding a long stick in his hand.

"Who is that?" I whispered to Elaine.

"That's our conductor."

Wow, I thought, that stick he's holding is really powerful since just one tap got the entire orchestra to stop and pay attention. When all eyes were on the conductor, he began his speech.

"Good morning boys and girls. This is the beginning of our new year and I expect great things from you. We will work hard and give a great concert at the end of the semester. Let us first welcome our new students and hope that soon they will be playing with us. For the new players, this is the Third Term Orchestra. As you progress, you will move from the third to the fourth and up to the Senior Orchestra." Everyone started to applaud.

"Congratulations on being accepted into The High School of Music and Art," the conductor continued. "May this be the beginning of a wonderful career in music. Some of you may now want to return to your practice room or stay and listen for a while. In either case, if and when you leave, please do so quietly."

Some students left, anxious to get their instruments to begin practicing. I was more curious about listening to the orchestra. This was so different from what I experienced when I sat and listened to the band in Barbados and the drum corps! The conductor opened a big book, which I later found out was called "The Score." He looked at the orchestra.

"Okay, boys and girls," he said. "Today, we'll read through *The Caliph of Baghdad*." All the players stopped practicing, opened their music and sat ready to play their instruments.

The conductor gave a downward motion and the music began.

What magic! I thought. I could feel the music in the pit of my stomach. I loved the sound. I hated to leave to go back to the practice room, but I did. On the way, I thought to myself, this is far more exciting playing music in the orchestra than playing the piano all alone in a room. I'm gonna work hard to practice and get good enough to play in the orchestra. As an only child, I was eager to do something so enjoyable with other people. So, on that day, I embarked on the beginning of my career as an orchestral musician.

I practiced and learned my rudiments earning the praise of Mr. Weiss. He always told me how proud he was of my progress. As well as practicing the drums, I continued playing the piano, and attended classes in music theory and music appreciation, although that might be better called music analysis.

I began to discover that even though this music was new to me, there were times I believed there was really nothing new in our world. It's just that we subjectively ignore our perceptions of things around us. Previously, I had only listened to the music of my peers and my era. Even though I had no contact with classical orchestra music in the past except for little excerpts I heard at piano lessons and recitals, I was beginning to recognize that these pieces came from a larger source. Before Music & Art I had no interest in finding out about the larger source, but at Music & Art, I did. My first day in music analysis brought me into this realization.

"Hello boys and girls," said our music appreciation instructor, a pleasant woman with a "musical" smile. Music seemed to emanate from her smile. "I hope you will enjoy this class since all you have to do is to listen."

We listened to the music and especially to her description of the music from all symphonies that she played. We learned about the composers and how they constructed the symphonies. I'll never forget the first symphony she played for us: Schubert's *Unfinished Symphony*.

But, something strange happened to me in that class. As I listened to the symphonies of Schubert, Brahms and Mozart, the music didn't seem foreign to me at all. I felt like I had lived it. Was I a reincarnation of those composers? Were they in my life subliminally?

I did well in music appreciation class. Did the teacher find that surprising? Obviously, she did, because at the end of the year when she handed out the grades, she said to me, "I have to tell you that you scored the highest in the class. You really surprised me."

That news shocked me as well as my other teachers and my friends. Although I was from Harlem with swing and calypso in my background and minimal exposure to classical music compared to all the European students, *I* made the highest grade. My classmates were expected to excel because they came from the classical culture. Perhaps my understanding and appreciation expanded each time I experienced and progressed from one style of music to another. I loved music, but unlike most of my peers in my neighborhood, I readily accepted classical music.

I couldn't say I loved one musical style more than another.

Whatever was being played, I enjoyed. Playing in the orchestra though was a different dimension. No matter how much I listened to music, it was nothing compared to being in the midst of a large orchestra. The different voices coming from the strings: the high, melodic sounds of the violins, a melody taken over by the sultry, sounding violas, the low flowing song of the cellos and the supportive deep hum of the string basses. Just being with a string quartet can open up so many tones and textures.

Now add the woodwind instruments: the flutes, which often double the violins' voice with a much brighter timbre like a bird in a tree, the oboes with their nasal sound and giving the "A" note to which everyone tunes their instrument, the mellow sounding, versatile clarinets whose range covers several octaves, the rarely seen saxophones with their funky, strutting sound. The colors, ranges and sounds can be awesome and spell-binding.

Wait, there's more! I haven't forgotten the brass instruments. They are the instruments which competed with the percussion for demonstrating the orchestra's volume of sound. The French horns, trumpets, trombones, and tuba together could drown out the strings and the woodwind instruments, but when they played pianissimo, or soft, like a choir it raised the hair on my skin. These players generally became my friends because they sat toward the back of the orchestra in front of or to the side of the timpani and percussion.

I did well in Music Appreciation class, but I struggled terribly with other academics in my first year at Music & Art. The academic reality of being at such an excellent school hit me straight on with my first report card. I had gotten a "D" average. I dropped from being a 98- percent student to a 50-percent student! How could this could happen? I was devastated. I always thought I was smart, and I had the grades and ranking to prove it all throughout elementary and junior high schools. I was upset, my parents were upset, and the guidance counselors couldn't understand what happened to me. My parents didn't wait for answers. They immediately talked to friends who pointed them toward getting a tutor for me. They did, and slowly, but surely, the tutoring would pay off as I carried a heavy load of classes in the next two years.

At Music & Art where the other students came from better junior high schools, I had to make a huge adjustment coming from a school in Harlem. However, when it came to the color of my skin, I actually didn't feel as rejected by the white kids as I did by other blacks in Harlem. At Music & Art, the other kids were white, I was black. They were Jewish, I was West Indian. The "accepted" girls in Harlem were those who looked almost white. I was black and West Indian. Socially, there was not much difference between being rejected by blacks or by whites. In some ways, at Music & Art I felt less rejected in its "white" environment. It didn't matter to my classmates where I came from or how I looked because all blacks looked the same to whites.

Initially, I was too shy and didn't really approach anyone, but two classmates came up to me. One was Adelaide Robbins, a young girl smaller than me. She played the piano like she was a part of its existence. I thought she could play anything she heard or any music put in front of her. I loved watching Adelaide play because she could make you believe that playing the piano was the most important thing in her life. Her father was a club date musician who played the accordion at gigs. I knew nothing about "gigs" and people looking for work at the floor of the musicians' labor union. I would soon learn.

Because all the students entering Music & Art had auditioned on the piano also had to play an orchestral instrument. Little Adelaide was introduced to the string bass. How she ever played it being much smaller than the bass was a mystery to me. Everybody joked calling her bass and her the musical "Mutt and Jeff."

Adelaide became a friend who led me into another new world. I was happy, but ambivalent about moving into it. I had already begun to feel separated from friends in my Harlem neighborhood. One day as Adelaide was eating lunch after a rehearsal, we talked about where we lived and our friends there. It turned out that she was an only child like me. I felt strange about the two worlds I was experiencing, but she had the same problem. While commiserating with each other she said, "How about coming up to my house for dinner? I'd like you to meet my parents."

"Where do you live?" I asked. She said she lived up in the Bronx off Fordham Road.

"Fordham Road!" I exclaimed. I remembered when not too long ago I had gone up to Fordham Road where my mother worked. I couldn't imagine going back there as a visitor when my previous experiences had left such a bitter taste in my mouth.

"I don't know if my mother would let me," I lied, scared to say yes.

"Oh, come on," Adelaide coaxed. "My parents would be happy to have you."

I did have to ask my mother to get permission. There was no way I could go anywhere at that time in my life, without Mum saying I could go. So, when I got home I asked her. Then she proceeded to ask several of her own questions.

"Who is she? Where does she live? Will her parents be home? Who else will be there?" I had to say, I didn't know to most of these questions. I was reluctant to go back to Adelaide and ask her all Mum's questions because I believed only my parents were so strict and that everyone else would laugh at me because their parents were more lenient. However, after giving it much thought and asking my dad if it was okay, Mum surprised me by saying I could go to Adelaide's home. I was both thrilled and apprehensive.

With trepidation, I set out for my first venture into the world of white people as a *guest*. It all felt so strange to me. I rode the same subway I used to travel with my mother, but now, I was a teenager on my own.

Because Adelaide's father worked in a profession usually not known for making big wages, their apartment was a walk-up like mine. Her parents were nice people. Her father was a typical type club date musician with his smart-aleck jokes and frivolity. I found myself laughing with him, totally forgetting that I was in a white home.

Dinner was different than the dinners I had known my whole life. Spicy Bajan food was seasoned with herbs, mostly thyme, marjoram, and lime juice. All topped with the Bajan Hot Pepper Sauce. My mother's friends always said the West Indian people who worked in Jewish homes taught them how to cook. It seemed like Jewish meat was boiled as was almost everything they cooked. The only seasoning was a little salt and maybe some black pepper. I thought the meal at my friend's table had no character, but I ate it and thanked them for inviting me. The food was not important. The opportunity to visit with people from another culture mattered most to me. It was amazing that although we lived only blocks apart, we were worlds apart.

When I left Adelaide's apartment, I worried that the women hanging out in the neighborhood would approach me when they saw a black youngster walking through the streets. Fortunately, no one paid any attention to me.

Adelaide would not be the only classmate whose home I'd visit. Eventually, there were Audrey and Else. They lived up in Washington Heights, another community more or less off limits to blacks. Both lived in tall apartment houses where I had to take an elevator to get to their apartments. The parents of these classmates were more professional. I had no idea what they did, but where and how they lived indicated they had well-paid positions.

I was uncomfortable when I saw that my other classmates

had maids in their homes. Other than when I went to Barbados on the ship and was served by the waiters, I was never waited on in a private home anywhere by a maid. I thought to myself, they will be telling their friends they had to serve a black child.

After visiting my Music & Art friends in their homes several times, I had not yet invited any of them to my house. I imagined they would not want to come to my home in Harlem. My classmates, however, were the budding liberal protagonists of our generation. Although we lived in communities mostly separated by race, they were sensitive and were beginning to make their ideas about racism known. One classmate, Audrey, pushed me into inviting her to my house. She brought it to my attention when I mentioned going to the Savoy on Friday. In those days, it was known that white people loved to go "up to Harlem" to listen to the great swing bands at the Savoy. My classmates were no different. They saw the opportunity to go up to Harlem with me.

Audrey and her cousin, who was also a music student in our class, loved swing music. I was beginning to move away from my childhood friends, but I still went with them on Friday nights to the dances. I talked about it with Audrey, and soon, her curiosity and desire to go were getting the best of her and me.

One day in class, she leaned over to me and said, "I would love to go dancing with you some Friday night." I knew she was interested, but I didn't know how I would deal with bringing a white girl to the Savoy with me. After thinking about it, I decided to first bring Audrey to my house for dinner, then afterward, we could to the Savoy.

The day before, I casually asked my mother, "Mom, is it okay to bring my friend, Audrey, home for dinner tomorrow night?"

"Tomorrow night?" Mom said.

"Yeah, she wants to go with us to the Savoy, and I thought she could come here, have dinner with us, and then we'd go to the dance."

"Oh, no," my mother protested, "I'm making coo-coo and salt fish, so how can you invite her here?"

"What difference does it make, Mom?"

"What difference? How can I give her coo-coo?"

In Barbados, there was a tradition of having coo-coo, every Friday. Coo-coo is basically an African dish made in Barbados with yellow cornmeal and okra, served with meat or fish and lots of gravy.

"Why can't she eat coo-coo?" I protested.

"Because that's a Barbadian dish, and she wouldn't like it."

"How could you say that?" I pressed Mom.

"I know because most people don't like okra, anyway, and I know she wouldn't like this."

"That's unfair!" I protested more strongly. "I have been invited to other homes and ate their native food, so why can't they come and eat our native food?"

"Because they're white. I don't want anyone making fun of our food." Mom was adamant; I couldn't bring Audrey or any white classmate to our home.

I had to go to my friend the following day and make up an excuse why she couldn't come to my house. It was too embarrassing to tell her the truth. During my three years at Music & Art I was not encouraged to bring white friends home, and certainly not on Friday.

I lived close enough to Music & Art to walk to and from school without having to ride the subway like all the other students. I stayed after school only to participate in sports. There were term parties but I didn't attend them. The parties at school were different from those I went to in Harlem. We danced "the Lindy;" they danced what they called the "Lindy Hop." Although the music was swing to them, it was not Duke Ellington or Count Basie. I listened to Tommy Dorsey and Glen Miller, but there still was a racial divide. At Music & Art, I began to develop a love for Brahms, Bach and Beethoven but I couldn't give up completely the ties I had to my black community. I had my feet in two worlds. My social life remained in Harlem and I religiously went to all church functions.

Music was my major love but as a teenager, I needed to have a boyfriend. It never entered my mind that I could have a boyfriend who went to Music & Art; they were white or Jewish. At home, my mother didn't let go of her reins on me. I did, however, briefly have one boyfriend.

Tommy or Tar, Jr. as I used to call him was my first serious and only boyfriend. He lived in the Harlem River houses, one of the first public housing projects built in the early 1940s by the government for poor and working class families. How I wanted my parents to move into these apartments with *real* refrigerators. Every Saturday I had to go to the corner of 153rd Street and Bradhurst Avenue to order a 25-cent piece of ice from the Italian man who later brought it to our apartment. The ice would last just about a week. I was so impressed that each of the Harlem River apartments had a box in the kitchen that kept food cold without having to buy ice. We thought everyone living in those apartments was special.

At one Saturday night church dance, everyone was talking about Frank Sinatra singing with the Tommy Dorsey Band at the Paramount Theater on Broadway, and who would be going. While Tar, Jr. and I were dancing, he nonchalantly said that he was going. Then he said, "Would you like to go?"

"Would I?" I said without blinking an eye. I liked Tar, Jr., but he had never paid any more attention to me than he did the other girls. So, it was a huge shock that he asked me. I hardly knew what to say. I couldn't believe my ears.

"The show will be in New York in a couple of weeks," he continued. "I'll talk to you."

I really wanted to go, but I was afraid of asking Mom if I could go with Tar, Jr. to this special occasion. In the next few days, I would experience another happy shock.

When the dance was over, friends of my parents took me home as usual. I was so thrilled inside but I still had to face getting my mother's approval to go with Tar, Jr. to the show. If she said yes, which I prayed she would, it would be the first time for me to go anywhere without her except for when I went to the baseball game. This would be the absolute first time to go anywhere with a boy! For days, I framed how and what I would ask Mom. I also had to make sure she was in a good mood before saying anything. Finally, the time was right when one day Mom was sitting at her sewing machine most likely making a dress for me. She made all my clothes, as most women sewed, especially those from the Caribbean.

"May I go to hear Frank Sinatra at the Paramount with a boy named Tar, Jr," I said.

Like every other time that I asked Mom for anything the first thing she said was, "Hi Laney, did you practice today?"

"Yes," I assured her. As always, she wanted details, and I was ready. She was impressed that Tar, Jr. lived in the Harlem River Project, he went to DeWitt Clinton High School and he was going into the service. And then, she said yes! I breathed a deep sigh of relief and joy that I could go on my first date. The show was an exciting experience never to be forgotten. I heard the young Frank Sinatra live on stage.

Before Tar, Jr. went off with the army to the Pacific, we went to see the great Billie Holiday on the famous Fifty-Second Street. I loved being with him. At 18, he was tall and good looking, but he was never fresh with me like I heard most of the other boys acting. When he was gone, he wrote to me and sent his picture from Iwo Jima. Fortunately, I was a very occupied senior at school, yet Tar, Jr. was always in my dreams. Then came the letter telling me he was coming home on furlough for a couple of days. All I could think about was being with him. How could I spend time with him if I was in school?

I shared my dilemma with one of my close friends, Audrey

who unlike me, was all about having fun. She told me about cutting school. I had never missed one day of school. My mother couldn't get me to stay home even if I had a cold. Having no siblings, it was no fun staying home. Well, believe it or not, the first and only time I cut school or anything in my entire life, was when Tar, Jr. came home on furlough. I left home that day and returned at the end of the day with my parents never knowing I hadn't been in school. I would even be lucky that for some reason, my absence never appeared on my report card!

Audrey instructed me on how to arrange for meeting Tar, Jr. He and I spent that glorious day walking along the Hudson River, and sat and ate lunch under the George Washington Bridge. The unusually warm day embraced us. Tar was concerned that I get back to school in order to be at home on time. He was that kind of thoughtful person. I loved him; I hoped he loved me, too. After his short furlough, he again went off to the Pacific. For several weeks, we wrote each other regularly, but his letters became sparse. I thought it was due to the irregularity of mail coming from the Pacific. When he returned from overseas, I never saw him again. The beautiful day we enjoyed under the George Washington Bridge was our last date. Our budding romance never bloomed. Tar, Jr.'s mother saw that we would never be together. It was strange how I heard about her objection to me.

While sitting on a stoop one day, someone who I thought was a friend said that Tar, Jr.'s mother didn't want him to see me because I was "too dark." In my aloof fashion, I pretended not to be hurt, but such a stinging rejection deeply hurt me. Getting publicity for attending Music & Arts and not too long afterward, winning the Duke Ellington Scholarship wouldn't be enough to heal my broken heart. For Tar Jr.'s mother and too many others, having skin that was too dark canceled out all my other attributes. The experience could have destroyed me, but instead, I was determined to be successful.

Music & Art was an academic college prep school. Everyone I knew was concerned with getting top grades in the Regents Examinations so they could be accepted at the college of their choice. I was just hoping to get a good enough grade to go to Hunter College to be a math teacher like my aunts. My entire family in Barbados expected me to follow in their footsteps. My mother, however, left her sisters and brothers who were respected teachers to pursue music as her career.

One day following all the end term exams I arrived at school and heard someone yelling at me, "Hey, Jonsey, go up and look at the Regents score." I was scared to death to go and look at my score.

I walked up to the bulletin board outside the grade guidance office where many other students were already eagerly looking for their scores. Some let out sighs of relief while others looked disappointed because they got only a 97 score. Then everyone surrounded one boy in the class, an art student, who earned a perfect score! He wouldn't have to worry about getting his choice of college because all the Ivy League schools would pursue him. He was a young man who had migrated to the United States with his parents escaping persecution of Jewish people in Germany. He went on to become the much sought after graphic artist, Wolf Kahn. I couldn't help thinking to myself the difference between his family migrating to this country and ours as black immigrants. I made my way up to the bulletin board and looked for my name. E. Jones, 86. Wow! I was happier with my score than those who were unsatisfied with their 95 score. I got past the cut-off and could attend Hunter College. Little did I know at that point I would have the last laugh.

The success I vowed to achieve in my life began that senior year. I practiced diligently enough to become a member of the Senior Orchestra, was admitted to the honors music society, was voted the most athletic girl in my class and then won a three-year scholarship to attend the distinguished Juilliard School of Music. I had raised my grade average by at least 30 percent, giving me an 85 percent average. Three years earlier, I entered Music & Art feeling insecure in a foreign land in every sense. Many probably had considered me the least like to succeed. By graduation time, however, I emerged at the top.

Graduation day was such a joyous day. My parents were the happiest people on Earth. Their daughter had not only graduated, but had won the three-year Duke Ellington Scholarship to attend Juilliard. Everyone in the neighborhood was invited to the celebration at our house.

There was no thought at that time as to exactly where I was headed. It didn't matter. I had won the scholarship playing piano and timpani and could go anywhere. The wonderful news stretched clear across the sea to Barbados. I was in America but that didn't matter. Barbadians love to celebrate the success of their natives so my story made the front page of their newspapers.

I would learn that the most difficult part of my success would be living up to the expectations of my adversaries. It was one thing to *get* there, but could I sustain being in this environment? I would no longer be with high school students in our city, but with students from around the country—North, South, East and West—the majority white. My experience with white people was only in Music & Art and they were mostly Jewish. I hadn't completely severed my relationships with my community. At Juilliard, would I make a complete break?

Chapter 4

POLITICAL INVOLVEMENT
Taking a Stand

I remember how I hated going to the movies, seeing the way whites live and they not being aware of how we lived in Harlem. I disliked the difference to the point that I disliked my own life until I got into The High School of Music & Art. It was there that I was introduced to a specific political action which represented to me, possibilities for changing that which I disliked.

After getting into Music & Art shortly after becoming a freshman, I was eating my lunch alone in the lunchroom during lunch period. A student came over to me and asked to sit with me. There was no hiding the fact that there was a degree of cliquishness between the freshmen, juniors, sophomores and seniors also between the music students, the art students and even between the string students, the wind and brass. It didn't take long for me to learn about this. Being a freshman in the percussion section and not even riding the subway home because I lived close enough from Harlem to walk home, made me a total outsider.

Those early days were very difficult trying to belong somewhere. To a great degree, I was alone except in sports. So, because of the environment it was unusual for this young white boy to come and sit next to me.

"Hi," he said in a friendly though not fresh manner.

"Hi," I answered.

He was bright and sensitive enough to realize I would be puzzled by his coming to sit with me, which of course I was.

"Hi," he went on. "My name is Marty and I would like to talk to you."

I'm thinking to myself, what's there to talk about? I couldn't tell if he was a music student, senior or anything as he had nothing to distinguish him.

"Yes?" I answered suspiciously.

He continued. "My name is Marty and I thought I'd like to tell you about a club we have here in school that many students belong to."

"Yeah? What kind of club?"

"Well," he said, "we're a club interested in working against segregation and racial prejudice."

At this point I sat up and paid attention to him for the first time. He was a white male with dark hair and probably Jewish. Most of the students at Music & Art were Jewish. I also assumed all Jewish people had dark hair making them look like fair-skinned Negroes. We used to joke and say the school was like the Ivory Soap commercial, 99.44 percent pure, Jewish. On Jewish holidays, which I knew nothing about, the school was almost empty since the Jewish kids stayed home . They had an extra advantage because they also got to stay home on traditional holidays.

Eventually I became an "honorary" Jew and could stay home on their holidays.

He continued oblivious to my thoughts.

"We're a political club."

Schools always have clubs and sororities for social activities, some exclusive and some opened to all. Basically, what I heard from my friends was that they didn't like these clubs because they tended to discriminate in the selection of members. They were above all, racists. So, when he said "club" I was ready to get up and walk away.

He then anticipated my thoughts and actions and said: "I know how you feel, but our club is not like that. It is a club that fights against that old concept. We study how to eliminate prejudices. We Jewish people have been discriminated against and have had to endure all kinds of prejudices. So, we know the struggles of Negroes."

This confused me. I looked at him and said: "You know the struggles of the Negro? Do you live in the city?"

"Oh, yes," he said. "I've lived here all my life."

"Do you live in the Bronx?" I asked, challenging him. It never occurred to me, from experiences with my mother, that Jewish people actually knew anything of the struggles of Negroes because they treated us with such disrespect.

"Yes, I live in the Bronx."

So, I started to walk away and he came after me.

"Wait!" he called.

"Wait for what?" I countered. "What could you possibly know about Negroes' struggles? My mother works for Jewish people in the Bronx and I have grown to dislike them." And I walked away.

"I don't blame you," he said to me as I was leaving. "That's why we created this club. It's made up of those of us who have observed what is going on in our communities and want to talk, discuss and analyze what we can do," he said, following me out of the cafeteria. "At least we want to do something about it."

"Let me think about it," I said.

"Can we talk tomorrow or someday soon?" he asked.

"Let me think about it," I reiterated as I walked away.

And think about it I did. He touched a chord that was music to my ears. I hated these people who were always treating us as maids. Yes, many black women worked as maids and like my mother had no choice to do what they really wanted or for which they were qualified.

My anger about this prevailed in my young life day in and day out. But doing anything about it? All I knew was that black people went to church and prayed to make life better. Having lost the sibling that I so faithfully prayed for, I had doubts about depending on prayers and God to change life. But at the same time how could I trust this person who comes from them, to think differently?

At this age, I was still under the influence of my parents' beliefs that children behave in accord with what their parents taught them. Confusion reigned in my head. In order to make a change, he, as well as I, would have to defy our parents' beliefs in tradition, prayer and God.

I went home; saw my parents as good people. It was through their efforts that I was able to go to Music & Art. Everything they did was for me, "the spoiled only child." How could I go against them? Yet, I doubted prayer and God.

I agonized for days and days. I also did my best to avoid seeing Marty as I wasn't ready to make a decision. I had other demanding concerns pressing in on me.

As I was going through the turmoil, I found that what I was confronting would affect my entire life. Was I wasting time practicing the drums? There were no blacks or women in any classical musical organization that I knew of. So, I was practicing for the joy of it, playing the music of Brahms, Schubert and Beethoven. The more I practiced and played at Music & Art, the more my eyes were opened to the fact that this music was played by whites, whereas the music I heard and danced to was played by Negroes. Yet, once introduced to the symphonies, I loved it. There were so many sounds, not just a song that lasted for several minutes. Every song I heard previously was 16-32 measures A.B.A. form. Nothing as complicated as a symphony all composed and performed by old white men which could go on for hours.

Of course, at this time in my life, I had no idea that this would become my profession and joining this club would become the training ground for the struggles I would be in to become a professional musician. The decision to join with Marty and his club thus loomed big in my future. It also was the beginning of separating me from the beliefs of my parents.

Many years later, in retrospect, I was thinking about my mother with her reaction to the path our decisions had taken me. She confessed her disappointment with me for having turned away from the church and God. That seemed to be more important to her than the success I had achieved with my career. So, knowing how she felt and not wanting to hurt her, I had to think of the best way to show her my love and respect in spite of the path I had taken. So, I wrote her a letter.

Dear Mom:

I thank you for all you've done for me. I could not have done it without you and Dad. You made me practice, you made me study, you even went against your religious beliefs when I confessed to you that I was pregnant. Instead of condemning me to a life with a child which could impede my career, you said to me, "Nothing will stand between you and your career." Instead, you went out and found a man, Dr. Hunt, to perform an illegal abortion. You never mentioned it to Daddy. I am eternally grateful to you as it allowed me the opportunity to be who I have become and which has exposed me to the world in the process. How I think is a result of you giving me the freedom to explore ideas beyond the boundaries of our beliefs. What I have learned was only to make a better world without the restrictions of racism and exploitation of workers.

With love and respect,
Laney

My dad always called me "Laney." Although he was a deacon in the church, he was not a devout believer. He attended to all the traditions but somehow indicated that he had some doubts of creation and GOD. But we never talked about it.

I did go on and was confirmed in the church when I was 16 to please my mother. At the same time, I had joined the club which was the Young Communist League. I then joined everything including the American Youth for Democracy, Young Progressives of America and the American Labor Party.

The next time I saw Marty after confronting all my profound thoughts, I didn't avoid him. I was ready to take this step into a new world of people and new ideas. I was introduced to the other members—all white, all Jewish, all Music & Art students. The first meeting was so strange. I had no idea what they were talking about. But whatever it was caused everyone to be paying serious attention to the tall strange man who spoke without interruption. I thought to myself: Why am I here? I don't understand a thing he is saying. When he finished his dialogue, the students, realizing my discomfort, gathered around me. My recruiter said, "Hey, gang, let's welcome Elayne into our ranks."

"Yes, we're happy to see you," said one guy.

"Don't worry, you'll get adjusted and become one of us," said one of the few women present who noticed my discomfort.

Marty went over to a table in the back of the room, picked up some pamphlets and gave them to me. I looked at them and saw words I have never heard of. Communism? Socialism? Marx?

"What's this all about?" I queried.

"It's the basis of our philosophy in our fight to end racism and exploitation of the working classes."

"Working classes? What did that mean?"

They didn't stop to explain any further as they had their club meeting affairs to take care of. They ended the meeting, agreeing on a date for the next meeting to which I was invited to return.

I couldn't wait to return. What role is all of this playing in my feelings about the unequal differences I was aware of, especially with race?

In the meantime, I had to put this club behind me as I had to study, get ready for upcoming Regents, and I was also participating in after school sports, which resulted in being chosen as the most athletic girl in the senior class at graduation. The most athletic boy was Ted Israel, a viola player who got into the New York Philharmonic right after graduation from Music & Art.

The next meeting which I was able to attend was the initiation and beginning of my path to what was called Left Wing or Progressive activity. By now I had little or no time for any friends or activities in my Harlem neighborhood. I did continue going to church for Friday night chorus rehearsals and Sunday morning service because I loved singing in the choir. It also afforded me an opportunity to play timpani accompanying the chorus in the "Hallelujah" of Handel's *Messiah* at Easter. Singing in the choir and playing timpani exhilarated me. I loved it.

There wasn't a day in my week that was not filled to the brim with music, sports and politics. I was also playing in the school orchestra every day, eventually reaching the senior orchestra. Added to that, I was playing Saturdays with the All City High School Band.

Mom and Dad's friends began asking them if I still lived at home as no one ever saw me. My days were spread out beyond 24 hours with minimum sleep.

Once a week I met with my "progressive" friends for learning and understanding the history of Communism, socialism and Karl Marx's *Das Kapital*. Already it appealed to me. The members, unlike my other classmates, were concerned not just with music but to make a better world for all people to live together. It stoked my thinking and I visualized colored people enjoying the benefits of life that the whites had.

The expectations made me happy and, as a result, I immersed myself reading the writings of Karl Marx's *Das Kapital*. Now I was being introduced to what progressive activity implied. There was much to learn, but also much to do. We joined together with organizations whose theories involved activities towards implementing what we studied. Not wishing to alienate my parents I did go on and was confirmed in the church when I was 16 to please my mother. At the same time, I had joined the club which was the Young Communism League. I then joined everything: American Youth for Democracy, Young Progressives of America and American Labor Party. Election time was imminent and that meant we were given information about candidates and their platforms. We set out to campaign for those candidates whose philosophies were compatible with progressives.

Living in Harlem, I had minimal involvement or understanding about campaigning for election.

I knew there was the Great Depression as I remembered hearing that my father was lucky to get a job, though that job was less than anything he felt qualified for. Mom supported his meager wage by doing domestic work, certainly not what she expected when migrating from Barbados.

It wasn't until I was in this club that I realized how knowledgeable and conscientious about the election my father was. I recalled how on election night he stayed up with a huge sheet of paper in front of him and sat next to the radio. He recorded by hand (my dad had an incredible Spenserian handwriting) the results of the election from every state. The results came in, in increments, as it was all reported manually. He kept track because he was interested in Roosevelt winning the election. I knew nothing that went on in the campaign up until Election Day.

Whatever there was that made Franklin Delano Roosevelt special, attributed to my crying when I heard of his death. He was an icon since as we came of age, we only heard about FDR as our President. I couldn't miss hearing his speeches because my father never missed his speeches or "fireside chats," as they were called. Vividly I remember President Roosevelt saying "The only thing we have to fear is fear itself," only because it was repeated over and over.

I was now in my graduating year (1945) from Music & Art and so much to be done. Finals and Regents exams were very crucial for me. I started out at Music & Art with my grade average at 55 percent, which was a severe disappointing drop from the 98 percent I had in JHS 136, which enabled me to be accepted in Music & Art. How tragic to my self-esteem and a disappointment for my parents. They came to my rescue by getting a tutor for me. With their help, I was able to raise my average to 85 percent. So, I was working hard to raise my academic average along with all my music and other activities.

Music & Art was an academic college bound school. So, everyone I knew was concerned with getting top grades in the Regents so they could be accepted at the college of their choice. I was just hoping to get a good enough grade so I could go to Hunter College and follow my family's objective to be a math teacher. This was the expectation of me by my entire family in Barbados. My mother left her sisters and brothers who were respected teachers, to pursue music as her career.

One day following all the end term exams when I arrived at school, the first words I heard were from someone yelling at me. "Hey, Jonsey, go up and look at the Regents Score." I was scared to death to go and look at my Regents score.

There on the bulletin board outside the grade guidance office, were many students eagerly looking for their score, some with a sigh of relief, some a little disappointed because they only got a 97 on the Regents! Then there was the boy in the class, an art student, everyone surrounded because he had a perfect score! He didn't have to worry about having his choice of college because he was pursued by all the Ivy League schools. He was a young man who had migrated to the United States with his parents escaping persecution of Jewish people in Germany. He went on to become a much sought after graphic artist Wolf Kahn. I couldn't help thinking to myself the difference between his family migrating to the United States and ours as black immigrants. I then made my way up to the board and looked for my name. "E. Jones 86." Wow! I was happier with my score than those who were unsatisfied with their score of 95. I got past the cut-off and could attend Hunter College. Little did I know at this point that I was going to have the last laugh.

During this critical period for my future, I had to cut down on some activities until the death of President Roosevelt. That night we regrouped—John, the brains of the group said: "We have to think of what direction we will take now that Roosevelt is gone. We must be aware that Roosevelt was successful in maintaining capitalism by initiating some socialist programs. We have to be diligent in moving his programs forward toward socialism and not retreat. The VP will naturally take over the presidency and fill out the unfinished term. In this time, we have to prepare for the 1948 election, there will be local elections which we will analyze and support. The American Labor Party will provide leadership."

With Roosevelt gone, every political ideology from left to right emerged to be ready to promote and take their ideology, into the next election.

It all began with local candidates for me. 1945—what a year for me. So many new adventures and expectations.

I graduated Music & Art with awards and recognition of my athletic and music abilities; and now in my hands, the three-year scholarship to Juilliard, not Hunter College, but Juilliard, the most prestigious music school in the world.

There's no doubt that I had come to a fork in the road of my life. I thought I was headed on the road to being a math teacher, the path all my aunts took except my mother. I followed the path that gave her joy and fulfillment of her own dream of being a musician. I was ever so happy. The difficulties of taking this path were not visible to me, yet. Only a rainbow was on the path.

My rainbow path had another little road that I had to include in my journey, the work of politics. As my journey took off, an incident along the way made it apparent that I would need help and support to continue the demands made on me and my schedule which made club meetings complicated. Although I attended Juilliard, many of the friends I made in Music & Art went to other colleges, mostly City College, which was accessible with minimum or no tuition fees. But that didn't stop us from getting together. For me the action I was to become a part of was the election of Ben Davis, an African-American man, to city council.

I received a phone call one day soon after we were settled in our school schedule.

"Hey, Jonesey, how yah doing?"

"Wow," I exclaimed, "I am in way over my head—too much to learn. Too much of everything—but I love it!"

John had gone to City College. He wanted to be an attorney and music wasn't as dominant in his life as it was in mine.

"Well, it's okay, very academic with no sounds of music wherever you go. But I'll be so busy studying and writing papers that I won't have time for music. But my political activity will complement my law courses. How about you?" he inquired.

"I don't have to tell you. Music is all I want, after my experiences in Junior High School and playing catch up with academics in Music & Art. I will avoid any subject that has nothing to do with music. I just don't feel qualified for science, history and all that jazz."

"But what about your degree?" he interrupted.

"Haven't thought it out yet," I said, feeling uneasy.

This entire neighborhood that Juilliard was located in was an intellectual, educational oasis, I could never think of myself as being in that class. This was the residue of how my junior high school experiences framed my thinking. No way would I subject myself to humiliation. Music was my forte and I'd have no problems doing well.

My days were full even without the academics. To make up

for it, I scheduled myself for any and every subject related to music. At the same time however, whenever a message was sent to me about a meeting. I manipulated to have it at a time I could attend.

I was apprehensive of getting involved initially. But as I got immersed in the meaning of socialism and communism, I saw these ideologies as being the answer to what plagued me all my young life, the discrepancies between black and white, rich, poor and religion. So convinced was I about this ideology, that I was willing to sacrifice all my free time to study Marx and Lenin and be politically active. My first experience combining schedule and campaign was going out evenings, foregoing dinner, to go door to door to get voters out to vote for Ben Davis for councilman.

I had developed a close relationship with one member of our club, a Jewish viola player, Arnold Brown. Although he was a string player, our schedules were basically the same, playing in the orchestra. So, we were able to go together on the electioneering campaign that was the extent at our "dating." However, the gathering place for all students to study, debate or just frolic was the Juilliard student lounge.

One day, in the midst of a stimulating debate, not about music, but about the pros and cons of the political climate, I turned to Arnie and said, "I must leave because I remember I have an important exam tomorrow, so I must go home to pray and get ready for the exam."

"Pray?" exclaimed Arnie. We had never spoken about religion but it was apparent from comments he made that his Jewish parents were non-practicing socialist Jews.

"Yes, I have to pray." Even though I questioned prayer, God and Jesus, this was the belief of my parents and friends. I had divided loyalties and still clung precariously to the belief in prayer.

"Prayer?" Arnie continued. "What good will praying do?"

"Praying," I defended, "so that I'll do well on my exam."

"That's ridiculous," he continued. "The only thing that will help you is to study and practice more in the time you spend praying."

"Well I dunno, I have to go." So, I ran away from him, feeling uneasy. I thought about it as I went home to pray or not to pray. That's the question I was scared of and worried about, I thought of all the questions I've had in my mind over the years. Maybe he's right. So, I didn't pray. Instead I studied and learned my music theory. The results were better than I could have expected. That experience put the lid on whatever religious belief I still maintained.

Not only was I active in political activities, but there was another activity which emerged at Juilliard.

I was the only black student in the orchestral department. There were several other black students with majors in piano and voice. They were all facing the subtleties of racism and all felt a need to support each other by forming a club with the slogan "In Unity there is strength." At our meetings, we spoke of our aspirations and focused on the racist incidents that popped up which tended to stand in our way.

The fact that almost all of us were accepted in Juilliard, on scholarship, indicated that we were qualified, so why the problems? Must have been racism!

The racial and sexual specter was fast coming upon me.

I, like the others, was uncertain about what the future held. What were the expectations for the voice students? Concertizing in a chorus or a church job? But lastly, opera? And the expectations for piano students? Teaching? Accompanying? Orchestra? Concert pianist?

I had no idea where I was headed. My friends could focus on teaching and took classes in pedagogy. Many took classes towards a degree at Columbia University. They were realistically preparing for their future. What did I schedule? Conducting! Composition! Realistic? No, I knew of no black conductor and was not aware of black composers other than in jazz and swing. The history of black classical composers was not readily available, so in a sense, I was swept up into a journey in unchartered waters. These waters were leading me towards dreams I had. I remembered lying in bed and visualizing myself on stage. I had no idea what stage or where, but I felt myself being there. Deja-vu?

One day a friend of Mom's, Mrs. Ferdinand, who worked for many years for a Jewish family and lived with them in the Bronx and spent every summer with them at a place in Far Rockaway, came to me out of the blue and asked. "What are you doing this summer?"

I was surprised that she spoke to me or even asked me a question. Whenever she came to the house, all she ever talked about was Mrs. Gutterman. She was an immigrant from some strange sounding island in the Caribbean—called Montserrat. Why she was even in America I had no idea, but her entire life evolved devotedly around this family. She was at the beck and call of their young son, Morty. She often spoke about the way these families doted on their young progenies. Many families were so protective of their little inheritors that they did not send them to camp or day camp during the summer months. One such family had a young son who was the apple of their eyes. The mother was a stay-at-home mom, who had to have her own life and free time from the care for this child. Thus, she had to look for the perfect person to leave him with when school was out since they didn't trust sending him to camp.

My mother's friend thought highly of me and thus approached me and asked if I would be interested in having a job for the summer. A job? Yes, taking care of this boy while the family was spending the summer in Long Beach. This would have been my first opportunity to work and be away from my parents as this was a live-in job.

Mom thanked her friend for asking me and said we'd think

about it.

When Mrs. Ferdinand left, Mom told Dad about the job and they both queried me about taking on such a responsibility. This would be my first year in high school. The summer was always a problem for my parents since I too was never sent to camp. My best summer so far was when we went to Barbados a couple of years earlier when I was eleven.

"This would be a good opportunity for Elayne spending time at the seashore and making a little change for herself, reasoned my parents.

Since I didn't know what to expect, I trusted my parents' decision and took the job in Long Beach. I was introduced to 10-year-old blonde Joshua. Immediately I could see that he was bright, spoiled and precocious.

"Are you going to be taking care of me?" was his first words to me.

"Yes, I'm looking forward to it."

"My mother says I'm a handful" he challenged me already.

And a handful he was. His favorite word was "why?" Everything I asked him to do was a challenge. I wasn't prepared for this being I was a child of the West Indian parents. WE were raised with "Do as I say." I would never think of saying "why" to them.

So, this was an education for me of other cultures and behaviors.

Breakfast and dinner was had with his indulgent parents. Although I wasn't a maid, I did have to wash the dishes, feed and bathe Joshua, then take him to the beach.

The first time I walked with him to the beach I was astonished. I grew up going to Rockaway Beach each Sunday with my parents and friends. It was generally very crowded and quite dirty. This was a section of the same beach reserved for Negroes. There were bath houses for bathers to change their clothes. I never liked going in them as they were always smelly.

I never noticed that these were houses that people lived in. All I remembered were shacks selling all kinds of beach wear. I really hated it although I was not aware of there being anything better.

What I discovered about the beach where I was now employed was that the only similarity to Rockaway Beach was the ocean. Otherwise, we were miles apart, literally in every aspect.

There were no shacks, no bath houses, no rotten smells and no garbage. The most glaring, no black faces. This neighborhood had neat little pastel cottages with petunias springing up from every little patch of dirt.

I never knew beaches could have clean white sand and not have people almost sitting on one another because it was so crowded. When we went to the beach it was an all-day event. Thus, every family came with enough food to keep appetites, which the sea seemed to encourage, satisfied and filled.

No such thing on this pristine beach. Each family had their spot with all kinds of signs, "Do not eat, sleep, drink or make a loud noise," visibly displayed. In small print at the bottom of the sign was a statement that affected me like a kick in the face. **Household help may use the beach only after sundown or 6:00 p.m.**

I could be on the beach only with my charge. Who wanted to be on the beach at sundown? I was happy to have a job with a satisfactory pay. But I could not be like my mother and her friends to idolize their charges as they work in this menial racist situation. So, I quit after three weeks.

As if this was a lesson, my mother's words were always ringing in my psyche when she made me study and practice. "No way you gonna clean white people's floors." But I didn't count on the actions of my ward. I didn't have to cook and clean the floors, but I was still a maid. I had to bathe little Joshua, which was always a battle. I fought with him each night.

"Joshua come take you bath."

"I don't want to," he'd scream at me. This went on until his mother interceded. "Come Joshua darling. Take your bath." He continued, "I don't want her to bathe me."

"Why not, my darling? His mother pleaded.

"Because she is dirty, she looks like the dirt!"

I couldn't cope with this, so I left.

Mom did not have to worry about the possibility of me doing domestic work, or, as it turned out, any job other than music. The political activities and friends I made musically took me far away from that possibility of domestic work. The political left was much attuned to using music to further their ideologies and activities.

I had never learned anything political in school other than democracy. We knew that Hitler's domination was based on fascism as was Mussolini's control. The United States was the good country. But simmering below the surface were those people, workers and Negroes, whose lives were not benefitting from migrating to the great America's democracy. Immigrants entering the country along with their desire for having a life better than what they left in Russia, Germany and Poland fared better than coming from even the West Indies. When they came, along with them came their culture. You could listen to the music and identify immediately where their identity, culture came from.

I loved classical music but these cultural political songs aroused a sense in us all of being in this struggle for a more egalitarian life. "Oh, you can't stop me; I'm working for the union I'm working for the union till the day I die."

I was enjoying my life, musically, politically and even economically.

Winning the Duke Ellington scholarship made me highly visible to all in the music world as well as the political world. The political Left began to find occasions to use me for events. I could say they were exploiting me, but the events I was called for supported the issues which were always forefront in my thinking—eliminating racism and inequality between rich and poor.

In my musical growth, Juilliard exposed me to invaluable experiences, very similar to what I had to go through. The difference, this was Juilliard, the top music institution in the country. Unlike Music & Art students, the Juilliard students were serious about their desire to have music as their profession. The competition became fierce in desire to land a quality job in music. Obviously, to be qualified you had to be proficient and you had to study, practice and play. You needed to study with the best teachers and, at this time, the best teacher for me was Saul Goodman. Everyone vied for his attention and to extract from him any and everything he had for their purposes.

I inadvertently had a leg upon them having gone to the summer school session and taking lessons with Goodman. So, he knew me and sometimes called on me to demonstrate to the new students how to execute a particular passage. This did not sit well with my classmates who began to think of me as "teacher's pet."

Understanding the phenomenon that this little black girl was upstaging the big guys was almost impossible for them to tolerate. It all came about at our final concert just before graduation. We were told the great conductor, Fritz Reiner of the Pittsburgh Symphony, would be guest conducting this concert. We would play Brahms's First Symphony, a work which featured the timpani at the opening measures. We all practiced this symphony diligently, listening to and playing along with the recording of the symphony. We wanted to familiarize ourselves with the music not only on the score, but in our being by memorizing the crucial phrases. There were rehearsals leading up to the momentous final concert. Goodman would come and listen to us at rehearsals as we took turns playing the timpani part.

A critical decision was going to be made, not only in the percussion, but all the sections, string, woodwinds and brass by the respective instructors. After the final rehearsal, on the bulletin board was posted the names of the players who would play for Fritz Reiner. We all looked and, lo and behold, under timpani was "Elayne Jones." The body language and sounds emanating from the guys clearly demonstrated their dissatisfaction with the decision.

After the concert, Fritz Reiner told the orchestra manager he wanted me to come to his dressing room. Scared to death I went. He had a notorious reputation of being very demanding and hard on the musicians. So, since this was after the concert, I didn't know what to expect. It was with heart in hand that I went to the maestro's dressing room. There he sat with a seemingly scowl on his face. Yet as I approached him the scowl softened and he reached out and held my hand.

"Young lady, you make beautiful music with these hands." I was so stunned all I could do was to stammer "Thank you, Maestro," and left the room weak with joy.

To add injury to insult, I was chosen in another prestigious performance. I was also playing in the Juilliard Opera Orchestra. A grand announcement was publicized throughout the music world. The great composer Igor Stravinsky was going to conduct the premier of his opera *Orpheus*. I was elated to be the person selected to play with this great world renowned composer.

I graduated in 1949 but in 1948 I was hired as a result of my progressive friends and contacts, to play a weekly syndicated radio program "Labor USA" on WJZ-ABC. This was a 15-minute program sponsored by the AFL-CIO. It was a political program about workers' struggles, with music interludes between dialogues.

Something was happening. I was getting a reputation. Playing with the musicians on "Labor USA," because of the content of this program, musicians were chosen from the progressive community. On this job which paid well, was a very warm, sensitive, aware cellist, Vic Sazer. He was the first to come over and introduce himself to me. One by one, the other musicians were curious about my presence. Within the next few weeks during the run of the program, I got to know these men, each telling me how wonderful it was to have me on this gig. Idle compliments, I thought. But the compliments were genuine as I was about to find out.

This was an election year and all political parties were vying for support of voters. I was, of course, supporting the progressive party candidate, Henry Wallace. As usual, in between exams and concerts, I managed to find time to participate in the political activities. I got involved with the musicians who were the men I played with in the labor radio program.

"Hey, Elayne. It was wonderful having you play with us. But we had no idea you would be willing to join forces with us, politically."

Although I had been meeting with our little club from Juilliard, I was now meeting with larger groups from all over the city. Musicians who were from schools like Manhattan School of Music were all organized by the cellist I had met on the "Labor USA."

The project of these progressive supporters of Henry Wallace was to form an orchestra which would play for the third-party convention in Philadelphia. My new friend Vic explained to me. "This orchestra will be conducted by a young choral director, Bob deCormier, and we want you to play with us if your schedule allows."

I was happy to be asked and happy to be playing with these musicians and for a cause I wholeheartedly approved of.

In the next few days I was given all the particulars for this concert.

Although I had a busy schedule there was no problem as the

rehearsals were on two successive Saturday mornings.

There was not just the orchestra, but also a chorus. We were performing *Alexander Nevsky* by Sergei Prokofiev.

How happy I was to be a part of this monumental event. Even though I was 20, Mom and Dad were a little apprehensive at my involvement.

"Laney, I'm happy you're taking a part in this convention although it's politically controversial," said my Dad. "It's for a good cause so go with our blessing."

Early at seven o'clock in the morning, Vic came to my house in his 1947 station wagon. We left and he stopped to pick up Nina, who later became his wife, plus two other people.

Our participation was for only one day, the day of the nomination of Henry Wallace for President. We were the highlight of the convention with our stellar performance by our orchestra and chorus.

This really launched my career politically and musically. Another path was being opened for me.

Progressive people were always looking for and supporting the struggles of black people. One such person who caught the eye of progression was a young black conductor, Dean Dixon. On the agenda of one of our meetings was what we can do to promote this talented musician.

This was the continuation of a period in African-American history known as the Harlem Renaissance, the artistic endeavor of Negroes, as we were known in those days. It was making itself known. There was talent abound which in many areas was being used and exploited by the white arts community. They saw material coming out of the black community which was rewarding financially for them.

With all the talent coming out of this community, the doors to the hallowed halls of classical music remained closed to those of African heritage. It was okay to play piano as well as trumpet, trombone and saxophone in a jazz arena. The saxophone was not appropriate in a symphonic setting until Gershwin wrote for them in his music.

Black people were kept out of the classical orchestras as it was believed blacks couldn't play or were not interested in "European music."

Although there was nothing written, there was an understanding that musicians were not encouraged in conservatories and in employment to venture into this "sacred world." Thus, black music students turned instead to jazz with the pronouncement, "They don't want us, and we don't want them."

Dean Dixon defied this unwritten law and had the audacity to try and be a symphony conductor. Of course, he had to be supported. The union didn't support him wholeheartedly as evidenced by the fact that in major cities in the United States, there were separate unions. One for black jazz musicians and one for white classical musicians.

Dean Dixon was exposed to classical music in his native country of Jamaica and, like all foreigners, immigrated to the United States, the land of opportunity, to pursue studying music as a career. But like all expectant foreigners of color, they found racism instead of opportunity. He was meeting not encouragement but resistance to his desire to conduct.

I met him in his last year at Juilliard as steadfast as ever in his dream to be a conductor. Fortunately, my eagle eyed progressive friend Vic happened to be in a class with Dixon in conducting strings. Vic happened to be chosen to be in this class to play for conducting students.

Dixon played a low profile at school. Either he didn't know about our group of black students or chose to go it alone. But once Vic got a whiff of his presence he would no longer be in the shadows. Vic latched on to him and made everyone aware of his presence and his aspirations. It was thus that Dixon's career took off.

With the ideological belief in racial equality, in no time at all like minded forces joined together, and the America Youth Orchestra, with Dean Dixon, conductor, was formed.

The orchestra was made up of students from all the music schools in and around New York who were sensitive to the fact of having a black conductor. I, however, was the only black player in this orchestra. I loved playing with Dean Dixon. He was smart and so knowledgeable. Knowing the resistance that he would face from the audiences, especially to seeing a black conductor, he initiated playing for school children particularly. His objective was to create and build his own audience from scratch.

He was so successful at this idea, that soon there were many copy cats. The most known was Leonard Bernstein's Young People's Concerts. Unfortunately, when people speak of concerts for the youth, there is no mention that Dixon was the initiator of this idea.

By this time, I was leading a non-stop life of playing. One of the highlights was when I was called by a contractor, who became a lifelong friend, Arthur Aaron.

I was getting many calls for jobs, at meetings, demonstrations and other events. Unexpectedly one day a call came, and when I answered a voice said, "Elayne Jones?"

"Yes," I answered.

"You don't know me, but I was told to call you about a job."

"Oh? Who are you?"

"I'm Arthur Aaron. I am a cellist. I hire musicians to play in orchestras for a variety of occasions. I'm in the process of hiring special musicians for a very special concert, and I was given your name to hire."

"Oh, well what is the concert?" I questioned.

"Next week Paul Robeson will be singing at Town Hall," Arthur explained. "The sponsors of the concert would like to have an orchestra made up of the best musicians as we want the best to accompany Paul."

"Paul Robeson?" I repeated.

You could not be a part of the Progressive Movement and not hear about Paul Robeson. He was an actor, a singer, a four-letter athlete at Rutgers University and a fighter for blacks, working class and all disadvantaged people. He was a giant in every way. But he was mostly known as a great singer actor.

Arthur Aaron went on. "You were recommended highly so I'd love it if you could play with us."

"Wow," I said, "this sounds fabulous. When are the rehearsals and performance?" Arthur then gave me the dates, place and times of the rehearsals and the day of the concert.

I was so honored to be asked to play a concert with this great man. This was one of the numerous memorable events in my musical career that was emerging.

At the same time, I was also playing in the National Orchestra Association. This was a training orchestra for musicians who were preparing to play with a major symphony orchestra. The conductor of this orchestra was a very unique man who was both educator and conductor. How I even became a member I cannot say. Again, I found myself the only black musician playing with the same guys from other orchestras in the past, some who tried to make it difficult for me. Many percussion players may not have found my presence among them comfortable when competing for recognition and hiring. It wasn't my playing but my being black, female and little.

These progressive musicians, who were not in competition with me, were just the opposite. I was no threat to them. They did much to further my career. My tomboy days actually framed my personality to being easily getting along with the guys. I could banter with them and their language didn't offend me.

They loved making fun of conductors. I didn't have to play with reputable conductors to know that for the musicians, conductors were less than reputable. No musicians, no matter

how great, he was, be he Jascha Heifetz, the great violinist, or
any other, escaped the harsh criticism or joking by them. In other
words, a picture of the ins and outs of what was going on in the
music business contributed to my "musical career." I learned it
wasn't so much what you knew but who you knew. Over the
years, I was referred to as "one of the guys."

Chapter 5

THE DOUBLE STANDARD
Youth

I can start from my toes up. Here I go in Physical Education (Phys. Ed.). I was always an athlete, due to being a "tomboy," a term not used much today, but which was used to refer to a young girl who loved playing in sports with the boys. There was another reason for my athleticism; it got me closer to the boys, especially since I did not think I could attract the boys competitively with girls.

I was a natural athlete and did very well and felt confident of my ability. During my years in Junior High School 136 in Harlem I excelled in sports and won the Police Scholastic Athletic League Award when I graduated.

When I went to The High School of Music & Art, I was confronted with unfair competition out of racism. Not the hateful cross-burning KKK type racism but the kind which makes anything European acceptable as opposed to anything of African origin. I am very definitely of African origin—with hardly any hanky-panky in my family tree—meaning no rape by a white man which would give me residue from the rape such as fair skin color, straight nose, thin lips, straight quality of hair, as my hair was very kinky or nappy, a term we used to each other.

This salient fact was brought home to me the first week of our Phys. Ed. class. I really looked forward to the period which was called "GYM." I was soon to realize that there was more to GYM than just throwing, catching, and hitting a ball or any of the other aspects of sports. Here, added to that, was the body beautiful.

I had no idea what a "high instep" meant prior to attending Music & Art.

I had studied tap dancing along with my friends at the neighborhood recreational center, due of course, to the popularity of Bojangles in all the Shirley Temple movies and because there was no such thing as a person of dark skin in ballet where so-called, beautiful feet and body was the emphasis. Whereas in tap dancing, rhythmic ability of the feet and body was highly regarded. I was good at tap dancing and felt confident about that talent. Why didn't I pursue it as a career? My practical and realistic parents realized there was no future in tap dancing except as a novelty. Considering the fact that every black parent with any cultural drive sought to introduce their children to tap dancing—the number who became famous—or who could just make a living was less than .01/2 percent of the population. I saw that the success of an art form was dependent on the attribute of the European body and frame.

"Point your toes, curve your arch," my gym teacher challenged me. She thought I was being obstinate and lazy, not following her commands. I couldn't understand because I was trying my best, but my feet were flat, and since in that particular group all my peers were white and had more or less the approved feet, I began to feel that there was something wrong with me.

Going to an all-white school emphasized my differences because I had developed white relationships which exposed me to the "positive" features of their feet. Shoes were made to emphasize the high instep with high heeled shoes—and even the loafer. Ballet, rather than tap dancing, was the desirable medium. Ballet emphasizes for one, the high instep and the pointed toe. This coupled with a few other features, tended to exclude the black foot, body and color.

Many years later, I was playing timpani in the orchestra with

the American Ballet Theater (ABT). I happened to be friendly
with our concert master who was married to one of the principal
dancers of ABT at the time. The company had just returned from
an engagement in Hawaii, and during a rehearsal break, he
spoke about their experiences playing in Hawaii.

"How wonderful it was to be in Hawaii but strange if you
can't take advantage of its jewels, the sand and sea," he moaned.

"That's a strange thing to say," added one of the musicians.
"Didn't you have a ball in Hawaii?"

"Not really, because we had to have many rehearsals and
didn't have much free time. We were obliged to work with the
local musicians, leaving us with very little free time. But the
worst part was when we did have a couple of free hours, I was
dying to go on the beach and soak up the sun and go for a swim
in the beautiful blue sea."

"Sounds great to me even if for just a couple of minutes!"

"But that was the problem, I could go, but Nora Kaye
couldn't go."

"I guess she had a lot of practicing to do. I know those ballet
dancers sure do work hard."

"Oh no, that was not the problem. The problem was the sun."
"What?"

"Yes, it was the sun! Management did not allow the girls to
go out during the day for fear that they would get a little dark
from the sun and spoil the picture. They had to look white on
stage and management couldn't take any chances."

The so-called "flat" foot of those of African origin has never
been regarded as being attractive or desirable. Barefooted
dancing of Africans was not given the sort of interest and
credentials which could provide a positive image of this style of
dancing and the form of foot needed to dance this style.

Isadora Duncan was considered a rebel, daring to dance in
Russia without the traditional dance slipper. Many dancers have
followed in the tradition, among them Martha Graham. As I

have followed the dance scene, it is apparent how the standards, superior and sub-superior take shape. Barefooted dancing is fine for Europeans as long as that foot has the European shape.

All my life I have been overly sensitive about my feet partly because I am a musician with a great amount of sensitivities in many areas.

I was always conscious of the imprint left by wet feet in the wet sand. I would find myself not allowing my foot to press too heavily on the sand so the flat-footed imprint would not leave that flat outline.

When my son Stephen was born in 1954, he was beautiful to me in every aspect but one. I worried about his feet which as he grew, they developed no arch. Not only did I feel flat feet to be ugly, but was brainwashed to believe that not only were flat feet unsightly, they were unhealthy and they led to many physical problems. Being a parent concerned about her child's health, I trotted my son who was about three years old into the pediatrician's office to consult about exercise to help his feet and the best shoes to wear.

My children's father George, my husband, was a physician as were all of his friends, yet when I got pregnant, I went to a female obstetrician-gynecologist, Clementina Pallone, who I believed would be more sensitive to my needs. At the time, she was not only an ob-gyn physician, but a politician who ran for councilwoman in 1953. After the children were born I chose a very talented young black woman for our pediatrician, Dr. Yvette Francis, also with the belief that she would be more sensitive to my children's physical and emotional needs.

The day I took my son to her concerning his feet, my choice paid off. She too had lived her youth like me under the adverse reaction of our feet. She was a mother and had the same concerns about her children's feet, therefore, as a concerned mother and doctor, she pursued the true facts behind this myth and did her own research into the matter.

She came up with information never widely disseminated that "black feet are best suited for walking as they can support the body better." Those "beautiful" feet with the high arch instep, break down because they do not support a heavy body as well. The people of Africa on the whole did more running and walking to reach their destinations than the Europeans. Their feet developed to make their travel less wearisome. The shoes they wore were basically fitted around the foot and therefore flat like sandals. The European foot must conform to the shoe.

"Don't worry," Dr. Francis consoled me. "Your son's feet, though not pretty by European standards, will never cause him any difficulties."

I can't say that I wouldn't like to have beautiful feet, but I thought beauty is a contrived concept. Anything which is healthy and strong should be considered beautiful.

I now regard my feet with respect and love them.

One day, after playing tennis, I was sitting around with other players discussing our various muscle aches and cramps. Feet were the biggest culprits simply because they are too fragile to sustain the beating they receive. As a result, shoe manufacturers have amassed billions of dollars creating shoes for sports to support those feet. That is one area that I can sit back and feel superior about my ugly feet because I was able to wear the least expensive sneakers without problems because my feet were evolved to support my body and its activities.

Chapter 6

DUKE ELLINGTON
An Experience to Remember Forever!

While I was attending The High School of Music & Art, I also played with the All City High School Band. Rehearsals were every Saturday morning at Commerce High School at Sixty-Sixth Street and Ninth Avenue, the site of the present Juilliard. When most other children wanted to linger in bed at that time, I was rehearsing with the band. I never missed a rehearsal. The spirit of the music always called me. Out of bed, I'd jump, get dressed and off I went. My mother no longer asked if I was going. She had already learned that I was not a person to stay home if I had to go to school or rehearsal. As an only child, I preferred being in school with my classmates and friends than at home alone. That pattern would follow me throughout my 50-year career.

In my senior year, the band director recommended that I try out for the Duke Ellington Scholarship, a three-year grant for tuition at the Juilliard School. His recommendation was partially due to how conscientious I was in attendance as well as my musicianship. This was intimidating for me because although I loved playing, the violinist seemed to get all the attention. I was filled with self-doubt.

I clearly remember the night when I told my parents that I was reluctant to audition for the scholarship. We were sitting in the kitchen eating dinner and apparently, I was looking very glum. My dad loved to eat and usually buried himself in devouring his rice and peas. So, it was quite startling that he noticed my mood. He and Mum had obviously been discussing the possibility of what could happen if I got the scholarship.

"What's wrong with you tonight, honey?" Dad said. "You aren't as lively as usual."

"I'm trying to decide if I should take the audition for the scholarship," I confessed.

"What?" he exclaimed.

I continued. "I just don't think I could compete with the white kids. They take private lessons and are already giving concerts. I don't take private lessons"

"Are you crazy?" my mother chimed in. "You've been playing and taking piano lessons since you were knee high to a grasshopper."

I interrupted her. "But I'll be taking the audition on the timpani because it's a scholarship for orchestral instruments," I lamented.

"So, what if they've studied?" Mom responded in her lovely West Indies accent. "You have nothing to lose. You were invited, weren't you? So, I don't want to hear anything about not going, girl. Go, the lord will take care of you." End of discussion.

I couldn't let down my parents, but I didn't feel confident. That feeling, however, wasn't much different than how I felt about taking the exam to get into Music & Art three years earlier. Was *this* any different? Well, as Mom said, I have nothing to lose. If I don't make it, I could still follow my first career choice to be a math teacher. I loved math and it was my idea to follow in the footsteps of my aunts and uncles in Barbados. Again, however, my parents desired for me to prevail. I took the audition and was admitted into Music & Art. I would audition for the Duke Ellington Scholarship no matter how I felt about myself.

The preliminary auditions took place at Brooklyn Tech High School and I passed the preliminaries on to the finals held at Juilliard. I can't remember what I played on timpani but I played "Claire de lune" by Claude Debussy on the piano. I just focused on doing my best. When the auditions ended, we waited for the judges' decision. After their deliberations, the names of the three winners were announced. Then the unbelievable happened.

I heard the name, "Elayne Jones." I couldn't believe it. Was I dreaming? I who had to compete with the hot shot white violinist couldn't emerge a winner. It couldn't be possible, but it was not only possible, it happened. Along with two white boys, Paul Rudolph on French horn and Ross Norwood on flute, I won the Duke Ellington Scholarship for three years study at Juilliard! I wanted to scream. I kept pinching myself because I didn't want to take the audition when I heard about it. I couldn't wait to let my mother and father know that their belief in me had proven right.

The press must have been notified of the scholarship because it was associated with the great Duke Ellington. So, photographers and reporters appeared and swarmed all around us. They hadn't expected to have a such newsworthy story—a Negro girl competing on piano and drums winning a coveted scholarship. They focused their attention on me, throwing questions at me so fast I couldn't think straight. "How were you able to beat out all of the other outstanding music students?" "How long have you been playing the piano?" "When did you start playing the timpani?" Still in the zone of disbelief, I struggled to formulate an answer to, "How did you manage to win?

My parents didn't seem surprised at the results. They must have known something I didn't know about myself. Years later I would learn that Mum viewed my success as my own inspiration, but I thought differently. If she hadn't made me practice, I would have been out on the streets. If it weren't for my parents, I would not have become an outstanding musician.

As I became professional, playing in symphonies, ballets, Broadway shows, I encountered many types of conductors. Some were great, some mediocre and the average. Playing in these venues, I began to hear and be aware of the pecking order of how musicians were type cast depending on who they were, where they played and what they played.

The symphony orchestra musicians considered themselves superior to all other musicians. The conductor was the chief and had to lead the musicians who could not play without him. He gave the signal to start; he kept them together during the playing of the symphony or orchestral music and gave them the cut off to end the piece. As I got older with more experience and confidence, I found myself thinking back to the incredible day I spent with Duke Ellington and his band of musicians. It was a day never to be forgotten and to be used as reference.

I have been privileged to play over the years, Broadway shows including *Carnival, On a Clear Day You Could See Forever, Greenwillow* and a couple of others which didn't make it to Broadway after the out of town previews from the first composed note to its opening on Broadway. I could not help but remember how Duke operated as a composer and conductor. I compared him and his style to the top of the line, Broadway or Symphony and so on. Let me tell you what that day was like.

I was 18 and in awe of the opportunity to be in the presence of the great Duke Ellington.

As a scholarship winner, I was invited to observe and sit in a rehearsal session with his band which he would be different from when I auditioned for the scholarship. The day of the scholarship audition, the Duke was present for the final round with Dr. Peter Wilhousky, the director and conductor of the Juilliard summer school program. He sat quietly as an observer, while Dr. Wilhousky put me through the rigors of the audition.

Weeks later at the rehearsal hall, here he was with his own band, he was "Duke" the leader. His entourage included the band members, Billy Strayhorn, the famed arranger, and another man who sat at a table always with his hat on, a half-smoked cigar hanging from his mouth, and a pen in his hand. Reams of music paper were laid out on the table. All kinds of sounds from the band members playing and tuning their instruments filled the room. Then the Duke walked in. He looked taller than I had remembered from the scholarship audition.

After bantering with various band members, he strode over to the baby grand piano waiting by the bandstand. He sat down and began playing. The look on his face told me he was in his own world. Having no idea of what I was supposed to play, I sat quietly in the back of the room. The timpani were there, but no music yet.

With what seemed like magic to me, Duke was concentrating composing music while Billy converted the musical sounds coming from the piano into musical notes on paper. In what seemed like minutes, Billy had taken Duke's music, arranged it, and passed it over to the man with the cigar in his mouth who then gave the music on music paper to each musician.

Duke got up, joked with everyone, and then in a very relaxed tone said, "Okay boys, let's hit it." He gave a punching kind of down beat and the band started playing. He set them in motion without anyone first saying, "Someone play an 'A.'" There was no such step for those pros. After Duke gave the downbeat, he wandered away and just listened. Then he went to the piano and along with the band, played the new music he had just written. Whenever we played new music in the symphony orchestra, the parts were offered to the players to study days or weeks before the first recording or rehearsal. Rarely would the parts be given to musicians right before a recording or performance began, but this was what happened with the Duke and his musicians. The music just written, was passed out, looked over and played for the first time!

All the musicians in Duke's band were so in tune with one another that for the entire day, I never heard him ask any section to play softer or louder. They seemed to instinctively know how to play as a whole. At the time, I wasn't as impressed with their playing and discipline as I would be later when working with other conductors who got in the way of the music. Duke, however, would never have been asked to conduct a symphony orchestra except if his band was making a guest appearance.

As a professional playing in symphonies, ballets and Broadway shows, I encountered many types of conductors. Some were great, some mediocre and average. Playing in these venues, I became aware of the pecking order of how musicians were typecast depending on who they were, where they played and what they played.

Symphony orchestra musicians considered themselves superior to all other musicians. The conductor was the chief and had to lead the musicians who could not play without him. He gave the down beat signal to start, kept them together during the playing of the symphony or orchestral music and gave them the cut off to end the piece. As I got older and gained more experience and confidence, I often thought back to that incredible day I spent with Duke Ellington and his band of musicians. It was a day I'd never forget and would use as reference for what I thought makes a great conductor, composer and musician. I compared the Duke and his style to the top of the line professionals whether on Broadway, with a symphony or with any other production.

Observing him at that rehearsal in 1945, it was clear to me even as a young student how much Duke respected and trusted his musicians. He did not let his ego interfere with the art of making outstanding music. Unlike many conductors I would play under, I would always see Duke Ellington as a truly great musician and person!

Chapter 7

JUILLIARD TEACHERS

I had won the Duke Ellington Scholarship. I pinched myself not once, but over and over for days, weeks, because I could not believe I was going to go to Juilliard. Mom and Dad were ecstatic. They had worried first about what high school I would attend, hoping I would not have to go to the local high school, Wadleigh. Then I got into The High School of Music & Art. When I was graduating high school, they worried about what college I would attend, hoping they'd have the money to help me through school. I had expressed a leaning towards following in my aunt's footsteps and become an academic math teacher. But now their worries were placated. I was going to the most prestigious school and there would be no financial problems. I had a three- year complete scholarship!

I loved music, but never thought I would pursue it any further than high school and community music involvement. But all of a sudden I was catapulted into thinking along a different path. Not towards being a teacher, but into a school of outstanding aspiring musicians.

When I got into Music & Art, I was not as aware of the nature of the challenge facing me. This time however, I was very much aware of what was ahead of me. I was overwhelmed with people calling and writing to congratulate me. Everyone knew about my winning since it was the Duke Ellington Scholarship, the publicity was intense in every area of the media.

Only the best were accepted at Juilliard, so I felt I would have to live up to the reputation. As a result of talking to many people,

I was led to think I'd better attend the Juilliard Preparatory Summer School Program. So, I enrolled and took my first classes at Juilliard.

My first and primary class was with Saul Goodman, my teacher and timpanist with the New York Philharmonic.

There were six floors to Juilliard which was located on 122nd Street and Broadway. I was able to walk from my apartment on 150th Street and Eighth Avenue to school, although I did not do it often. The surrounding of Juilliard's location was across from the Jewish Theological Seminary and on the other side, and six blocks south was Barnard College for girls and Columbia University. An environment of learning and inspiration, and inspired I was.

I registered for the summer session. I had a timpani class, a George Wedge Theory class, and orchestra. I could not wait to get started and above all to meet Saul Goodman. The first day of the summer session, I went to the sixth floor and the percussion rooms.

I was familiar with the huge rehearsal room since that was where I played for the audition. The back of the rehearsal rooms was where all the percussion rooms were located. I went into the rooms with a sort of reverence. The rooms were decorated with pictures of almost all the percussion instruments with various men's pictures holding the instruments. There were tables with various size drum pads and in the corner, one kettledrum.

The smell of smoke permeated the room. Saul Goodman was a cigar chain smoker. There was no ban on smoking in those days—anywhere. I was to discover that Goodman always had a cigar lighted or not in his mouth, and I was soon to meet the man who was to be responsible for furthering my career. Goodman was generally late for lessons, and this the first day for my lesson he was late.

But he showed up and although I had seen him play many

times at the New York Philharmonic concerts playing the timpani, I did not realize how short he was. He entered the room through the open door. "Hello," he said, "you must be Elayne," and he held out his hand to shake mine.

"Hello, Mr. Goodman."

"Oh, you can call me Saully," he urged.

"Okay, Mr. G."

I never called him Saully or Saul, as all his other students did.

He was even shorter than I thought he would be. It was just like with me. People always thought I was taller because in the orchestra, all the other players were sitting and we stood behind our timpani so there was no way to compare us as if we were standing side by side. People just looked at where our heads were which of course were above all the others.

So here I was about to take lessons from the great Saul Goodman. My teacher, Bernard Weiss, at Music & Art was a trumpet player but was also the instructor for percussion. Therefore, a trumpet teacher studied also the trombone, tuba and depending on the person, also the French horn and included was some percussion.

My teacher had some percussion lessons, so I would imagine he was maybe a step or two ahead of me. He taught me enough however that I was able to progress at music and art and eventually played in the senior orchestra.

Here at Juilliard, I was now with the real teacher. So, in a sense I was a beginner, and he treated me thus. But I thought to myself that since I had played in the senior orchestra and the All City Band, I knew a thing or two.

What was my first lesson going to be like? All the instruments have scales to play or a piece of some sort to demonstrate their level of ability. What we had as percussionist were the rudiments—all 26 of them. This I had learned and practiced faithfully. It was not difficult for me because as a pianist, I had developed the discipline of practicing my scales and exercises.

So, the first thing Goodman asked was, "How are your rudiments?"

"Not so bad, I think."

In this room was a table with the drum pad, which we use to practice on. Whenever a child says to the parent "I want to learn to play the drums," the first thing the parent says is, "What! Play the drums with all that noise and banging?"

Well, what they do not realize is that when you are learning, you play on a piece of very hard rubber which is glued on top of a square piece of wood. It gives almost the same feeling as hitting a drum without the sound. With this the student is able to practice without disturbing anyone.

So here in this room was a drum pad plus a set of timpani, but playing on that came later. I brought my mallets with me but Goodman gave me a pair of his mallets. "Here, play with these, they are mine which I am developing. Here, try them," he urged. So, I took his drum sticks which were indeed different from what I had. I played around a bit with them at the same time warming up my hands.

Goodman, in the meantime, waited and watched me warming up. Then, he said, "Okay now, play some paradiddles going from slow to fast, then piano to fortissimo." I played what he asked and he shook his head in approval. Then he said, "How's your roll? Play the roll open, then closed, piano to forte."

This I did with no problem, to which he said: "You have good hands and good dynamic control. Let's see now how you read."

Then he put some snare drum music on the stand and said, "How about reading this for me?"

It so happened that I was familiar with the book, but none-the-less, I would have had no problem reading the music. After all, I was a pianist and reading music presented no problem for me, unlike the other drummers who had no piano background.

After playing, Goodman was very impressed with me. By this time, our first hour together was over in what seemed like minutes. I was very happy because I made a good impression, and Goodman was obviously pleased. This was the beginning of a very successful relationship. The other students would claim that Goodman taught me all he knew unlike the other students. I did not think there was anything wrong with that until one guy said Goodman feared competition from the male students so he held back, but did not fear that I would be competition because how could I compete when there was no place for me to go as a girl? But later, he played a major role in my winning the job when I auditioned to play with the New York City Opera. We might all had thought there was no place to go, but I absorbed everything he had to offer.

Saul Goodman became the timpanist of the New York Philharmonic when he was a teenager. His teacher, Alfred Friese, became ill and Goodman had to sub. Story goes that Goodman played so well that Friese took an early retirement. Goodman proved to be not only a fine player, but also a musician. He had perfect pitch and he was innovative and creative. He developed a style of playing in which he eclipsed the timpanist in all the famed orchestras.

Goodman taught his style of playing which became the premier style of playing. The first thing he taught was how to hold the timpani mallets and how to strike the drum. Prior to Goodman, the stroke was a downward motion, Goodman's concern was getting the best sound out of the timpani. He experimented with the best way to make a distinctive sound. His method of attack was upward rather than downward. You rebound the mallet as you struck the drum. His objective was to put the vibrations of the drum in motion. If the contact of the mallet on the drum head lasted too long—a period of split second—it would interfere or muffle the vibrations. As a result, the drum had a resonance that was deep and penetrating. Essentially what he was doing was stroking the drum rather than just banging. As a result, the discerning musicians listening

to his playing the timpani, heard a unique sound. Every one
began to pay attention to the timpani not as just another drum
in the percussion section, but a musical instrument providing
not only rhythm, but melodic resonance.

I practiced very hard to execute the Goodman style. I also
worked hard to hold the mallet, gripping it between the thumb
and forefinger. After years of playing, I developed a very special
muscle at the base of my thumb and forefinger. Goodman
devised exercises for me to develop my arms for power. The
male students loved to kid me, that I was too skinny and little
to be able to play forte on the timpani like a man. It was a
challenge for both Goodman and me. Thus, his creation of
exercises which he later composed and compiled into his first
Exercise Book for Timpani. Whenever I had a problem executing a
passage, he would write an exercise for me.

Goodman gave the timpani the respect comparable to the
concertmaster or even all the principal players of the other
sections, such as the principal oboe, flute, clarinet and so on. His
playing took on such a dominance that it was called the "second
conductor." Because of its size and sound and the way he
played, the timpani took on a dominant role in the orchestra.
Players began to watch the conductor and listen to the timpani.
In order to lead enough to be followed, you had to know the
music. Goodman created another exercise—listening to all the
music that we would play in the orchestra. One day he brought
in to the school a record player with a Beethoven symphony. He
said, "Today we are going to learn this symphony just by
listening and looking at the music." So, he put the timpani part
to the symphony which he brought from the orchestra on the
music stand, and put on the record. What I had to do was listen
and play along with the record. There was no conductor to keep
the beat, or indicate the sections which were going slower or
faster, louder or softer, or give you the cue when to play. When
the record started, you had to hear the tempo and listen for your

entrance, then play along.

It was a marvelous exercise. It taught you to listen, to keep your rhythm—because if you played too slow or fast, you did not keep up with the record. Then you really had to learn and memorize the music. We went through all the symphonies of Hayden, Beethoven, Schubert, Schumann and Brahms. So that by the time I had to play in the orchestra, I was able to go through with no problems.

Goodman was also responsible for creating ensemble playing for percussion. Everyone is familiar with chamber music which included strings, woodwinds and brass ensembles. But there was nothing written for percussion. There were compositions in which there were more than two or three players. These compositions were of Berlioz, Stravinsky, Tchaikovsky. So, Goodman took these works and made them into ensemble for us. Over the years, this led to composers seeing the vast possibilities of the percussion with so many sounds and instruments that the repertoire now is vast. Goodman did much to make percussion have musical respectability. We were no longer seen as just "the drummers."

It was required that all students who are percussion majors would have to learn to play all the percussion instruments which are in groups:

(1) the tuned drums - the timpani

(2) the mallet - which has a keyboard like the piano but is played with mallets, the xylophone, marimba, glockenspiel

(3) rhythmic instruments - snare drum and all related instruments

(4) All others, like bass drum, cymbals and the little sound effects like triangle, wood block, tambourine.

Each of these instruments had a specific way of playing them, which we had to learn. There was another teacher who taught everything except the timpani. He was Morris "Moe" Goldenberg. He was a fabulous mallet player and played mallets for almost every top orchestra in New York. I took lessons from Moe on xylophone. He was a very loose-limbed person in playing and discipline. You can really only play mallet instruments if you are loose limbed, and precise at the same time. It required very concentrated practicing because it was hard to be precise and accurate. I had again, one advantage over the other students. I was a pianist. Piano was my major but over the years, it took a back seat. But I was very proficient in the familiarity with scales and keys. So, Moe was very lenient with me. I never excelled at playing xylophone although I did play xylophone and glockenspiel in many B'way shows.

But it was the ensemble classes that Goodman set up which with Moe's input we learned to play all the percussion instruments. Moe also had great technique playing the tambourine which he taught all of us. All the percussionists who came out of the classes and ensemble of Goodman and Goldenberg eventually landed jobs in the major orchestra. First, however, we had to apply what we learned in ensemble in the orchestra.

It is amazing how we grew. When I attended Music & Art, I progressed through the levels of orchestras. There was an orchestra for every year: Third Term Orchestra, Fourth Term, Fifth, Sixth, Seventh and finally the Eighth Term or Senior Orchestra. That was what we all aimed for. I went from Third, Fifth to Eighth. When we got into the Senior Orchestra, we felt very important. Our conductor, Mr. Richter, taught us all he knew and made us feel as though we had already reached being professional. Then, I was confronted with reality of the Juilliard Orchestra, a step up from both the Music & Art experience and the other group I played with, the All City High School Band. The thing is to go in with confidence that you know what you are doing, but at the same time, be humble and ready to learn that you really know nothing.

I had attended the Juilliard Summer Program before

beginning my first-year semester. I played of course in the summer school orchestra with the teacher and conductor, Peter J. Wilhousky. He was the examiner when I won the Duke Ellington Scholarship. We spent almost the entire summer on one program. This orchestra was made up of high school students who went to academic schools and studied music privately. They needed to get orchestral experiences to improve their grades and then there were a few like me who were getting advance experience before Mr. Wilhousky treated the orchestra more like a class of instrumentalists. We went over and over passages with every section. For me, it was very boring. The pieces we were playing had very little timpani and when I did not play timpani I just had a note or two on the triangle.

Goodman used to joke with me and say, "Get used to hanging around waiting to play," but this was Mr. Wilhousky's style since I could not remember going through so many starts and stops at Music & Art. This Juilliard summer school orchestra was almost the same level as the Music & Art orchestra. But conductors are really like teachers. Each teacher has an approach to the students in preparation for an exam or a concert. I actually liked Mr. Wilhousky. He was very sweet but pedantic. We repeated it so much that to this day I still remember "Goldmark Wedding Music" but I blocked out the rest.

When the school year semester began officially, I could not wait to experience Juilliard and what it represented. Going to summer school put me at ease with the rest of the students. I can only say, it is a good thing I went to summer school. I did not have to cope with both the new school, new teachers and new students. I just had the students and that was more than I could handle.

I had a major adjustment when I went from junior high school to Music & Art that was from all black, girl students to all white, very smart children. I did not really begin to catch up until my senior year. My music ability and athletics prowess, kept me on balance (I was voted the athletic award when I graduated along with a young boy). I got a special award from the Police Athletic League (PAL) and was in the ARISTA for music. But in everything else I did not feel equal in any sense. I sat in the back and kept my mouth shut. For the most part, I was ashamed of how I spoke, the way I looked and my lack of academic skills. Perhaps if I had that I would have felt better about myself. But it was music that opened the door to the world and gave me a sense of pride. Then I won the Duke Ellington Scholarship and I put everything behind me. My picture was in the papers and I was being applauded by the world.

Here I was at Juilliard registering and getting my program. The teachers at Music & Art were kind to me, seeing I was, to them, a very conscientious student. So, they gave me in the end very respectable grades which followed me to Juilliard. But in spite of that, the damage was already done. I saw myself as being capable only in music. We were given an outline of Juilliard and what it had to offer. It was known, of course, as a premier school for music, second only to Curtis Institute of Music in Philadelphia. But it did offer a credible academic curriculum.

We were assigned teachers or counselors to guide us in mapping out our design for our expectations and goals for graduating. I have no recollection of the teacher assigned to me. All I know is that we did not understand each other. She was not prepared to understand where I, a black youngster from Harlem was coming from emotionally. Basically, I was scared to death. Although Juilliard was a small school compared to most colleges and universities, it was larger than Music & Art which it too was smaller than most public high schools. But I felt very small and insignificant until I received some special attention, being the winner of the scholarship. The two boys who won the scholarship with me did not seem to have the same concerns. They could blend in.

The teacher guiding me did not have a clue of how to put me on the right track. So, she gave me overview of my class requirements and what were the requirements. I was at Juilliard, but here she was giving me languages, math, history, science. I thought I had left all that behind me. That was not what I wanted to pursue. I struggled at Music & Art and did not think I could face it again. I wanted to go where I was better suited to being comfortable.

Though she was a guidance counselor, she was not a psychiatrist. She could not understand me and the miscalculating I had of myself. It was not until many years later, that I came to the realization of what my fears were and how they developed. I did very well in academics at Junior High School 136. My parents, being strict, made me practice and do my homework. The teachers at the School were all white and we were all black. More often than not, they did not extend themselves to teach us, and if there were discipline problems, they taught nothing while commenting that we would amount to nothing but maids anyhow. The combination of their limited teaching and my parents' insistence of me working hard at what little they offered made me appear to be very smart. I had an average of 95 and that plus my music ability got me into Music & Art High School. The requirement for Music & Art was, outstanding grades in academics and talent in music. I made both getting into the school. I was then faced with students who had the high grades, but theirs were legitimate. They had gone to schools which, to them, they would say were lacking in quality, but their teachers did what they could to make up for the lack . Therefore, my 95+ average did not measure up to their 95+ average. As a result, my first year at Music & Art, my average dropped to 50. I unfortunately, interpreted it as meaning I was not smart. That stuck in my mind and contributed to my lack of self-confidence in everything but music.

As I sat that day going over my graduation requirements, I

resisted taking any course that involved academics, my nemesis. Most of the academic classes were held a few blocks down from Juilliard at Columbia University at 116th Street. Even that scared me. I did not want to be embarrassed going to Columbia, whose reputation was to enroll the brightest students. I then opted not to go that route. So, to guarantee I would have the necessary credits to graduate, I made it up by taking every course Juilliard had to offer in music. If my guidance counselor was aware of the rationale behind my rejecting taking these credits which would lead to getting a B.A. instead of a diploma, I would have succeeded. How I regretted not taking the required subjects and getting a degree, because racism had invaded my self-image and belief in my intelligence.

Once I rejected the academics, I made out my schedule with a full load of subjects in music: timpani and percussion, theory, ear training, sight singing, piano (which by now became my minor, rather than my major) conducting, music history and composition.

Students at Juilliard came from many states in the country. They all had an attitude of being special. There appeared to be a hierarchy with the piano and string players supposedly the top musicians. So, I found myself taking a back seat in all my classes. I hardly remember my teachers. It was very much the same reaction I had to the teachers at Music & Art. As we keep moving up from one stage in life to another, we encounter the same fears on a higher level. I was coming into Juilliard with credentials from an outstanding school and a scholarship winner—enough to make one feel good about oneself. But I was not a pianist, a violinist or voice major. I was a black woman in the percussion section, who was considered neither outstanding, unique or odd. So, I had to start from square one in proving myself to me and to them, that I belonged among them as I have had to do all my life, so far.

It is interesting that I do not remember my teachers from

Juilliard, other than those connected to my instrument. I loved the subjects that I was taking and looked forward to going to classes every day. I even managed to find a reason to go on Sunday. I had to practice, I told myself and others. I could not miss a day of practice. Neither did any of the other students. Practicing was important to almost all of us. So, there were many students in the practice rooms. They had to sign up for rooms. I was fortunate. Since there were fewer percussion students, getting to practice was not as combative.

The assignments given by the teachers were not as demanding as Music & Art. The teachers were very conscientious and made demands on us. Now it is quite possible that they were not so tough, when I later compared them to the uncaring teachers I had at Junior High School 136. I got together quite frequently with my classmates from Music & Art, and of course, somehow at some point, the experiences we had with our teachers, varied significantly. They did not think the teachers were demanding, and depending on what junior high school they came from, some of my classmates—those who came from communities in which the expectations were very high—did not feel as though they derived much from their Music & Art academic education.

There was a similar interpretation about the music instruction. Again, some kids entered Music & Art having had already advanced study in their instrument. Those of us who were beginners with their instrument like me, who was a piano student, who were required to take an orchestral instrument, looked to our instructors through different lenses. My past experience, made everyone I came in contact with, seem like the highest in authority, so I looked up to everyone. I questioned very little, so by the time I reached Juilliard, I had become a little more knowledgeable. I learned from my Music & Art teachers, but I was also learning a good deal from my classmates. They had tread along paths I knew nothing about. There was a world out there way beyond anything I could imagine, living in Harlem. Going to the movies was the closest we got to that world, but it was more like a fantasy which never entered our reality. I grew away from Harlem and its limitations and absorbed the new world opened to me on this new path of life. I left my Harlem friends behind.

Stepping into Juilliard opened new paths. Many years later when I was playing in Leopold Stokowski's orchestra, he gave us a philosophy that explained the nature of life. He often said, "Life is not a plateau, you are either growing, developing and getting better, or you are deteriorating." Although I was not aware of it, I was growing and was aware of it when I had difficulty relating to my friends in my neighborhood.

My time spent in Music & Art was extremely challenging and I worked very hard to catch-up. So, going from Music & Art to Juilliard was not as big a leap as it was going from Junior High School 136 to Music & Art. I did not feel the pressure which might have accounted to why my relation to the Juilliard teachers was different.

Chapter 8

TANGLEWOOD
One of the Happiest Times in My Life

High in western Massachusetts, the Berkshire Mountains created a magnificent natural site that looked like a scenic movie backdrop. Deep green pine forests, azure skies, ice blue lakes. Impressive for a person coming from an environment where "mountains" were made of dirty red and gray brick, the asphalt jungle. . As I stood gazing at this marvel of nature, I couldn't believe how events had unfolded to bring me, at 21 and still a skinny little girl from Harlem, to Tanglewood, one of the most prestigious music camps in the country.

I had first heard about Tanglewood during a concert at Carnegie Hall. I found out it was a program for music students who, by passing an audition, could spend the entire summer living and working with members of the famed Boston Symphony Orchestra. Being at Tanglewood meant being totally involved in and surrounded by music, music and more music. Intrigued by the prospect, I discussed the possibility with my teacher, Saul Goodman, who surmised it would be an invaluable experience for me. My parents were delighted at the idea and encouraged me to try out since they knew how much playing in an orchestra meant to me.

Right away I wrote to the Boston Symphony Orchestra for the particulars: the date and place of the audition and the music we would be required to play. Timpani repertoire is nowhere near as wide as that for strings, but the musical demands are equally great. As the appointed day arrived, I became more excited about going and more apprehensive about what I was getting myself into. The auditions were regional with some prospective students auditioning in cities other than New York.

I ended up playing well enough to be accepted and to receive a scholarship! My parents and I were overjoyed. Unlike the other kids in my Harlem neighborhood, I had never been to summer camp. My parents said it was because they couldn't afford to send me, but I always suspected the real reason was that they didn't want to let me out of their sight. Tanglewood would be different; it was a study camp and for music at that. They were proud their daughter would be spending a summer at not just at any camp, but with renowned musicians. By the time the day of my departure rolled around, everyone at St. Luke's Episcopal Church and everyone else in the neighborhood knew about my upcoming adventure.

I traveled north with Nina Lugavoy and Charles Libove— two talented musicians; she was a pianist, he was a violinist, and both were students. At the end of a four-hour scenic drive, we got lost after reaching the small town of Lenox, Massachusetts. The directions said the Tanglewood grounds were located down the road about three miles. We drove back and forth several times but couldn't find it. Perhaps it was in the opposite direction, we thought. So, we took the road towards Pittsfield, but it wasn't there either. Between Lenox and Pittsfield, we saw nothing but woods and an occasional house. Whenever we stopped anyone to ask for directions to Tanglewood, they said, "Oh, it's back down the road that-a-way" and pointed us in the opposite direction.

The residents of Lenox weren't all that enthusiastic about the music camp. They were mostly annoyed about the invasion of their privacy during its six-week tenure, even though not enough cars drove through there to cause even a minor traffic jam. Eventually their attitudes would change as the Tanglewood festival became a major event and brought with it increased revenue and vast development or, some would say, destruction of the beautiful woods.

We finally found Tanglewood by a beautiful coincidence. While driving back down the road for the third or fourth time we noticed a snazzy red Plymouth convertible with New York plates cruising ahead of us. The handsome driver looked familiar so we followed him more for the fun of it than anything else. He led us right to the Tanglewood entrance. We had passed it several times, but because it appeared to be a private estate we made no effort to trespass.

Once we got through the gates, no one stopped us, much to our surprise and relief. We continued following the red Plymouth that brought us to the west green field. It turned out that our leader was Leonard Bernstein, who would later lead us in concert. As a result of following Bernstein, we were among the first to arrive on that late Saturday morning. It seems that all the other newcomers also got lost until a direction sign was placed at the entrance.

I was at Tanglewood! The atmosphere was different from that at The High School of Music & Art with its white intelligentsia. At that time, I had felt uncomfortably inferior to those around me. At Juilliard, I had continued the Herculean effort to climb out of the depths of my inferiority complex while mingling with those considered the cream of the crop. At Tanglewood, though, I was transported to a heaven where I could interact with the kind of people I had long respected and idolized. I took a deep breath of pure, country air and felt that I was exactly where I was meant to be at last.

After several hours as everyone staggered in, we were given our room assignments and maps of the grounds. In the distance stood a large white structure called the shed which would eventually be the auditorium for the concerts by the Boston Symphony Orchestra and the Tanglewood students. Schedules of rehearsals, lessons and performances were handed out by section: strings, woodwinds, voice, piano, brass and percussion. We were not to live on the grounds of Tanglewood. Instead, our accommodations were about five miles outside Lenox. The women's dormitory was set up at what was the Lenox School for Boys, a boarding school for young boys during the regular academic year. The men's dorm was a magnificent estate turned over every summer to Tanglewood's sponsor, the Berkshire Music School. Most of the chamber music performances were scheduled in the impressively large Victorian style living room there.

The remainder of our first day was devoted to learning our way around and meeting our roommates. When I got to my room, my roommate was already there. She was a tall, intense and obviously nervous young woman with a caramel-colored complexion.

"Hi," she said as I walked into the little room we were to share for the next six weeks.

"Hi," I answered, also feeling apprehensive.

This was my first experience at living away from home and sharing my room with another person—and me a sibling-less, 21-year-old! Although all my student activities and musical experiences since entering high school had been with white students, this was my first time actually *living* in a white environment.

"Hey, I'm glad we're together," she said, appearing to relax a little, seeing I was the same skin color.. "What's your name?"

"Elayne Jones—and yours?"

"Julie Perry. I'm from the Chicago," she volunteered. "I plan to write the great Negro American Symphony," she quickly informed me. "What do you do? Are you a voice student?"

"No, I'm in the orchestra."

"You are?" she exclaimed with great interest and surprise. "What instrument do you play?"

"Guess," I challenged mischievously.

"Well, I don't know where to start because I've never seen a black person in any orchestra, that is, a symphony orchestra, but I would guess first the piano since every Negro child I know takes piano lessons. But," and here she seemed to reason with herself. "You don't find that in an orchestra. I must admit, I'm puzzled — tell me," she finished.

I briefly toyed with the idea of continuing the guessing game, but chose to reserve that for whites. I revealed to her, "I play the timpani. Kettledrums."

Julie was startled. "You are a girl and black, too, playing an instrument like that? I just don't believe it. I have never seen a Negro and a woman playing timpani. You are so little," she went on. "How can you play those big instruments?"

"Well," I informed her, "it has been an uphill battle." Then without yet unpacking our bags and getting ourselves settled into the room, I heard myself recounting to her the events that led to my being there. "Sure, I am little and all the boys in my percussion classes throughout Music & Art and Juilliard continually challenged my ability to play the timpani and especially, to execute the dynamic range of fortissimo because that required power and strength. But look at my muscles." I held my hands out to Julia. She touched the well-developed muscles at the base of my thumbs and first fingers and then gingerly tapped my forceps.

"Wow!" she exclaimed. "That's beautiful."

"Muscles aren't the most important criteria for playing timpani," I hastened to add. "Since for the most part you and I know you don't have fortissimo continuously. That usually only happens during the climax of the piece. So for the most part, they only used 'string it' as a way of keeping me out. It's ironic because I didn't choose the drums. I was given them at Music & Art by teachers who jokingly said that since all blacks have rhythm I should take the drums. Little did they know I would pursue this as my profession. So here I am in spite of all the efforts of so many to discourage me." I paused, feeling like I'd talked a lot about myself. "Tell me, how did you become a composer, Julia? I know how difficult it must be to submit a composition which would reward you with admission to Tanglewood."

"Well, as you know, most of us Negroes get our music in the churches," she explained. "Both my parents played for our little Sunday church services. They directed the choirs and each took turns giving music lessons to the adult and young people's groups. I went along with them to everything and absorbed lessons from them. I say absorbed lessons because like the cobbler's children who don't have shoes they never had time to give me music instruction. I played the piano by ear, picked up theory and harmony and just found myself making up tunes. Writing music for instruments other than the piano came about by listening to Duke Ellington, but one time our class was taken to hear the Chicago Youth Orchestra. That had a profound impact on me, and I've often wondered whether that was because all the kids in the class said they hated the music."

Julia took a breath. "I loved it," she said with deep reverence. I nodded quietly and smiled to show that I understood. "Hey," she laughed, jumping up and breaking the moment of silence. "We'd better start unpacking. The jitney will be here pretty soon to take us back to the grounds."

"Yeah, you're right," I agreed, grabbing my suitcase. "But don't leave me hanging. Where did you study composition?" As we quickly unpacked, Julia continued her story.

"My parents began to take my creative venture seriously and consulted with other choir leaders from larger and more influential churches. They recommended the Chicago Institute of Music. I went for a test and received a scholarship. That was the beginning of my torment. I had to persevere because the instructors who were white weren't at all tactful in trying to discourage me. They naturally assumed I didn't have the cultural background to understand much less write for classical groups. They wanted me to write for gospel or jazz." Julia stopped unpacking and looked at me with determination in her eyes.

"But I *wouldn't*," she continued emphatically. "I intend to write about what I feel! Here at Tanglewood with Aaron Copeland as head of the composition department, I intend to learn as much as I can, so let's get settled and go and face our challenges."

"Yes!" I agreed, even more inspired to make the most of this experience.

We spent the next few hours meeting the other students. We exchanged names, instruments, ambitions and goals. Then we investigated the acres and acres of Tanglewood. We learned that the shed was the center of the grounds. Its enormous stage could accommodate up to 200 orchestra musicians and 200 chorus members if necessary. Around the shed was seating for about 2,000 with an unobstructed view of the stage.

There were many rooms backstage where all the theory classes were held, and rooms where we could practice. Best of all, we could practice out in the woods that surrounded the grounds. Imagine going over your part for Beethoven's Sixth Symphony, which we were scheduled to perform that summer, with real honest-to-goodness birds to accompany you.

The main grounds rested peacefully about a one-mile walk from the serene Lake Housatonic. A stream gurgled near the rear exit of the shed. When I followed that brook, I went along a path surrounded by the heavy branches of overhanging weeping willows. Not only was I going to learn much about music, I was quickly adding more to my knowledge of nature than I ever imagined. Born and raised in the asphalt jungle, I knew little about trees, birds and flowers so it was all so refreshing and new. The path ended suddenly in a clearing with the expanse of the lake peacefully rippling before me. I had made that first adventure by myself because I was in the habit of going off on my own. Perhaps due to being an only child, the years of going to baseball games and other places by myself, or still being shy about initiating activities with white people.

I didn't see my two driving companions the first couple of days and made no attempt to seek them out since they were "going together" and I didn't like being the odd person. Actually, I was glad to be alone. I didn't think anyone else would be as awed as I was at the sight of the lake and I didn't want to be embarrassed. As others came down the path, though, I discovered I was wrong. The beauty of the wide expanse of water was incredible even to them as well whether seeing it for the first or the hundredth time.

When the jitney returned us to our quarters, Julia and I discovered something distressing. The rooms were extremely sparse with two cots, a foot locker and no mirrors. I assumed boys never required such mundane things as mirrors, but we women being what we are had to have reflections of ourselves. The only place for that was in the bathroom. But it wasn't a typical bathroom, at least not for us and especially for one as shy as me. The large room had six sinks, and over them the much-needed mirrors. Three shower stalls without curtains stood at the far end. Not a bathtub was in sight. And lo and behold, six toilets with no doors took up the rest of the space.

It didn't take long for our anxieties to surface. Julia had also spent the afternoon exploring alone. Our aloneness brought us together, less as close friends—we never did become close—but more as two people lost in a foreign world together. That bathroom was frightening to us. It was obvious we had to share it with several girls housed in neighboring rooms.

Julia came from a black ghetto in Chicago, which meant living in a small apartment with her mother, father and brother. Their apartment included a bathroom with a toilet and a bathtub. And, of course, I only had to share my bathroom at home with its sink, tub and toilet, with Mom and Dad.

"Isn't it interesting," she said, "that in the slums there was never any such thing as a shower." She furrowed her brow as contemplated. "I wonder why showers enjoyed by whites were considered too good for us. Is taking a shower a luxury?"

We stood there facing the prospect of exposed toilets and showers. The thought was devastating. Since my high school days, I had never been able to stand in front of a mirror when white girls were present, always primping and combing their hair. After all those years, I was still self-conscious about my hair and face and I knew Julia was too even though we never admitted it to each other. But by some deep secret understanding, she and I managed to avoid the bathroom in spite of any discomfort we might suffer, until no one else was there. As the weeks sped by during which time we each developed friendships among the white female students, we would never feel comfortable with them in front of the mirror.

The next day after arriving was Sunday with Tanglewood's formal opening exercise which took place on the manicured lawn. By then all the faculty, made up primarily of players from the Boston Symphony Orchestra had arrived on the grounds. It was awesome—and totally unlike my introduction to either Music & Art or Juilliard. Here were college graduates and young adults ready to take that all-important step across the threshold into the professional world occupied by the top people in the profession. The Boston Symphony Orchestra was ranked among the top four American orchestras the other three being the New York Philharmonic, the Philadelphia Symphony and the Chicago Symphony. Only the Boston Symphony Orchestra, however, had a program that gave perspective musicians the opportunity not only to be coached by them but to live with them and see them as human beings pursuing their professional and personal lives.

We were introduced to members of the staff that included:

Boris Goldowsky, opera director; his assistant, Sarah Caldwell; Eleazor de Carvallo, conducting teacher; Leonard Bernstein, conductor; Irving Fine, composition; Aaron Copeland, composition; Zvi Zeitlin, violinist; Lucas Foss, pianist and Hugh Ross, choral coordinator.

Copeland rose to speak. "We are told that you were all especially chosen from throughout the country representing the best talents," he said. "We are sure each of you will continue not only to fulfill our hopes for your success as professional musicians, but could make your own name as well. Everyone here is dedicated towards this end and we expect a superb summer of music." He continued.

"We have accepted each student based on ability, background and experience. There are some of you who showed great talent and musicianship and although you did not have much training or experience, we thought you would grow in this environment. Some of you cannot really be considered students anymore since you may have already played professionally, but I feel a musician is always a student. I assure you that this kind of balance will certainly benefit all." I listened closely to Copeland's every word.

"Monday—that's tomorrow—just before the full orchestra rehearsal, each instrumentalist will meet with the head of their section. During that time, it will be determined what level you are and you will be seated accordingly. Now, I can just hear some of you worrying about being stuck in one position without a chance to move up. Don't fret. No seating assignment is permanent. So those of you on first stand must work to stay there and those of you in the back can work to move up. It should be fun and enjoyable for all."

When Copeland finished, we orchestra students were called by sections and introduced to our coaches, as were the singers, both operatic and choral. The warmth of the whole occasion melted any of my remaining apprehension. Despite the air of seriousness and high expectations, the calm, tranquil country atmosphere prevailed and I felt no pressure. Five white male students and I were assigned to Boston Symphony Orchestra timpani player, Roman Schultz. Once, while I was a student at Juilliard, I had observed him playing during a concert of Beethoven's Ninth Symphony and noticed a difference in style between him and my teacher, Saul Goodman. I was singing in a chorus made up of students from Juilliard at the time, who were not necessarily voice students but who loved the music whether singing or playing.

The other percussion players said hello to me as we gathered around Mr. Schultz. Their greetings were cordial but noticeably quizzical. "Hi, are you playing timpani or percussion?" came a query from a tall, heavyset New Yorker.

"Timpani!" I replied emphatically. The fellow New Yorker knew me, so his question was totally unnecessary. I knew what he was up to. He just couldn't face my presence because of our past confrontation at Juilliard. The incident was unfortunately repeated here in Tanglewood and would be repeated all my professional life. At the time, in those beautiful surroundings, it never entered my thinking that I would have to cope over and over again with the negativity of those colleagues.

Mr. Schultz welcomed us, not at all aware of the beginning of dissension in our ranks. He made no issue of my presence so I liked him. He was German and I figured he was in his sixties. He motioned us to come close and said in halting English with a German accent, "I look forward to seeing you tomorrow, Monday morning. We shall have sectional rehearsals for the first hour then we shall all get together with the whole orchestra for rehearsal." He anticipated our next question.

"Yes, I see there are six of you and only one timpani part. Each of you will have a chance to play and can observe one another before the rehearsal. I will appoint who will play. I will try to be fair and judge only on the quality of your playing during the week."

My work was cut out for me. I must challenge those individuals who already seemed to be smug and bent on ignoring my presence as some sort of threat. I felt very much alone.

When Mr. Schultz said, "I will appoint who will play," a chill ran through my body. I feared having a similar incidence happen here in this beautiful environment. The scenario regardless could be repeated. There were six of us who wanted to play but there was one player for every composition. Unless the composition had percussion, this relegated the other players to standing around watching, listening but not playing. I remembered Goodman referring to this dilemma by telling us, "You will just have to consider this a part of your training."

This might have gone by with no real obvious dissention. What emerged however, was resistance the first time. Goodman selected me to play timpani ahead of the other students. They couldn't really challenge Goodman's decision, but they made it clear to me that they didn't approve of his choice.

I caught the eyes of some of the players in the other sections. They seemed more receptive to me perhaps by not being in the string, woodwind or brass section I wasn't a threat to them. Some people even seemed genuinely glad to see a young Negro girl in the orchestra.

"Hey, what's your name?"

"Where are you from?

"How come you play the percussion?"

But the strangest question of all was, "How come you're here?"

Would they ask that of a white student? Certainly not. But I got it continuously. How to answer? Should I respond seriously, frivolously, facetiously or angrily? They also asked, "How did you become a musician?" and even more so, "How did you become a timpani player?" I had to acknowledge that I was an oddity and that I was dealing with honest but limited people, in an obviously non-traditional situation. Whether I liked it or not, it was my job to educate them whenever and however I could. I had to look on my questioners as unenlightened babes in the woods. They saw themselves as the epitome of musical erudition but I saw them as lacking in perspective.

From opening day on at Tanglewood, cliques immediately fell into place. String players gathered together as did woodwinds and brass. In my section, the five white guys formed their own group. As the only girl and the only black, I didn't fit in. After the ceremony, the jitney arrived to return us to our rooms. I couldn't find Julia so I climbed on and sat in the first available seat on the jitney. Everyone aboard was excited, animated and singing. It turned out they were girls in the chorus. I was drawn in immediately to the laughing and vocalizing. Their cheer was infectious.

I sat next to a girl who right away said to me, "I didn't see you in the church."

"Right you are," I confirmed. "I'm in the orchestra."

"Oh," she said. "What is your name?" without asking what instrument I played.

"Elayne, and yours?"

"Norma—I'm impressed that you're in the orchestra. You must be a serious musician."

"Well, aren't you?" I questioned.

"Not really," she admitted. She volunteered that her parents manufactured shoes in Boston and had a home in Cape Cod, but they wanted her to have some culture and encouraged her to attend Tanglewood. They attended concerts of the Boston Symphony Orchestra and heard about the summer and thought it would be good for her.

"I decided to come just so I could get to meet different people," Norma said. "It wasn't expensive for my parents so it wasn't important how good I was because they could afford to pay for me and also contribute to the school fund."

I liked her immediately even after she told me of her background. It was diametrically opposite to my life. I had gotten a scholarship and knew I couldn't have spent such a summer if I had had to depend on my parents' contribution. By the time we reached our dorm, a five-minute ride, Norma and I had become friendly enough to want to continue our encounter.

Our friendship began there and would continue for years to come. At first, it seemed like a strange relationship. She had money but no talent; I had talent but no money. Her parents were upper middle class Jewish business people who owned a shoe factory. My parents were middle class Barbadians who worked at menial jobs beneath their station. Norma had never ventured outside her environment which traveled with her each summer when they went to their Cape Cod retreat.

"I grew to hate going there," Norma confided weeks later. "The only thing we didn't take with us was the names of the streets in Haverhill. It was the same dishes, same people, and same arguments. It was almost impossible to escape the clutches of these insulated over protective cultures. My parents naturally believed they had my best interest at heart. They went from one generation to the other—never changing. It was clear to all of us that they could feel safe with their old friends and customs. Anything from the outside was a threat."

Following that first meeting, Norma and I saw each other every day and had the opportunity to exchange many ideas in great depth. The initial question in my mind was how she broke away. Her explanation added to why she and I developed our friendship.

"All the households in their little community had maids and my home was no exception. Matty, the girl who worked for us, was around ever since I could remember. She gave my brother and me breakfast, dressed us and took us to school, picked us up from school, gave us dinner and put us to bed."

As Norma related this life, her eyes glowed warmly the way people's expressions soften when speaking of a very special past love. As she went on, it was obvious she felt a great deal of endearment for this woman. "Matty used to sing to me every night. I didn't know what kind of church she attended but I loved her singing. Now I know she was singing spirituals but at the time all I knew is that she opened my ear to other singers and I found I loved not only listening but I, too, wanted to sing."

Norma explained to me the difference between Jewish synagogues and Christian churches. "The cantor does most of the singing and very rarely were women allowed to participate in the choruses in temple."

This was interesting to me because although I had gone to Music & Art with most Jewish kids, many did not attend synagogue or temple. Norma was really the first person I got to know well who came from a traditional religious Jewish household. I was the first black person she ever got to know well who wasn't a maid, even though at some points in her life she met the children of black women who worked for her mother's friends.

A strange and ironic bond indeed for the daughter of the maid and the daughter of the madam to find ourselves drawn to each other at Tanglewood, brought together by the warm care and loving singing of another black domestic. Like sociologists, we both observed the relationships we had with our respective roommates. We each had been paired with girls from the same backgrounds. Yet I never got close to Julia, and Norma didn't feel a kinship with her roommate.

"Shari is so unlike me even though we come from the same city with similar Jewish backgrounds," Norma observed with disappointment after several days. "She has very little interest in the music program and only attempts to exploit her looks to hook a guy. I really can't stand her. Lucky for me I met you?" I, too, found it easier to talk and confide in Norma than in Julia.

Apparently, similitude was not necessarily conclusive to being simpatico.

I couldn't wait to get to the first orchestra rehearsal, being singularly nervous about working with Schultz, the Boston Symphony Orchestra timpanist. The only timpani teacher I ever had was Saul Goodman at Juilliard. I had grown up with him and he too grew up with me. He never really said directly to me that he didn't think I would make it through the college. But every time I executed some difficult passage, he called the other percussion teacher, Moe Goldenberg, a highly respected and the best mallet player, to come and hear me play. He continued bringing attention to me until the day I graduated, four years later, a practice which would turn out to be to my advantage.

The date of my graduation exam on May 17, 1949, was posted. This would definitely not be like my first graduation exam when I was getting my three-year diploma. I had performed well at that time and received grades high enough to be recommended for one more year on a full scholarship as offered by the trustees of Juilliard. Goodman, as we all called him, took obvious credit for my accomplishment and was as proud as any parent. After all, I had achieved the unusual: the first black student to graduate as timpani-percussionist—and female, at that. Now, there I was six weeks later facing a new challenge with Schultz. I had had four years to work with Goodman. Could I rise to the circumstance with Schultz in six weeks?

Suddenly I became aware of my train of thought and scolded myself. "Why are you even thinking this way?" I asked myself. "After all, you're a Juilliard graduate?" Yet, a woman's instincts can be ever so dependable and somehow my feminine intuition coupled with past experiences warned me to be prepared for anything.

Despite the best laid plans of man, disorganization always reigns supreme at the onset of any project. The first rehearsal of the student orchestra at the Berkshire Music School in Tanglewood in 1949 was no exception. As I arrived at the designated rehearsal location, I saw everyone scurrying around with their instruments looking for the coaches and meeting places of their sections.

It didn't take long for me to know which direction to head in. Already some of my colleagues had arrived and I heard para-diddle practiced on an available snare drum. On the right side of the shed, someone else was pounding noisily on the timpani the famous excerpt from the opera *Samson and Delilah.* Trumpeters blared scales up and down as loudly as possible. It always seemed strange to me that members of symphony orchestras, famed for their cooperative execution of some of the world's most beautiful music, warmed up without being sensitive to the cacophony they produced or even how they competed for the highest noise level. I stood aside and waited until someone in authority appeared on the scene to put an end to the disorder. The noise was becoming unbearable when three gentlemen strode into the room.

"Hey people—have a heart—save your enthusiasm. You will need your lips for the long day ahead planned for you!" A tall pleasant looking man perhaps in his thirties approached the stage holding a trumpet under his arm. Following him was Mr. Schultz, the percussion teacher. As he walked over to the other trumpet players, the Boston Symphony Orchestra trumpet player said, "I know we generally play together in the orchestra but it is a little impractical for us to practice together. So, since it's a beautiful morning why don't we go out to the woods and leave the stage for the percussion."

The 10 or so trumpet players packed up their instruments and away they went into the woods for sectional orientation and distribution of parts. The competition would be fierce I thought as they strolled off, with ten guys trying to play music generally written for a maximum of three players. Well that's their problem, I reflected. I have my own to deal with.

In the meantime, the percussion players had stopped assaulting drums as Mr. Schultz walked in. Now that the trumpeters were gone, I was able to discern how many percussionists were there. Oiye, I thought. Problems again. Too many players for too few parts. I hoped I wouldn't be subjected to the harassment I had experienced at Juilliard.

"Good Morning," Mr. Schultz said interrupting my apprehensive thoughts. "I'm happy to see so many of you. Ah, let me see" —he looked around and started counting and asking names. At this point, the names meant nothing and had no identity to me other than the fact that there were five guys standing there. I remained more or less in the background until Mr. Schultz looked over at me and beckoned.

"Young lady, do you care to join us? Come tell us your name, we won't bite you."

I moved forward, not really feeling shy or apprehensive. Two of the percussionists were from Juilliard, including the one who had asked me that unnecessary question the day before, and as far as I could recollect, had not graduated. I remembered some nasty incidents that happened during Juilliard orchestra classes. I walked forward in front of the other players and informed Mr. Schultz that my name was Elayne Jones.

"Ah, I remember you my dear. You played a lovely audition. You are very talented and I am happy to have you with us."

I looked at the two from Juilliard and they silently acknowledged me by eye contact. I moved back to the background and allowed two other men to take a dominant position in front of me. But not for long. Mr. Schultz soon asked us to put all the instruments in order. As usual, the stage hands always managed to place the percussion instruments in the wrong order. I would learn that stage hands did this in every theater or auditorium.

The other percussionists bustled about putting the four

kettledrums in place. Then they lined up the snare drum and the bass drum next to the xylophone. I stood around watching the operation not because I didn't wish to participate but because they had taken charge of the set-up as though I was not in the room. As soon as order reigned, Schultz began to talk in a relaxed manner about our prospects and expectations. The crucial point he emphasized was how he could distribute the music in such a way that we would spend a minimum of idle time.

How busy the percussionists were depended on the music. Music of the sixteenth and seventeenth centuries generally involved one timpani player. Music of the seventeenth and eighteenth centuries like Mozart and Hayden involved timpani and sometimes one percussion. From the eighteenth through the twentieth centuries, compositions by Schubert, Beethoven, Brahms, Tchaikovsky, Dvořák and Berlioz included timpani and a variable number of players.

At Juilliard, Saul Goodman had been a creative and innovative person as well as a fine timpanist. All the instrumental students at Juilliard had to take ensemble and chamber music classes as well. Previous to that edict, an instrumentalist was only required to take private lessons and play in an orchestra. Over the years, it would become apparent that with the growth of the schools coupled with the greater demands being placed on musicians that another dimension was needed to satisfy all these needs.

I could still hear Goodman bemoaning his fate. "I can remember when I'd have only four students," he said. "I only had to come in two days, give my lesson and leave. Now it's 1949, the war is over and all the veterans are returning to school on the G.I. Bill. I have more students than I can handle." He blew a long stream of smoke from the cigar that always dangled from his lips. I thought the only time he didn't have a cigar in his mouth was when he ate and while playing on the stage of

Carnegie Hall. He was, however, a clever and innovative man who came up with the idea of the percussion ensemble which is what made him such a fine musical timpani player.

There I was at Tanglewood with the same scenario: more percussion students than ever before. Mr. Schultz was totally unprepared for such a large number of players and not sure how to handle this situation. Previously, Tanglewood had limited its student participation to residents of Massachusetts and surrounding states. But as the institute mushroomed, it expanded its facilities and the regions from which it chose students. Of course, when such things happen it is usually on the administrative level with the participating teachers the last to be informed.

The two guys from Juilliard helped to bring some order. I was aware of Mr. Schultz's dilemma but I didn't think I could tell him what to do and figured he wouldn't listen to me anyhow. Who would pay attention to anything coming from a little black girl among big men?

Finally, the day came for us to start rehearsing the Beethoven's Sixth Symphony. Serge Koussevitzky, the music director of the Berkshire Music School and conductor of the Boston Symphony Orchestra, was our conductor and instructor for the performance. The Sixth Symphony is often called the *Pastoral*. Considering where we were, there could not have been a more appropriate work to play.

The first movement, *Awakening of Joyful Feelings upon Arrival in the Country*, aptly described my mood. The second movement, *The Brook*, certainly conveyed the natural out-of-doors environment of the shed and the nearby burbling brook. The idyllic environment even invaded Koussevitzky's stern and scholarly directorship. During one rehearsal of the second movement of the Beethoven's Sixth Symphony, the day was particularly made to order. An extremely blue sky surrounded a brilliantly warm sun whose rays eased themselves into the shed. Birds chirped as though they were auditioning for the maestro. The fresh fragrance of the tall blue spruce trees mingled intoxicatingly with the small of freshly cut grass. Koussevitzky stopped conducting frequently to make comments and corrections about phrasing, dynamics or an errant note.

At one point, he stopped the cellists and caught us all off guard by speaking to one of them in his familiar voice with its heavy Russian accent. "Young lady," he said, "eet iss beau-ti-ful day out, we play beaut-ti-ful music and you sit there with beau-ti-ful instrument between your legs and all you do is scratch." Laughter erupted from the orchestra which up until that point found itself so tense that awareness of the surrounding atmosphere was blocked out. That spontaneous comment not only broke the ice and uplifted all of us, but soon became the quote of the century.

The clearing outside became the afternoon meeting place for all the students and Boston Symphony Orchestra players for sunning, swimming, boating or just relaxing. Many of symphony members kept a range of sail and motorboats at the lake. They graciously and generously shared the boats, and by the end of the summer we were almost like one big happy family. Except for these treks down to the lake to enjoy one or two hour retreats, our every waking hour was spent practicing, playing, or listening to music.

Those six weeks at Tanglewood were one of the happiest experiences of my life. When it ended, I knew I had to return to New York and find employment. As I drove back with Charley and Nina, I girded myself for the job hunt, wondering whether I would meet the same kind of stereotyped reactions I had encountered in high school and college. What happened next would surprise me and my erstwhile colleagues. I would get a job far sooner than I expected.

After returning from Tanglewood, I felt lost and unhappy and felt like crying most of the time. I missed everything about being away. Mom and Dad never came up to visit me at Tangle-wood. They always gave excuses why they couldn't come and it pained me. I wanted them to see where their daughter was spending the most glorious musical experience of her life. It had made me feel so isolated when other parents came to visit. Oddly enough, Julia's parents didn't come either, but they had an excuse—they lived far away in Chicago. Whether the other students who lived far away were visited by their parents I didn't know. I guessed that my folks were shy being in the company of white people. All of their friends worked for white people but once they left the job, they disappeared into another world devoid of whites. Yet, all their conversation was about those white people. My parents not visiting me would stay in my mind. I vowed to myself that when I had my own children, I would do everything in my power to always visit them at school, camp or anywhere.

Chapter 9

NEW YORK CITY OPERA
Tackling a Job "Cut Out for a Man!"

In September 1949, I began my first major job with the orchestra of the New York City Opera at City Center. What an important challenge that was to be for me. At that time, there were no blacks in this or any classical orchestra; there was resistance even to considering me. After all, "She's not Italian, so how could she play the operas which are predominantly Italian?" and "She's not French or German." On top of that they said, "How could she tackle a job cut out for a man?"

When I studied at Juilliard with Saul Goodman, who was the principal timpanist for the New York Philharmonic, he often encouraged me to keep going. Whenever I went into lessons feeling blue because of remarks like, "She's too small, she can't play a fortissimo," made to me by my fellow percussion students, Saul told me, "Don't let anything or anybody stand in your way." He was Jewish and not very tall so, he obviously had experienced discrimination because of his religion and height.

I had auditioned for the position of timpanist with the New York City Opera, but I couldn't start immediately because my predecessor, Alfred Howard, was allowed to remain until he had to leave to fulfill his commitment. In the meantime, while waiting patiently but anxiously for his departure, I had to attend all the rehearsals and performances and learn the music by looking over his shoulder because by the time he was to leave, the rehearsal period would be over. And so, it ended. Al left and I took his, *my*, place in the orchestra. That job would not only expose me to opera, European musicians and conductors, but to East Coast cities.

I soon learned that playing opera presents many problems unique to this form of orchestral repertoire. I am in a dark pit, many feet away from the conductor and most often to the side of him which means his beat is not as distinguishable as it is if I were on stage in the symphony facing him. Therefore, it is more difficult to see whether he is conducting in one, two or four. When facing a conductor, I could see clearly. From the side in the pit, everything looks like the same beat. If this isn't clear, it makes playing more formidable. In opera, there is never the steady flow of beats because we are accompanying singing dialogue. Therefore, a singer might start a note on count one and sing a recitative of words before arriving at count two.

Depending on how a conductor feels, he could and often does hold on to the note in order to allow a singer to express their feelings. He must wait on the singer and we must wait on the conductor. When you become an experienced opera orchestral musician, you know the music, the idiosyncrasies of the singers, the mannerisms of the conductor and the story. This takes time and many years of experience to learn.

My introduction to New York City Opera was putting all this together without the familiarity of the music, singers or conductors. I had jumped into the orchestral pool without knowing how to swim. The pool was the deepest ever because the first performance I had to play without a rehearsal for one of the most difficult in the repertoire—a Strauss opera, *Der Rosenkavalier* with a tough German conductor, Joseph Rosenstock. I was faced not only with all the obvious problems, but those peculiar to my instrument.

Timpanists must tune the instrument, hear the notes they need either by having absolute pitch, or knowing the music well enough to use relative pitch for chordal structure. If the music is unfamiliar, it becomes necessary to analyze the chord progression, otherwise I am tuning strictly by intervals. If I'm playing a "C" and my next note is "F," I sing to myself an interval of a 4th. While singing and tuning the note at the same time, I must keep the count of where I am. So, there I'm counting – 1,2,3,4 - 2,2,3,4 – 3,2,3,4 – any unlimited amount of measures and of rhythm since I could be required to count 1,2,3,4 – 2, 2,3,4 – 1,2,3 | 1,2 | 1,2,3,4,5 | 1,2,3,4 | 2,3,4,5,6 and so on. I am kept extremely busy and for the most part I am all alone like swimming in a sea of sharks waiting to devour me.

The orchestra family is made up of groups such as first oboe, second oboe, first clarinet and second clarinet, first and second trumpet, and 26 strings. The groups usually play together although they may not play the same notes but harmonize within a chord. Timpani is often part of a chord from any group, but you must count alone.

In October 1949, my historic debut night finally came. I walked into the pit with all the complexities of playing confronting me plus knowing that I was the first black person to play in an opera orchestra, and the only other woman in the orchestra then. There is no word in the English language to describe how scared I was that night. My heart was beating so hard and loud, I thought it was on the outside of my chest. The only thing louder was the pounding in my head.

I didn't get too much help from my colleagues sitting in front of me because we were playing such a difficult opera that everyone was too busy dealing with their own individual problems. Three-and-a-half hours later the final curtain came down. My skin was drenched with sweat.

The opera ended with cheers from the audience for the singers, conductor and orchestra and my new job which would last for the next 11 years. That performance certainly did not go without little errors, but under the extenuating circumstances, they thought I was outstanding. My first season with the New York City Opera was off to a grand start!

There was so much to learn. Nothing at The High School of Music & Art, Juilliard or Tanglewood prepared me for the demands and rigors of the opera company. Worst of all, I was riding on the coattails of Alfred Howard, the boy wonder. Everyone spoke highly about his playing; I had to fill his shoes. That would be truly only the beginning of the many hurdles to face me.

The opera schedule included going on tour to various cities after the final fall season performance. Chicago was in one of the cycles of cities where orchestras stopped during their tour of America. The first stop was generally New York City at Carnegie Hall. I made Carnegie Hall my place to go to so I could hear and observe musicians. More often than not I went alone, making it easier to sneak into the auditorium.

At 21, I had never ventured anywhere further than Staten Island on the ferry without my mother, except for Tanglewood. The tour took nine of my colleagues and me first to Chicago. To us in New York, the Chicago Opera House ranked third after the old Metropolitan Opera House and New York City Center. Every year the New York City Opera made this junket to Chicago in November when it was cold. The impending tour was both frightening and exhilarating for me.

"You'll be responsible for the entire percussion section on our fall tour," Joe Fabbroni, our orchestra personnel manager, informed me just prior to leaving on the trip. I was shocked.

"What? How can I take on that responsibility? I hardly know the operas myself."

"Well," Fabbroni revealed, "in the past year, Joe Volpe used to go along."

Joe Volpe was the percussionist who had been born playing operas or so it seemed because he knew them so well. I was indebted to him because he taught me and helped me through some of the other difficult operas with Puccini being especially difficult. My entire body went cold with the thought of having to play without his reassuring presence during the tour in strange cities, strange pits and unfamiliar musicians.

"This year," Fabbroni continued, "management has decided to travel with the complete chorus to save money on rehearsals rather than take the entire orchestra."

"Why did they have to choose this year to economize when I needed all the help I could get?" I lamented.

"Don't worry," reassured Fabbroni. "You'll do it."

I suspected however, this was just another test I was being put through before my complete acceptance into the orchestra. The first test, of course, had been playing *Der Rosenkavalier* without a rehearsal.

My major confrontation was knowing which instruments to pack to take. Having trunks for the timpani, Joe Volpe and I were introduced to two fantastic Irish engineers who were specialists in providing, repairing and selling percussion instruments. They had a shop in the basement of a brownstone on Forty-Seventh Street. When I knew of the tour I made many trips to their shop. Whenever I got there I met many drummers whose needs were filled by these men.

There I was on a Monday at 6:45 a.m. in November 1949 about to embark from Grand Central Station on the Zephyr for the 24-hour train ride to Chicago. We traveled by sleeper car in the Pullman car. The Pullman cars had seats by day and beds at night. The conductor went through the cars, upending the seats and in a blink of an eye the seats were transformed into bunk beds. Who slept? Not I. This was my first experience being away from home as a professional musician. No longer a student, I was on my own. The only members of the orchestra who went along were the first stands of all the strings: violins, violas, cellos and bass; one oboe, one flute, one clarinet, one bassoon, one trumpet, two French horns, one trombone, one harp and me. The remainder of the company of singers, dancers, conductors, stage directors and stage hands added up to our having three cars on the train for our exclusive use. That was the first of many trips I would make to play for audiences throughout the world. It would also mean meeting interesting people and musicians and having the opportunity to exchange views and experiences with them. There was partying from the minute we got on board the train at Grand Central Station until we arrived in Chicago early in the morning. We were met at the train station with waiting cabs which took our orchestra and chorus members to the hotel.

We arrived at the hotel dragging our tails behind us. It so happened that there was a convention in the city and all the rooms had not yet been vacated. Joe Fabbroni let me go ahead of the line.

"Elayne, you must get to the auditorium early to unpack your timpani. I'll tell Blanche the same thing."

So, the harpist, Blanche Birdsong, and I were suddenly paired because we had the big instruments which had to be unpacked. The two little women had the biggest instruments.

"What about our room and our bags?" Blanche and I inquired.

"Don't worry," Fabbroni said, "the rooms aren't ready yet, anyhow. The bell boys will put your luggage in your rooms when they're ready so we'd better get to the auditorium."

I would later be told that our orchestra personnel manager had a devil of a time getting me into the hotel. It was against hotel policy to register a Negro there. After much haggling, the hotel management was allowed to register me but only if I didn't have a private room. Since Blanche was the other woman, they figured we could room together. It seemed reasonable, except Blanche was from Longview, Texas, with all the ramifications of how Southerners felt about blacks. But that's another story.

Off we went to the Chicago Opera House. Blanche and I arrived at the theater before any of our colleagues. The two smallest and supposedly weakest members of the orchestra to cope with the two largest instruments, harp and timpani. Our colleagues carried their instruments with them because they were smaller and portable, so they could arrive later at the theater provided they allowed themselves enough time to warm up before playing. There stood before me a magnificent structure of stone on the banks of the Chicago River. We approached the building from the rear, of course, to enter by the stage door. It was really hard for me to assess my first impressions because my thoughts were on getting into the building and finding my timpani trunks.

I wasn't aware of what I was about to face. We reached the stage door which was as obscure as a bug in a rug. I would figure out after years of playing in theaters that stage doors were always hidden away in an inaccessible alley, generally smelly and dirty, sharing the passage way with the residue of garbage of the day. This way the artists were protected from their fans, or perhaps I had heard that historically performers used to be considered part of the help. Musicians were obviously considered the lower echelon judging by the place we had in the theater—all the way down in the sub-basement.

Blanche and I scurried through the ugly passageway and found the stage door. She opened it the and inside stood the usual sentry known as the stage door man. I have never figured out what kind of personality a person would have to possess to become a stage door man. They always appeared to me to be not too bright. This individual was true to type.

As Blanche walked through the door, he stopped her and inquired, "Who are you?"

"Blanche," she answered.

"What do you do? I don't recognize you."

"I'm from New York and I'm with the orchestra."

"What do you do?" he said.

"I play the harp." The stage door man gave Blanche one last look.

"Oh, okay, go in down the stairs to the basement," he

ordered.

"Do you know if the trunks are here?" Blanche said.

"I don't know ma'am, but look for Tom, the stage manager. He'll tell you." He turned around to face me as I stood right behind Blanche. "What can I do for you?" he inquired in a noticeable less respectful tone of voice.

"I'm from New York and with the orchestra," I repeated exactly what Blanche had said.

"Ya have any identification?" he challenged.

"Well, we're together," I said pointing to Blanche.

"How do I know you're a musician? I never saw no Negra in this theater before."

"She's with me and we're members of the New York City Opera Orchestra," Blanche interjected in her Texas accent. "I play the harp and she plays the timpani."

The stage door man looked at her disbelievingly. "A Negra girl playing drums in this here opera. I don't believe it. You have any proof?"

"Man, we have to go inside and get our instruments ready for rehearsal," Blanche urged.

"Well I can't let her in until I get an okay," he insisted.

"How come you didn't ask me for proof?" said Blanche.

"You're *white*, ma'am," he emphasized.

We had arrived at the theater early to be prepared for rehearsal, but this delay was causing us great distress. We would be late if we didn't have time to assemble and tune our instruments. It didn't matter one bit to an ignorant stage door man what could happen to us, since we were two young women with one who was black. After another tense moment or two, we were finally allowed inside.

It was a long day with rehearsals all day followed by the opening *Carmen* performance. We had no opportunity during that day to return to the hotel, so we ate our lunch and dinner nearby and didn't return to the hotel until after our performance that night. Exhausted, we got through the day on pure adrenalin. After the finale, we couldn't wait to get over to the hotel to rest our spent bodies and then go to sleep. Usually there was a company party after an opening, but that night was an exception. None of us had the energy to party after the all-night train trip.

Blanche and I were the only women who went on tour with the orchestra. I hadn't known much about her, only because she sat on the opposite side of the pit due to how the orchestra was set up. It was located below the stage. The length of the pit was generally the length of the stage and its width was determined by the seating arrangement of the auditorium. In some theaters, the stage was on the small side, reducing the size of the pit making the space to play in, very cramped. The first question we heard from the musicians when arriving in a city to play was "how big is the stage and the auditorium?"

Sometimes the pit was so small that instruments had to be eliminated—mostly in the strings. We could play with fewer strings, but it was almost impossible to eliminate a woodwind or brass instrument. Some percussion instruments could be eliminated, but the two instruments which were the biggest had to remain—the harp and the timpani. It was under these circumstances that Blanche and I got to know each other.

When I got into the orchestra all I could focus on was my timpani and my music. The faces of most of the players were a blur to me. I didn't know them so they had no identity in my life. I established a relationship first with the brass players because they were on my side of the pit which stretched from the right and left of the stage as did my sidekick and lifelong percussionist, Joe Volpe, but not on tour.

The string players and the harpist were on the other side of the pit. The conductor stood in the middle between the right and left side of the pit. The brass players, all Italians, acted as if that other side of the pit did not exist. They jokingly referred to the string players as the "MEECE" because they were scurrying around on their violin strings. I had distanced myself from the other side of the pit, so I didn't get to know Blanche and was hardly aware of her existence. Harpists are known for their total preoccupation of tuning their harp. They were so focused that they rarely interacted with anyone.

After our opening performance in Chicago, Blanche, or "Birdie" as she was called, and I went together, separately from the rest of the orchestra, to the hotel up to the desk clerk for our room assignments and keys. We expected of course to have our own individual rooms. I got to the desk first and asked the clerk for the key for Jones. The clerk turned around and returned with a key for Jones and Birdsong.

"Where is the key for Birdsong? I asked the clerk.

"There is one room for Jones and Birdsong, a double room," he said curtly.

"But we asked for singles," chimed in Birdie.

"Sorry Miss, but we had a convention which caused a shortage of rooms. So, it was decided that since you two are girls we assumed you wouldn't mind sharing a room until tomorrow when we'll have more rooms."

This, however, would not be the case because I was black. It would be made clear that I wouldn't have had my own room anyhow. We were so tired we didn't have the energy to protest. We took the keys and went to our room. It was indeed a double room, BUT it didn't have twin beds, just one big double bed. We didn't give it a thought. We just unpacked, threw off our clothes and got into bed. We both let out a sigh of pleasure that we could finally relax.

"Oh, how wonderful it is to be in bed," I said gratefully.

Then all of a sudden Birdie sat up in bed and exclaimed, "Jonsey, I never thought I'd be in bed with a Nigra!"

"What's that you say?"

She repeated, "I'm in bed with a Nigra."

I didn't know what to say. I was dumbfounded. I couldn't believe my ears. Fatigue escaped me at that moment. "What are you saying?" I asked again.

"Well, I'm from Long View, Texas," Birdie explained. "We never mixed with the Nigras. My brother was on the basketball team and they had one Nigra player, but he had to stay separate from the team when they traveled, and here I am in the same bed with you." Although we were tired, we sat up and discussed how irrational prejudice was before we could go to sleep. From that day on, we became best friends.

Our arrival in Chicago was greeted with frigid zero-degree temperatures and an icy wind blowing off the river where the Chicago Opera House was located. The other iciness was the initial reaction of the white male musicians hired to make up the balance of the orchestra. They had not been given any advance word that there was going to be a black female musician coming from New York to play percussion and the timpani! Then the questions came at me again.

"How did you ever become a timpani player?" That question was often asked especially at that time because Birdie was the only other woman in the orchestra and she was white. Their curiosity about me kept me talking almost every night, all night.

The other iciness was due to the fact at that time there still existed a musician's local union for black musicians and a union for white musicians. I presented a serious dilemma to them. The Chicago Opera House was under the jurisdiction of the white local.

"We never had any such problem before," confessed the white musicians' local representative. "Our Nigro boys play over on the south side where they belong and play the kind of music they know. Ain't no colored boy ever played opera."

"What we gonna do?" said another musician. "Who should she pay her work dues and traveling fees to?" When a musician from one city goes, and plays in another city, that musician must pay a penalty to the musician's union and its city called work/traveling dues.

The president of the black local contacted me. "You're one of us and we're proud of you," he said sincerely. "Problem is, you are not allowed to play without paying those fees. How can you pay those fees to the white local when they would not even accept you as a member?"

What a situation to have to think about just before going into the pit to play *Der Rosenkavalier* with a percussion section made up of three guys who had never played the opera. It was a strange happening. I was aware that all eyes were on me, not the fellas who hadn't played. If they goofed, they'd just brush it aside. If I goofed, that would be all they'd need to prove I was a misfit. I was determined when I walked into the pit that night that I'd settle all the problems. From the first downbeat to the last note, I not only played the hell out of my part, I was able to guide the other percussionists through with cues, nods, and sufficient help to lead them to a proud performance. I won their respect, but there was one more hurdle.

The following day just before our rehearsal, the white local representative approached me. "Well, we still don't know what to do about you," he said. "You sure make things difficult for us."

"*I* make things difficult for *you*?" I said. "I'm a professional musician, a graduate of Juilliard with probably a better education than you. If I lived in your city, I would not have had the opportunity to be of help to these guys, last night. You have a preconceived idea about what we can or cannot do. Do you think I am the only black classical musician in the world? You will have to change your policies and your outlook on life."

In a typical gesture of white men to black women, he patted me on my face and said, "Honey, you ain't like all the others. You're different." Anger rose inside me, but I said nothing.

How often I heard that statement, and each time I had to

quell my anger because my instinct was to punch them in the stomach. I also got the same reaction from some of the men in the orchestra at various times.

The problem still remained, however, as the two unions fought back and forth about who should get my money. I decided I did not want those white folks to get my money. So, I called the black local and told them they should make every effort to collect my dues and taxes and begin negotiations to have the two locals merge. Just before we ended our engagement in Chicago, I was notified I had to pay the white local. It was agreed that I was a New York musician playing in the territory of the white local of Chicago. Therefore, they were due the assessment. I didn't approve but I had no choice but to pay.

During the course of the two weeks we spent in Chicago, my presence became known to Grace Thompson, music editor of Chicago's famed black paper, *The Chicago Defender*. She was a dynamic energetic black woman who, as soon as she found out about me, contacted me for an interview and to meet other black Chicagoans, influential in changing the attitudes entrenched in the city. This was the beginning of a campaign to alter the separate but unequal status of the musicians' union. I was really furious having to pay the white union, but attention was brought to the black community which put pressure on all sides. The musicians' union would become integrated. The battle had just begun and I would believe it was the only one which was won. Chicago was still considered a southern town, even though it was north of the Mason-Dixon Line, so it's bound to be hostile to Negroes, which is what happened. I wondered at the time, what will happen when I go to the hotels, to the restaurants, to the opera houses in other cities?

I was delighted, though, when arriving in Chicago to see posters for the London Symphony Orchestra competing with those of the New York City Opera in proclaiming their gala appearance at the Civic Auditorium. My initial feeling was happiness in performing in the same city with the world-renowned London Symphony Orchestra. When I looked at the schedule, I saw that they were playing the same time as the opera. Inasmuch that the operas were always longer than the symphonies, we began our performances one-half hour earlier. With this schedule, we would be performing at the same time! I was disappointed that I wouldn't be able to attend the London Symphony Orchestra performance.

Fortunately, as I was walking into the Opera House I overheard some of the local musicians talking about looking forward to the London Symphony Orchestra performance given for the school children. Hearing the news, I was determined to get to that performance, and that's exactly what happened. Although there was no time to cultivate a relationship with my colleagues, I got to tag along with them anyway. I can't remember what the orchestra played but it didn't matter. My primary interest was watching the timpanist, Richard Bradshaw, and his style of playing.

We left soon after the last note was played. As I looked behind us, I happened to see a violinist emerging from what we discovered was the artist exit. My colleagues stopped to say a word or two to the violinist. I walked on and somehow got the courage to inquire of the next player emerging if the timpanist was also leaving.

"Yes mate, he's coming just now," said the friendly musician who then waited to point him out to me. I was surprised at how accommodating that musician was to answering me. He even went over to the timpanist saying, "Hey mate, the young lass over there asked about you."

"Oh yeah," he responded and walked over to me.

I had no idea what I was going to say to him but I blurted out: "Mr. Bradshaw, so happy to meet you. I'm a timpanist from New York at the Opera House with the New York City Opera."

He more or less interrupted me saying, "New York? We will

be playing in Carnegie Hall in about one month."

"We'll be back in New York by then also," I said. Again, he jumped in asking if I knew Saul Goodman who plays with the New York Philharmonic. "Yes," I said proudly. "He was my teacher."

"Oh, wonderful I would like to have a word with him," said Bradshaw. "You think you could arrange it?"

"I'll arrange for him to meet with you."

"That would be jolly," he said, scurrying off with his orchestra mates. But, then he stopped and reached out and shook my hand.

He was so warm and friendly to me that it was shocking. Thinking about that meeting made me happy at his response to me, a black woman who played the timpani. I didn't tell anyone but let the memory move to the back of my mind.

The remainder of the tour occupied my thoughts which blocked out any thought of arranging a meeting between Saul Goodman and Richard Bradshaw.

One day after returning to New York City from the tour, I saw the posters outside Carnegie Hall announcing the performances of the London Symphony Orchestra. From the deep recesses of my mind emerged the incident with the timpanist, Richard Bradshaw. I had to contact Saul Goodman. After leaving a couple of messages we at last got to speak to each other over the phone. We went through the usual formalities, and I told him about my successful tour with the opera, which he was pleased to hear about. I happily said the highlight of the tour was meeting the timpanist, Richard Bradshaw of the London Symphony Orchestra. I told Goodman that Bradshaw wanted to meet with him.

"So, if it's okay with you," I finished, "I thought we'd arrange to meet for lunch as time permits."

Fortunately, the London Symphony Orchestra was going to play one concert in New York in three days. I was able to go to

Carnegie Hall when the they arrived and got their rehearsal schedule, then called Goodman. From taking lessons with Goodman, I was familiar with the New York Philharmonic rehearsal and performance schedule. How I managed it I don't know, but I arranged for the two timpanists to meet at Carnegie Hall.

The appointed day arrived and I went to the Carnegie Hall stage door just about when their rehearsal ended. I waited and out came all the men followed lastly by the timpanist, Richard Bradshaw. He greeted me like a friend which really surprised me. Almost immediately, Saul Goodman arrived. He saw me at the stage door and walked over to where we were standing. His first words shocked me.

"Hello Elayne. I heard you played that recording last week with Stoki? Do you know I have always played timpani on all his recordings?"

"No," I said, backing away from his startling assault. "I only know that Fabbroni called me to play the recording, so how could I know who was usually hired for these recordings?"

"Well that was *my* job," Goodman continued. I tried to stop him to introduce him to Bradshaw but he was going to keep talking. I looked over to Bradshaw.

"Oh, hello," Goodman said, changing the tone of his voice. The two men exchanged friendly greetings and arranged to meet again, before the departure of the London Symphony Orchestra or when the New York Philharmonic made their tour to London.

As Goodman walked away Bradshaw turned to me and said quietly, "I'd be so proud if a student of mine was so qualified that the great Maestro Stokowski would ask for him or her to play a recording rather than me."

Chapter 10

MEET ME IN ST. LOUIS
No Room for Your Kind

Happy to leave the great city of Chicago, I looked forward to moving on to St. Louis, Missouri—home of the blues! We arrived on December 16th, after stopping for a performance in Milwaukee, Wisconsin. Little did I realize I would get to know why the blues came out of St. Louis.

The soloists and the conductor arrived there ahead of us, enabling them to check the facilities and the time scheduled for the run through rehearsals. We, the orchestra members and the chorus, arrived two days later on a train reserved for us.

In spite of the fact the seats, on the first-class train, turned into beds, at night, we stayed up talking and exchanging our experiences with the opera singers as musicians. This was our opportunity to get to know one another. By the time we arrived, we were exhausted, having not used the time to get rest. Once we arrived however, tired or not, we were still ready for rehearsals.

We arrived in town early, for the reason that we had traveled from Milwaukee, with limited facilities for the orchestra. Our first performance was not until the following night, and we were not obliged to rehearse, with the local musicians. We were still traveling with a nucleus of an orchestra, to save money. To make a full orchestra, it was necessary to hire local musicians, once again, to fill out the required number of players. The entire company arrived together, and off we musicians went by cab to the hotel. As a rule, everyone stayed at the same hotel in the towns where we performed, and the lodgings, always respectable, were likewise as close as possible to the theater. The rooms were usually priced at group rates. Thus, they were reasonable. The company manager made reservations for everyone, so all we had to do was go up to the desk, give our name and get our keys.

I arrived in a cab from the train with a couple of male colleagues, and went into the hotel lobby to join the others already standing in line. I moved forward as everyone gave their names and received their keys. The fellow ahead of me had a problem. Seems his name was missing. The clerk apologized profusely, and darted round like a firefly looking in all the boxes to find an available key. The mix-up wasn't his fault, but he kept saying, "I'm sorry, I'm sorry. I hope this room meets with your approval," after he was able to secure a room for this musician.

"S'aw right," said my colleague, and he wandered off to his awaiting room.

I approached the desk and said, "Jones." The clerk who just a moment ago was so solicitous, suddenly changed his demeanor.

"What?" he asked, sharply.

"Jones!" I repeated, thinking he hadn't heard me.

"There must be some mistake," he articulated.

"Don't you have my name?

"That's not the point, Ma'am. We just can't give you a room."

Not understanding what was happening, I challenged him, "You must have a room. I just saw you give the fellow ahead of me a room."

"Don't you understand, Ma'am, we don't have room for your kind."

Still not quite getting it, I continued, "I'm with all the other people; a musician the same as the man just ahead of me that just got his room."

With obvious annoyance, he said quite emphatically, "We don't have rooms, for your kind."

I still pressed him, "What kind are you talking about?"

"Nigras," he finalized.

"What! You must be crazy!" I exclaimed, "I'll go find our manager!"

"That's our official policy, Ma'am. Next," he said, turning to the person behind me.

I turned around with anger, frustration and tears in my eyes.

The guy behind me—I forget who he was, said casually, "That's the South, for ya."

He gave me his name, got his key and disappeared up the elevator. I just stood there, unable to say anything, not knowing what to do. The next person in line, one of the chorus ladies, didn't hear what had happened, but she noticed I was in shock. She thought I was ill and asked if I didn't feel well.

"I feel fine," I snapped. "I'm just in a rage."

"What happened? What's wrong?"

"They won't give me a room. Where's the company manager?" I said, looking around the crowd.

"I don't think he's arrived, yet, but don't worry," she said, reassuringly. "He'll fix it up."

As she continued comforting me, I finally caught a glimpse of our company manager. He was an Austrian, Laslo Halasz, who spoke with a thick Viennese accent and who had thus far been cordial to me. I ran over to him, and recounting the whole, sordid story, indicated how indignant I was. In his heavy accent, he demanded to know why any member of the opera company would be denied a room. "We're artists!" he explained, "Not street bums!"

"I'm sorry, sir," said the clerk, backing away, "It's our policy."

It was apparent to me that if it had been possible, this little redneck clerk would have also denied a room to our company manager. "There's nothing I can do," he said and pardoned himself.

Our company manager wasn't satisfied and asked to see the manager of the hotel, who by now had heard the commotion and was already walking towards us with a solicitous look on his face.

"I'm sorry for the inconvenience, but we have a policy, you know, and we can't upset our other patrons by having a Negro here."

Our company manager half-heartedly threatened to withdraw the 50 or so opera-company people, from the hotel and to go elsewhere. But he was made aware, by one of the stage managers, the futility of such an action, since that policy existed all over St. Louis.

Someone then volunteered the information that the local YWCA had a non-segregation policy, even though it was the South. Our manager turned to me and said, "I guess you have no other choice but to go there. I'm sorry, but you see there is nothing I can do."

A couple of the girls heard this and said someone should go with me, so I wouldn't be alone. It was then that Lorraine, a sympathetic, sensitive new friend, and two other chorus ladies, Margaret and Mary, went to get their bags and said, "We'll go together."

By the time some of the others heard the story, they all checked out of the hotel and joined us on our way, to the "Y," which was several blocks away. Getting a cab was another problem, as several passed by us, before we found one that would take us.

When we got to the "Y," we discovered their room rates were even cheaper than the hotel's discount rate. The chorus members' salaries were not as high as those of us who played in the orchestra. So, by the end of the evening, there were 10 ladies from the chorus at the "Y" who, by responding to my problem, inadvertently got a break on their expenses. More than that, we discovered a camaraderie for each other as artists that superseded otherwise overwhelming racial barriers. Over the next few days, I was to find out, during the conversations I had with these ladies, they had no understanding of segregation as it existed in the United States. Through this experience, they began to see what black people had to experience for the first time.

The next afternoon when I arrived at the theater, for our *Madama Butterfly* matinee, Joe Fabbroni was already there. He had been summoned by the opera manager.

"Hi, Joe, how ya doing?" I greeted the personnel manager, at the stage door. "You here to help me with the timpani? Is Birdie here yet?"

"Hi, Helina," Joe answered. He was an elderly Italian violinist who also spoke with a very thick accent, and he had the manner of a very strict, old-world taskmaster, who ruled the orchestra, with an iron fist. He had quite an impact on my career during the 11 or more years I worked with him. He insisted on arriving at rehearsals not one minute before downbeat, or ten minutes, but fifteen minutes, early exactly. If your name wasn't signed in by then, he would shout you out with his typical, "God dammit, Geesy Christ—you no a work for me, no more!"

Well, he never had to shout me out because I always arrived at rehearsals early, to set up my timpani and practice after my first encounter with him. Besides, I knew the old myth about Negro people being lazy and always late. So, I took no chances at having that label tacked onto me or hopefully on any black person. At the same time, I made a point whenever I could of fighting however I could those racist myths. My parents were very strict with me, and I was one of those "obedient" children who always did what her parents wanted. Joe Fabbroni's approach was in keeping, with my background. Later in my career, these exceptional work habits helped to ingratiate me with the great Leopold Stokowski.

At this point, though, I had only been with the opera

company for two months. Joe was already obviously pleased with my work, having come in under the trying circumstances. When I had auditioned for the opera job, I was not accepted until my teacher interceded. I was not Italian, I was not a man and I was black. So, it was with genuine feeling that he asked me, "How are you? How do you feel, over at that 'Y'?"

"Well, it's not too bad," I said. "The room is clean—not as good as a hotel, but alright. The food is decent. I ate breakfast, this morning, in the "Y" cafeteria, so as to avoid the nasty scene that occurred, last night."

"Yes," he interrupted, "I heard from the boys about all of you going to a Chinese restaurant, with your friends from the St. Louis Symphony for dinner and not being allowed to eat because you were along."

"It's funny how first-hand experience can have an impact on you, even though you know about it, and god knows I certainly have read enough about segregation," I replied. "But meeting it face-to-face is something else. The St. Louis musicians were appalled because it was the one restaurant in town they assumed was not segregated, being Chinese. That didn't matter, as it was quite apparent the restaurant owners gave in to the racist policy, just to stay in business."

"Where did you go?" he pressed on, anxiously.

I told him that my friend, a member of the St. Louis Symphony, June Rotenberg, a Jewish bass player from New York, had picked me and some of the other opera company players up from the "Y"—all of whom were from New York, by the way. When we arrived, the others had already been seated and were waiting for us. June entered first, with me following behind her. When the maître d' spotted me, he walked over and said I couldn't come in "without a reservation."

"I'm with the other group," I protested.

"You can't stay here," he declared, then stepped in front of me to block my passage.

Suddenly, as if a command from heaven had been given, the entire group responded, like a well-trained chorus. "If she can't stay, then we won't, either," they all said, in unison. Then they rose from their seats, proceeded towards me, and swept me out the door. It all happened so fast, I was dumbfounded. Once outside, they asked each other the obvious next question. "Well, if we can't eat here, then where can we go?"

We first tried a black-owned bar, but we discovered the white musicians couldn't go there. We ended up at some dive of a joint, on the outskirts of town. This place allowed our integrated group to stay but only served drinks and sandwiches. We spent the entire evening drinking, and since I'm not fond of sandwiches, I didn't put any food in my belly. As a result, we all got roaring drunk, but we got drunk together.

"That's horrible," said Joe when I finished my tale. He bowed his head, as though taking the blame for what had happened.

"Don't worry about it," I reassured him. "I'm here to play music, which I will do, and that's all that matters."

But I was unaware that wasn't all that mattered.

"There's more to it than just eating," Joe informed me. "I was told the management and theater board don't want you to play or Camilla to sing."

"Are you kidding?!" I exclaimed. First lodging. Then dining. Now, this. It was all beginning to be too much.

"No, I'm not," he continued, "They don't like the idea of a white man and a black woman onstage, as lovers." Camilla Williams was the first black woman to sing a leading role, with the New York City Opera and perhaps even with the Met—she had preceded Leontyne Price, by several years. But just as the DAR, the Daughters of the American Revolution, hadn't allowed the great soprano Marion Anderson to sing in a hall, in Washington, D.C., back in the 1940s, Camilla was now being denied the opportunity to perform operatically on a public stage in St. Louis, Missouri.

The only role she sang was Madama Butterfly in Puccini's opera of the same name. Not because she didn't know any other opera role but because with the oriental-type make-up the part required, she appeared more white than black, thus not offending the sensitivities of the audiences. I argued long and often, through the years, about how the supposed need for authenticity and realism was used as a cover for racism in theater. How often had I stood in the pit behind my timpani watching robust, healthy women singing the role of poor, sick, tuberculosis-ridden characters like Mimi in *La Boheme*. One certainly had to stretch their imagination to justify that casting, more so if the singer or actor playing a European or Asian role had a black face but looked the part, in every other sense. Such was the case with Camilla. She fit the stereotype of a small, dainty, diminutive Japanese woman, except her skin was dark.

"Also," Joe went on, with obvious concern, "They don't want you in the pit."

While I attempted to absorb this new bit of intelligence, Joe continued puzzling over this strange turn of events. "But we have to find a solution," he muttered, "as there is no timpanist in St. Louis who can play both *Madama Butterfly* and *Carmen*." The problem was since two percussionists were required for both operas, the timpanist had to be someone familiar with the operas. I was relatively new, but part of playing in an orchestra is understanding the conductor's mannerisms, as well as the music.

Our conductor for *Carmen* was a very sullen Frenchman by the name of Jean-Paul Morel. In this era, tradition maintained only French conductors, singers and musicians could interpret French opera, German conductors, singers and musicians for German opera, Italians for Italian opera and so on. No wonder few, if any, black conductors, singers or musicians were allowed since there were no operas from Africa.

Jean-Paul Morel looked like Marcel Marceau. There was

always a cigarette dangling, lighted or not, from a pair of lips, embedded in a long, hard, but flexible face. When things did not go according to his taste, which was often, he mumbled under his breath, in French. One time during a performance of the opera, *Mignon*, by Ambroise Thomas, three singers were supposed to enter down stage. For some reason, these ladies made the unfortunate mistake of timing their entrance about two beats late. Morel couldn't ignore that slip, even if it was during the middle of the performance. The next thing we knew, he had thrown his baton clear across the stage at the already embarrassed singers.

You had to be on your toes, with Morel, because he conducted at a fast pace. You had to know your music so well, you could play your part without looking at it, while keeping your eyes glued to his hands, which bounced around like fireflies. Coming in to play under his direction without the benefit of rehearsal or previous experience under his baton, was tantamount to committing artistic suicide. I was deathly frightened of this man and of making any kind of error with him. He also claimed to be a percussionist, who had recorded the famed Stravinsky *L'Histoire du Soldat*. Under these circumstances no local musician would accept playing under Morel as it was more like committing musical suicide.

On the other hand, our conductor for *Madama Butterfly* was young and not too secure in his position as a leader. He was real sweet but not at all authoritative. Italian operas have big traps, which could cause serious trouble if you aren't experienced. It is not the kind of music you can sight read. The recitatives the singer sings are never measured. You can't just count 1-2-3-4 and so on, for chances are there may be many words sung on any beat, thus delaying the progression of the meter. Therefore, you may find your count more like 1…2…3-4…1-2-3…4. Eyes on the conductor, ears on the singer, but even that isn't enough. Knowing the opera securely makes playing less like walking on a tight rope, blindfolded.

With this in mind, Joe's reluctant revelation made the present situation very serious. The company, already forced to go without the lead singer, Camilla, wasn't about to jeopardize its performances for two days by having me, its principal timpanist, sidelined. "I don't know what to do," Joe said, "but we must find a way to get around this shit. This couldn't happen in Italy." He announced, "There, music is supreme!"

When Blanche and I arrived in St. Louis, the two of us walked first into the theater. As I looked around, the facilities were superb when compared to many of the outdated theaters we had played in. The first thing I looked for was if there was a women's restroom. After being assured it had a lovely "john," for the girls, we felt a little more at ease. Our next concern was the location and size of the pit. The space met my approval, being large enough to enable me to have room for my four timpani, and also have my percussion players next to me so that I could help cue them through different passages.

There was one other feature, which would save the day. The pit was on an elevator, which meant that after all the musicians entered the pit and were settled in their seats, the conductor pushed a button, and the entire pit rose to stage level! While I was investigating the working condition, and setting up my drums, Joe was busy trying to work out the problem of my unwanted presence. A short while later, he came over and announced triumphantly, "We found a solution."

"Really?" I said. "What are they going to do with me?"

"You notice, of course, that the pit goes up," he explained. "The solution lies in not having the pit go up to a height where the audience can see you. They'll just keep it down as low as possible so that you will be hidden."

The major problem with this ridiculous solution was the conductor. He had to be high enough to be able to direct the orchestra, while also being visible to the singers on the stage.

Normally, the musicians and the conductor would be at the same level on the raised pit, enabling the conductor to oversee both the orchestra and the singers simultaneously. But under these circumstances, the conductor's podium had to be elevated so that he could see the stage from the lower-than-usual pit.

It was all quite hilarious. With the pit lowered and the conductor on risers, his feet were nearly at the same level as our heads, making it almost impossible to maintain eye contact with him or see his hands. It made for a strange performance for us and an extremely tiring one for him. Usually, the conductor can see the stage and the orchestra, equally. In this position, he could see the stage, but we were about three feet below him. Those of us with the orchestra were familiar with the music by now, and the style of the conductor. The local musicians, however, were put at tremendous disadvantage. They had rehearsed before we arrived in town, but only with their parts. In addition, we never participated in rehearsals with the local musicians, because the company was not about to pay us to practice music we already knew. So, they had no way of knowing the mannerisms of the conductor. I had to help them and act as a conductor, a formidable job.

The opening of *Carmen* that afternoon was bizarre with the musicians complaining bitterly about the set-up and not being in the proper position to get the beat and cues of the conductor. The local musicians couldn't understand why the pit didn't rise to the right level. Some of the men were overheard saying they thought it was a plot to undermine them and to make them look incompetent.

The conductor wasn't too helpful either. Whenever there was a mistake—and there were many, he'd glare at everyone. He wasn't happy with the set-up, either, and showed his displeasure by being unpleasant. No one knew the reason for the unusual proceedings except the stage manager, the orchestra manager and me.

But the following evening, word had begun to get around the theater that St. Louis's policy of racial segregation had caused the famed New York Opera Company to recast its black soloist and keep its black musician out of sight.

Not all was lost, however. "I never worked with any Negroes, before," fessed one of the local percussionists. "You people are good at jazz, what with your natural rhythm and all, but I never thought you could play our music so well."

That night, we departed for New York on the express Pullman train immediately after the *Carmen* performance. The trip had been full of firsts, all of which I felt I had dealt with, successfully and professionally. I really felt good when I returned home from my first tour. It would be followed by many other tours, which would eventually take me all around the world.

Chapter 11

THE UNION
Reflecting the Cultural Divide

Although I was making a living wage as the timpanist for the New York City Opera, the opera season from September through December, including going on tour for a couple to several weeks. That left me without employment from December to May, and I found myself feeling restless. I wanted to play all year round, and I could stand more income. So, I kept my eye out for additional opportunities to work.

Most of the short-term gigs were offered by Musicians Union Local 802 working out of the Roseland Ballroom on Broadway and Fifty-Second Street. The facility, called by the members "the floor," was used by the union during the day. It closed at three o'clock only to reopen later in the evening for ballroom dancing. From mornings to early afternoons, professional musicians looking for gigs gathered "on the floor."

"The floor" contained scruffy folding chairs arranged haphazardly against the wall and a long, scratched-up wooden table at the back of the room. Hundreds of musicians congregated around this expansive room in cliques, some young, others old, but all male. They sat or stood around, talking and smoking, exchanging industry news and gossip.

The contractors, mostly independent but not necessarily union representatives, did the actual hiring by circulating among the musicians asking, "Hey, boy, you looking for work, this weekend? I have a club date for Friday night."

A club date meant getting a gig, a job, to play for a wedding, anniversary, debutante party or graduation. There were many ethnic gigs because music for a Jewish wedding was different from music for an Italian or black wedding, or a Bar Mitzvah or any other occasion. This scenario was often repeated between the contractors and the sidemen. The majority of the contractors and musicians, called sidemen, played accordion, trumpet, saxophone, violin, string bass or piano; many of them played several instruments. They were Italian or Italian-American and often referred to each other endearingly as "boy." Most of the remaining musicians were Jewish. If they didn't like the term boy, they never let on. There were few if any black musicians.

Although the pay was equalized, there was a national cultural divide there. Italian musicians usually played the accordion for Italian affairs; there were Jewish musicians for Jewish affairs. Interestingly, I observed that the white musicians were often asked to play a black gig—that was considered equality. However, I never saw a black musician get an offer to play for an Italian or Jewish affair. Black musicians were hired only to play black cultural gigs. Equality went only one way. I was never sure how a musician became a contractor. It had appeared that the contractor was not a quality player because I never saw any of them playing.

Al Manuti was president of the New York City Union Local 802 America Federation of Labor (AFL). Al Petrillo was president of the American Federation of Musicians. Neither thought black musicians were capable of playing anything other than blues and later, jazz. Whenever Broadway scores included blues or jazz, white men played, though most had very little feel for African-American-based music. The better wages and the greater respect inherent in jobs on "The Great White Way" were openly denied black musicians.

There was also a special breed of men; I didn't know who appointed them. They had a special position in the union hierarchy. They were the members who hired musicians for all Broadway shows. They were treated like gods. The two I knew were Morris Stonzek and Sol Gusikoff. They were called contractors and completely monopolized hiring musicians to play in the Broadway pit. They never hired a black musician, even though the music was scored for the instruments found in jazz and/or swing.

Leonard Bernstein composed *West Side Story* in 1960. I had first seen him when I was 21 and studying and performing at Tanglewood. I was fully aware of how Broadway shut out black musicians. Bernstein, a sensitive musician, conductor and composer, was aware that black musicians were denied the better jobs. He also knew that most white classical musicians played strict European style and didn't have the natural feeling for the blues the score required in *West Side Story*. So, he wrote the music in a way that enabled white musicians to "swing" to the ethnic rhythms.

Swinging the rhythm was determined by how you approached a dotted quarter note, followed by a 16th note. Instead of playing four strict 16th notes, for example, black musicians learned to "bend" the 16th note to give it the syncopated beat identified with the blues. Bernstein cleverly wrote in 12/8 time, which mechanically produced a beat similar to the bended 16th notes. By following the score to the letter, the white musicians created the sound, making it unnecessary for *West Side Story* producers to hire their black counterparts.

Just for the hell of it, I would go down to the union and stop at the floor, although I knew darn well I wasn't looking for a job and knew I wouldn't get one anyway. I was already playing with the New York City Opera and felt proud I had a coveted contracted job, so I didn't have to depend on the floor contractors. Almost all of them, like the union bosses, were racist, sexist and not very bright. But the way the contractors reacted to me, it was obvious they disliked that they did not have me at their mercy, bowing and scraping, and begging for them to throw me a bone of a gig.

Al Kimmel was different. A young Jewish man who played the sax, he was dark, intense and dedicated to the progressive movement. Al was involved in politics. I had met him when there were educational meetings for planning political activity in support of workers' issues. He also played an active role in the musicians' union. Fighting for higher wages, more respect and better working conditions, he was determined to depose the union's old racist leadership.

One day during the early summer of 1951, I dropped by the floor with no special intention in mind. All the guys I knew were hanging around, bantering with each other. Much to my surprise, Al moved away from the boys and called me over. "You want a gig?" he asked out of the blue. I was shocked.

"Well, maybe," I replied, hedging while trying to figure out the catch. Why would Al be asking me such a question? To answer my quizzical look, he told me the story about a band at Crystal Lake Lodge in the Adirondacks that needed a drummer. Crystal Lake Lodge was known as a progressive adult resort with a progressive hiring policy. I had to think fast. What would Mom and Dad think if I were to take such a job?

I had no trouble accepting this job even though I wouldn't be playing classical music. I was going to be in the country playing music every night for dancing and for the shows. Crystal Lake Lodge was part of the "Borscht Circuit." These were hotels north of New York City that catered to Jewish vacationers. Every hotel in the Catskills and the Adirondacks had a band.

It was quite unusual to get this job; few women played such gigs. There was the Sweethearts of Rhythm, an all-black female band. And there was the more commercialized all-white girl band called Phil Spitalny and his All-Girls Band. Other than those ladies, it wasn't a common sight to see women playing a gig with a group of men. If and when a woman did, she generally played the piano. Two African-American women,

Mary Lou Williams and Hazel Scott, did break the barrier. They were more like concert pianists and didn't play gigs such as I played at the resort.

Playing a brass or woodwind instrument was almost out of the question for women. I remember hearing that mothers then didn't like their daughters playing those "male" instruments, especially the clarinet because they looked too phallic.

The resort environment was unique for me, unlike the summer I spent in Tanglewood. At the resort, I was exposed to a new experience of learning to play dance or swing music; at Tanglewood I learned classical music. There was a qualitative difference playing classical music and playing swing. Classical music is written with every expression notated. You play from music with every note, tempo dynamics clearly written. You follow the conductor, while playing in an ensemble, with many other instrumentalists.

Playing swing was so different. There was no written music. The leader or conductor was generally a pianist. Good pianists have a vocabulary of music, which they are able to play when requested by anyone. The guest comes up to the pianist and asks, "Do you know 'Melancholy Baby'?" At that moment, the experienced pianist says yes, then turns around to the band and says, "Melancholy Baby" in E-flat. He calls out the key to let the instrumentalists know what key he is going to play in, because there is no written sheet music. As the band starts playing, the guests get up and dance. That is so different from playing with an orchestra. In the band, we had to be in sync with each other in order to play together. In a sense, we were all leaders. We had to listen to one another and to be sensitive to each other, whether we played loudly in fortissimo or especially when we were playing softly in pianissimo.

I am certain that playing with a band in such a way made me a better symphony player.

I loved playing and watching people dance. It brought me

back to the days when I was growing up and dancing at the neighborhood parties; in the band, I now sat in the other chair.

My experience with the union was heightened when I was in Chicago touring with the New York City Opera. It led me right into paying attention to the role of the union in which I was a member in New York. My involvement with the affairs of the union prompted them to ask me to run for office on the union board, but the rules at that time didn't allow a member to play and hold an office at the same time. As tempting as it was, I had no desire to give up playing.

Chapter 12

GEORGE KAUFMAN
I Couldn't Take My Eyes Off Him

Millions of tourists, hikers and outdoor enthusiasts from New York, New England and the Mid-Atlantic states took their summer vacations either in the Catskills or the Adirondacks. The summer season lasted from July 4th to Labor Day. There was plenty of room to spread out, since the mountain range covered about 12,000 square miles of Northeastern New York. The Adirondacks were famous for wild and beautiful scenery, rushing streams, splashing waterfalls and purple-tinted peaks. Glacier-gouged lakes dotted the region, among them Lake Champlain and Blue Mountain Lake. But of all the bodies of water, Lake Placid and Lake George were best known for their resorts.

Crystal Lake Lodge was on the northern shore of Lake George. I played there every night with the little dance band. Although I loved playing, there were nights when watching people dance made me wish that I was dancing, too. The guests came up to the band and requested we play a song for them. When we played their favorite song, I loved watching them swing romantically to our music.

Most of the guests came up for a one-week vacation. Yet at that time, I had seen romances blossom from the first meeting into sometimes a hot relationship almost every week. I observed this happening and often wondered what happened after they left. On Wednesday, August 6, 1952, however, the pattern changed.

As I was watched the dancers, I noticed a handsome young

man coming onto the dance floor. I don't know why, but I couldn't take my eyes off of him. He was good-looking with curly black hair. From where I was sitting onstage behind my drums, he looked Spanish. Not only did he look good, but he was a smooth dancer. This was his first day at the dance, and I noticed already him dancing with the same girl that evening. Every time the music began, he got up to dance with her; I felt myself regretting I couldn't dance with him. I always loved to dance, but for some reason throughout that entire summer, I was happy playing and never missed dancing, until I saw the man with the curly black hair.

There was one little problem. How could I dance when I had to play in the band? There would have to be a drummer on vacation who could sit in and play for me. The other problem was what if he didn't want to dance with me? That made me sad. All those thoughts went through my mind as I played that night. I had already played through the month of July and never thought of dancing. I felt safe behind the drums and enjoyed getting the kind of attention that made me happy. Everyone watching me play the drums seemed to admire me. I accumulated several friends and looked forward to the invitations I received every night. "Come and join us for drinks, after you finish playing," they said sincerely.

One night as we were leaving the bandstand, I got a note from Ruth and Leo, a special couple I had met during the afternoon folk-dancing session. Ruth was a beautiful folk dancer who danced like Isadora Duncan. I fell in love with her because of her dancing and her warmth. Our deep friendship began that afternoon, and we would become lifelong friends. I didn't see her after the dance session because I had a rehearsal for the weekend show. While I was playing that evening, she and her husband, Leo, came up to the bandstand and signaled to me to join them for drinks. I was happy and looked forward to being with them. Hopefully, that would take my mind off the little distraction I had on the dance floor. In the meantime, when I looked for that handsome man again, I noticed he had gone before the dancing had ended. I guess he left with the girl he had danced with all evening, I thought. Oh, well.

Ruth and Leo had rented a lovely little cottage just outside the entrance gate to Crystal Lake Lodge. They left instructions for me about how I could get there. I packed up and as usual, bantered around briefly with my colleagues. They also had somewhere to go. But before I left, I mentioned to our pianist Terry Carter that I wish there were some guests who could sit in for me. There was always a guest who played the piano and was always happy to sit in, but there was never a drummer.

Terry joked with me, saying: "You're happy doing what you do. You don't need a drummer to sit in."

"Yeah, you're right," I agreed. But there was a feeling I had when thinking about the man I saw that night. I dismissed the thought and went off to meet Ruth and Leo. When I arrived, several people were already at their cottage drinking and dancing. I walked into a happy group of guests.

"Come on in!" said everyone who saw me. "Join us! Have a drink!" They stopped what they were doing and greeted me like I was a celebrity. This was by far the warmest group of guests I had experienced all summer.

"Come meet our friends," said Ruth. "We all came up together."

Then the unexpected happened. Who should be one of the guests? The young man with the curly black hair! My heart skipped a beat. Ruth continued introducing me all around, and then she came to that man. "This is George Kaufman." Instantly, we began talking with great interest in each other.

It was as though George and I had already met, and were in a conversation we had started which we continued without a break. I never felt strange being with him that night. After meeting, we interacted with the guests as if we were already a couple. At about one o'clock in the morning, the guests began to disperse because most of the them had driven up for the weekend from New York City that evening after work.

As everyone was leaving, George said to me, "Would you like me to walk you to your cabin?" At that moment, I realized I had just met him and knew nothing about him.

Prior to meeting George, male visitors approached me and invited me to have a drink with them. I generally went because I loved being with people, drinking and having fun, especially after the show. But I didn't seriously interact with them. That evening with George, however, the same scenario was a little different. I wasn't anxious to leave him. So, when he walked me to my cabin, I didn't want him to accompany me because I didn't know him, but inside, my heart was pounding with excitement. As we walked, I still pretended to worry about not knowing anything about him in such a way to make him ask me again.

That time I coyly said, "I really shouldn't, but okay." It was close to two o'clock at that point.

I was certainly accustomed to going to my cabin alone. I had never let any man walk with me during the previous five weeks of working at Crystal Lake. Letting George walk me was the first of other incidents that made me know he was special.

We walked together through the woods, taking in the sights and sounds, which I had never noticed before. We headed toward my little cabin and talked on, hardly noticing the dawn creeping up on us. We shook hands and parted. George was a gentleman; he didn't touch me.

After we parted, I couldn't believe what had just happened. I was with that handsome young man. Well, of course, I would see him the next day, but he would probably not even acknowledge me. Conflicting emotions kept me up that night. Would he approach me or just exhibit behavior as though last night didn't happen?

As it turned out, George didn't forget me. He invited me to

join him and his friends to play tennis. I turned it down because I never saw black people playing tennis. But he insisted, and I joined the group. They put a racket in my hand and showed me how to hit the ball. Almost immediately they said I was a natural athlete. I fell in love with tennis that day.

Another unexpected event popped up. That evening, Ruth and Leo had a little gathering and drinks before dinner because it was George's birthday. He and his friends left the next day. Sadly, we never got to dance at Crystal Lake Lodge, but we were able to make a date to meet after Labor Day, the end of my summer engagement.

I returned to the city on the third of September. The next day, George and I went on our first date. We walked by Grant's Tomb on Riverside Drive. I was entranced by George's life story. He was too young to remember when his father walked out on his mother, but later on in our relationship he would tell me that she died of a broken heart. After her death, his father returned and put George and his younger brother William in a Catholic orphanage. When his mother's sister and her husband discovered where the boys were, they resolved to get them out. The only way to do that was to adopt them.

After fighting through a lot of red tape and bureaucratic hassles, the boys' aunt and uncle succeeded in adopting them. They gave George and William their last name, Kaufman. The brothers were raised with a strictly kosher kitchen and they received the best education in the Jewish tradition. The Kaufmans encouraged their sons to become either lawyers, doctors or accountants. They sent William to City College of New York where he became an accountant. George, however, had a love for music and told his father.

"What!" Mr. Kaufman exclaimed. "To be a musician is to be a bum."

Neither of them knew the world's then-greatest living musician was violinist, Jascha Heiftez, a Jewish boy from Russia.

Consequently, George obediently went to Chicago Medical School, but his heart remained with music.

All of George's friends at Chicago Medical School were nice Jewish boys. They came from various cities around the world because it was the only school at that time accepting Jewish students. Perhaps because of its liberal policies, the school's student body leaned to the left. The newly graduated interns eschewed the AMA (American Medical Association) as an elitist organization. Instead, they formed AIMS, the American Intern and Medical Students group. They were altruistic and wanted to practice in the ghettos to help the poor.

At the same time, they rebelled against their Jewish roots and defied their religion. Rather than returning to their native Jewish communities, all of them decided to remain in Chicago. All except George. Devoted to his parents, he returned to New York to begin his medical practice.

Of course, George's parents never dreamed their dedicated son would wed anyone other than a nice Jewish girl. When he told them that he was going to marry me, a "schwartza," a black person, they were stunned.

Finally, Mr. Kaufman blurted out to his son, "Does she look like Lena Horne?" Little did they know.

I remember my parents' reactions when I told them that George and I were going to get married. They were shocked, too. During the years, I had dated many white fellows that I met at school and with whom I played. It never occurred to my parents that I would actually marry any of these boys. My mother had also managed to keep it secret from my dad that I had gotten pregnant by one of those boys. Despite her religious beliefs, she went to great lengths to have me get an abortion for practical reasons.

Instead of condemning me to a life with a child which would impede my career, Mom said to me, "Nothing will stand between you and your career, Laney."

She found Dr. Hunt, a man who had gone to medical school but couldn't get the necessary credentials to practice medicine because he was black. As a result, he provided this valuable service for women who couldn't afford an abortion which was expensive as well as illegal. I was eternally grateful to my mother for her humanity.

George had visited our apartment and my parents liked him. Mum suspected there was something different about George when I had allowed him to have my car while I was away with the annual opera tour. Up until then, I didn't let anyone drive my 1952 gray, four-door Ford. I told everyone that I had two loves—my car, which was my "husband," and my drums which were my "children." That became my mantra. Neighbors, colleagues and friends teased me about it, but at the time that was how I felt.

Several days before I was scheduled to go on tour, and only three months after we met, George was sad that I had to leave. That would be our first separation since we met in August. I was surprised to hear myself say to him, "I won't be here, George, but you can look after my car in my absence." Later, he would always say to me that he knew he was special because I trusted him with my precious car. Marriage was something else, because he was white.

While living in the Caribbean, my parents didn't suffer from the same kind of racism that their black-American friends had to endure. Yet, living in America, and experiencing racism themselves, they were fearful that it would affect the future of my career. Their fears would be unfounded. We learn in life, that it is not only what you can do, but who you know. By the time that George and I were thinking about getting married, I had begun already to be associated with people who respected me and my talents; people in a position to support my career goals.

Chapter 13

AUDITIONS
Can They Be Fair and Equal?

When applying for a job we must go through certain procedures to get the job. Each job has special requirements that enable a person to qualify. Applications could be a written exam, oral presentations and/or experience. Recommendation and nepotism, however, can often bypass all the other apparent requirements. These last two can be detrimental to the applicant who passes all the supposed requirements.

I first became aware of "audition" at The High School of Music & Art. At that time, we thought of it as being promoted from third term orchestra to fourth and on up to the epitome of the goal, the Eighth Term (Senior) Orchestra.

What is this "Sword of Damocles" called the audition? Anyone who has ever had to try out for a position in a chorus, orchestra, a role in a play or movie against other aspiring candidates, had to go through the process. It means going in front of a jury and performing a solo. Some people excel at taking auditions. Yet, there are those who might be the best talent, but never do well in this environment and are never hired for any job. Prior to 1958, that was the situation with orchestra auditions. It was obvious that certain people were either not invited to audition or never made it through the preliminaries.

I played for five years with the National Orchestra Association, a training orchestra. This was an orchestra organized to give aspiring instrumental symphony players the experience to achieve their goal of symphony employment. Leon

Barzin, a conductor-teacher and a superb educator, led this orchestra. He had the ability to bring to us all the nuances of playing the music of Brahms, Beethoven and Bach up to contemporary music of this era. He had outstanding soloists perform with the orchestra for the experience of playing with a soloist. Something interesting happened to me as I was playing and listening to a soloist for the first time.

We were playing Dvořák's *Concerto for Cello* with Dimitri Rostropovich playing the cello. I wasn't aware of his greatness at that time. It was my first time playing this beautiful concerto. In the hands of Rostropovich, the piece was captivating. As I just sat there counting my measures until my entrance, I became so mesmerized by his playing that I counted past the amount of measures to start playing. Fortunately, we were rehearsing.

The conductor stopped the orchestra, turned to me and said, "Ms. Jones, you are being trained to play, *not* to listen and to enjoy." Boy, I was embarrassed. But everyone laughed and sympathized with my emotion.

Although many of us were attending conservatories or music schools, Barzin was able to expand whatever we had learned. As a result, almost all the players would eventually end up in a professional orchestra at that time, except me. Playing in an orchestra involved more than playing your instrument well. You are playing with other musicians whose attitudes and style of playing techniques could be completely different from your teacher's instructions. Yet, you have to play with them in making beautiful music. This isn't an easy task and it is what you learn in a training orchestra.

Playing in the National Orchestra Association for five years, I witnessed many of my friends and colleagues going for auditions with many eventually landing jobs. I thought something was wrong with me in not having the same experience. Under these circumstances, it was impossible for me to assess why at the time. Years later when thinking back on that time of my life   years later, however, I would begin to understand.

People look at an orchestra and have no idea how difficult it is to be able to listen to one another and be aware of the conductor's demands at the same time. All of this must be accomplished as seamlessly as possible. When you look at the orchestra, all you see are about 100 musicians more or less divided between the strings, woodwinds, brass and percussions.

Now, let's address all the team sports in which players have to play together. The team with the most players—football, soccer, baseball and rugby, don't really compare to the unity and togetherness of a symphony orchestra. The musicians almost have to breathe together as one and of course, we have to be in tune with each other. All of this applies when we are on stage. The minute we walk off the stage, that's a horse of a different color. Often, the musicians don't even like, speak or socialize with each other.

When I got into the San Francisco Symphony, I would not be aware of the intensity of animosity between the players. The other orchestras the New York City Opera, New York City Ballet, New York Philharmonic, American Symphony Orchestra and Brooklyn Philharmonic were home based for me—all from New York. But I had never played in an orchestra in which players auditioned to get into it from all areas of the world, except when I played with Arthur Fiedler and the World Symphony. The National Orchestra Association was the first orchestra that I auditioned for and got the position.

Even the word, "audition" struck fear and dread into every aspiring musician trying to get into a symphony or any orchestra or music organization. Musicians preferring chamber groups didn't have the same concerns because chamber groups were generally selected. The symphony orchestra, however, was something out of this world. Musicians traveled long distances at their own expense to try out with untold numbers of other musicians auditioning for the same position. It is torture to go through so much and to come away empty handed.

One day at the union hall, I met Harry, a young black man who had just moved to New York from Cleveland. He graduated from the Cleveland Institute of Music where he was informed about and joined the National Orchestra Association to get orchestra experience. An oboe player, Harry had studied with the principal oboe player of the Cleveland Symphony. We became immediate friends and talked about our aspirations and hopes for a symphony position.

I encouraged Harry to join the musicians' union in New York. After discussing the benefits, we went to a union meeting. The meeting was interesting in that it became obvious that members tended to gather together depending on their ethnicity and the type of music they played. There were club date musicians who played the weekend gigs like dances, weddings and bar mitzvahs. Then the commercial musicians who played shows. The smallest numbers were the classically trained and chamber music musicians.

It didn't take long for Harry and me to see the racial divide among the musicians. Italian, Jewish, Latin and black gathered along the club date clique as we moved from the club date to the symphony. The ethnicity thinned out to where there were only white males. At this particular meeting, there were three of us black musicians sitting among the symphony group. The other person besides Harry and me was a young man we didn't know. So, we approached him to introduce ourselves. As we reached him, he was as surprised to see us as we were to see him.

"Hey, how you doing?" Harry and I said to the young man. "How you doing? We're surprised to see you here on this side." We all laughed together without saying another word. We already understood.

"What are your names?" he asked Harry and me. We told him.

"What's your name?" we asked him.

"Alfred Brown. Where you guys from?"

Harry answered first saying that he was relocating from Cleveland and had been in New York for a couple of months.

"And you?" Alfred questioned.

I answered that I was a New Yorker, born, raised and went to school here. "What about you?"

"I just finished Curtis."

"Curtis!" Harry and I exclaimed.

Curtis Institute of Music was the premium music school in the nation, maybe even in the world. I never heard of a black person going near the school, never mind graduating. Only a select few of the top musicians went to Curtis in Philadelphia. Harry and I were really impressed. We thought that with credentials like that, Alfred would have no problem over the years making it into a major symphony orchestra. Whether by design or not, he would never play in any organized orchestra.

Harry and I, on the other hand, were motivated by the idea of playing in a symphony. Our teachers were principal players in their respective orchestra, and we wanted to be like our teachers. My teacher at Juilliard, Saul Goodman, played timpani in the New York Philharmonic. Therefore, I dreamed about playing in the New York Philharmonic Symphony. At that time, however, nothing existed to make that dream a reality. But dreams motivate us to do better whether they are real or not.

Harry, Alfred and I met occasionally and our talk always revolved around the machination of the symphony, especially concerning auditions. Alfred always brought up the subject of the unfairness of most auditions. His frame of reference was not with black or female musicians, but with nepotism. Curtis students were considered the cream of the crop. Yet getting a position depended on who you knew.

Alfred spoke emotionally: "I'm a graduate of Curtis, yet I have no guarantee that I'll get the job I'm qualified for. These guys spent more time cultivating their friends as much as practicing."

What could we do about such a situation that affected one and all? There had to be an answer and it was soon forthcoming. One day, Harry was invited to a party given by some native Clevelanders. The people at the party were sociologists interested in furthering opportunities for blacks. One guest was Douglass Pugh, a young man who had just gotten the position of director of the National Urban League. He and Harry hit it off and became friends. Douglass was young and bright and soon began to pick up on Harry's concern about auditioning.

A few days later, Harry called me. "Hey, Elayne. I met this young man, Douglass Pugh of the Urban League who is the director. He said he would like to get together with Alfred, you and me and discuss the situation with blacks in the symphony."

I was a bit skeptical because the Urban League was not an organization of the arts. Harry, however, was impressed with Douglass's perception and genuine interest in our plight even though it wasn't jazz music we played. I reluctantly joined Harry and Alfred and met with Douglass.

The meeting turned out to be productive and led to a series of meetings during which time we contacted other musicians for their input and ideas about blacks having opportunities playing music other than jazz. Many ideas came pouring in to Douglass with two concerns taking the top seat: auditions and orchestral classical experiences. There were many black musicians who were told they couldn't audition because they had no orchestral experience. Yet, I had more than adequate orchestral experience having played for five years with the National Orchestral Association with not one invitation to audition.

Alfred was a graduate of Curtis Institute of Music. Harry was a graduate of the Cleveland Institute of Music. How would we deal with these two major problems? We had numerous meetings putting our heads together to come up with answers.

In his wisdom, Alfred pointed out: "Yes, we have to be concerned about the audition, but before we audition, we have to know the repertoire. Most of the nation's black players don't have access to playing symphonic repertoires like those of you in New York. Harry and Elayne have had more experience than any of us and yet have difficulty getting through."

He was saying that I was lucky to have gone to The High School of Music & Art, then Juilliard and Tanglewood. What did this mean? I was incrementally living in a classical symphonic world. Most blacks were still committed to being in the black community playing jazz. My focus was more towards playing symphonic music rather than being committed to music in the black community. Since the black musicians were reluctant to move out of the community, we thought we would establish a venue in which they would feel comfortable. So, in this spirit, the Symphony of the New World would be eventually created. The enormous task began of scouting the city, state and country for shy black musicians who were studying but had no outlets for their efforts.

We had numerous meetings with Douglass to discuss strategy. Publicity was necessary and he had a great idea: "Let's start first by contacting all the orchestras in the United States and recording the number of black members. We would compare that with black musicians playing jazz." We discovered that even in the jazz and swing groups, there was subtle discrimination or ethnic separation.

Under the heading of the National Urban League, we devised a questionnaire which we sent to every musical organization in the country that their research could find to query them about hiring black musicians.

Although we didn't hear back from every organization, we got enough information to bring the issue to the attention of the media. There were no black musicians in any white organization with contract or guaranteed wage. Many organizations defended their policy by reiterating their belief that black musicians "were not interested in *this* kind of music."

We had our work cut out for us. Once the story broke, however, we began getting letters from all over the country. We were stunned. There were violinists who were discouraged; although they took lessons, they had no idea where they would go. So, they generally gave up the idea of playing classical and went in the direction of swing or jazz or gave up the idea of being a professional symphonic musician.

We were then faced with the next step of organizing the orchestra. It was amazing how many black musicians as well as white musicians came forward to assist us in forming this special training orchestra. Did we bite off more than we could chew? Perhaps, but the ground swell of interest and support propelled us forward.

We decided to get together and organize. On October 12, key people gathered at my house for our initial exploratory meeting. The first order of business was our name. We bantered around many ideas. I came up with "Symphony of the New World." It came to me when thinking about the comment that Antonín Dvořák was supposed to have made when he composed his *New World Symphony*, which he attributed to the blacks in the United States. Moved by the Negro spirituals, it was said that he based his second movement on them. I was delighted when after a little discussion, my suggestion was accepted.

We went on to the next order of business of finding a conductor. Choosing the right conductor was critical because we were organizing a training orchestra in order to give to black musicians the opportunity to play orchestra repertoire. We wanted a conductor and educator like Leon Barzin who could inspire and teach. Who did we know who could fit the bill? We preferred having a black conductor, but there were few, if any, of them. So, we had to look for a progressive white conductor who could meet with our demands. Who? We left our meeting with   the objective to find the right conductor. And, find one, we would.

In making inroads into the commercial world of theater and recordings, Alfred Brown had played a gig with Benjamin Steinberg, a violinist who also did some conducting. In chatting with Steinberg, Alfred was impressed with his outlook with the racial situation and his sincerity. Alfred approached him about our project. Ben listened, was flattered and pleased with the idea. Alfred called us with his "find" and then called a meeting to discuss the possibility of hiring Benjamin Steinberg.

Everyone involved with our venture came to the meeting which would be historic. We examined Ben's credentials and conducting experience. His positive attitude played a major part in our accepting him. By the end of the meeting, we appointed Benjamin Steinberg the music director of the Symphony of the New World. We were then able to send out a press release about the formation of a training orchestra for black players.

We didn't audition any of the players; we welcomed all. Our initial requirement was for black musicians. Much to our surprise, many musicians were attracted to us like a thirsty person dying for water. Nobody doubted the value of the new orchestra. Ben Steinberg was a perfect choice for us and in less time than we had planned, we gave a debut concert.

Now that we had the orchestra in motion, we reminded each other what prompted us to form the orchestra in the first place. We were concerned about the audition procedures. With the Symphony of the New World, we were providing the opportunity to play in a symphony and get experience learning the required repertoire. Then we had to make the effort to see that when these musicians were ready, they would have the opportunity to audition fairly and equally for other orchestras. This wouldn't be an easy task as the orchestra managers had to first admit that there was discrimination in the audition procedure. Proving racism was always difficult because their rationale was, "We don't discriminate. Blacks are just not capable or qualified." So, we had to have a test case; one unexpectedly presented itself to us.

We had good public relations and made it known that our Symphony of the New World was formed for the sole purpose of giving black musicians an opportunity to get experience learning the repertoire and to play in a symphony. The response was greater than we anticipated. We had young musicians, anxious to be in the Big Apple, indicate their desire to come and play in our symphony. Among the inquiries was a young man who also had recently graduated from Curtis Institute of Music in Philadelphia, Al Brown's alma mater. Unbelievable! Another black musician and from Curtis!

We almost felt like parents looking out for their young fledglings, which was a responsibility we hadn't considered. Coming to New York, these young musicians needed housing and of course, because they weren't working, they needed to earn some money. We tried to provide them with temporary housing with friends. As for money, they would have to get part-time work, but who would hire them? We were surprised to get support from various people in the community, whites even more than blacks.

Actor Zero Mostel was one of the first known personalities to come to our financial aid. Once he made the commitment, many other personalities followed in his footsteps. We formed a board of directors, a "who's who" in the arts, health and education. So, we started out with the financial support needed to cover our expenses making it possible to plan our first concert.

Running parallel with our plans to attract musicians and work on our first concert, was the young Curtis graduate, a cellist, expressing to us his desire to audition for the New York Philharmonic. He had all the qualifications to apply for an audition. Little did we know then that his application to audition would create a national incident. About the same time, another black musician came to us from California. He was a bass player who wanted to join our orchestra and also audition for the Philharmonic. We had two black musicians on our hands wanting to audition for the open positions in the Philharmonic. A cellist and a bassist both dropped right into our laps. Openings with the Philharmonic didn't come that often so this was special manna from heaven!

Al suggested that we have them play for us as a warm-up so we could assess their playing. He was impressed with the cellist, as was Ben Steinberg, our conductor, because they were string players. The bass player was good, but we felt not as talented a musician as the cellist.

Initially, the New York Philharmonic was reluctant to accept their applications, presenting us with our first hurdle. We had to convince them there was no difference between these two musicians and other applicants. Word soon got out about the problem and spontaneously, a committee was organized for a demonstration. Signs were made up declaring, "New York Philharmonic Unfair to Black Applicants."

The demonstration had lasted only a few hours when Leonard Bernstein interceded on our behalf, embarrassing the New York Philharmonic management. They jumped the gun and announced to the press that the only reason the two musicians' applications were delayed was because they were from out of town and their references had to be checked. The two young men eventually auditioned and not surprisingly, did not make it through the first round.

That was when Al jokingly said: "Suppose it was impossible to know if musicians were black or anyone else auditioning? Would they make it?" He was joking, but it triggered an idea in our heads. We took it, analyzed it and realized we had something to work on and present. The more we thought about it, the more we were convinced that this was the path to taking discrimination out of the audition procedure.

Our next task was to convince the entire music world. A master of strategy, Douglass of the Urban League instituted the plan. We all knew white and female musicians who auditioned and didn't make it, and then expressed frustration about not getting the job they qualified to fulfill. We would appeal to them. This would be a monumental job and we were well aware of the pitfalls of the auditioning procedure.

Douglass's plan was to create a screen behind which every applicant would play. They'd be given a number and that's all would be known about them. We had a meeting with the members of the orchestra and the conductor and, after giving it a minute of thought, they voted overwhelmingly to make it mandatory for every audition. Second, we took it to the board of directors and it didn't take much convincing to get them to go on record approving, "Audition Behind a Screen."

In a shorter time than we expected, the idea was accepted, although with reservations about it in some areas of the symphony community. Eventually, they were convinced that this system was indeed in the spirit of American democracy. However, an amendment was approved, making this procedure optional: "It would be required that the semi-finals and finals be open."

Chapter 14

HOW RACISM EXISTS,
OPERATES AND CONTINUES
Will It Ever Change?

In 1985, I was deeply moved to respond to the article, "What's Behind the Shortage of Blacks in Symphony Orchestras?" published in *Ebony* magazine. By then, I had been in the classical symphonic profession for 40 years. I knew that my experiences and insights could answer the question posed by the *Ebony* article. Below is my full response at that time.

I have read with professional interest the recent article in the *Ebony* titled: "What's Behind the Shortage of Blacks in Symphony Orchestras?" My particular interest is due to the fact that I have been involved with the classical symphonic profession for the past 40 years. I have been a player and also have taken a very active political stance to integrate the orchestras. Obviously, this is a subject very dear to me body and soul.

Through the medium of my career as a professional musician, I would like to utilize my experience to demonstrate firsthand how racism exists, operates and continues on. And, in my opinion, will basically never change. I must say that the majority of my colleagues will emphatically deny the existence of racism in their lives and on the job.

Presently, I am the timpanist with the San Francisco Opera Orchestra and have been playing with the organization since 1972. I have also been the timpanist with the San Francisco Symphony from 1972 to 1975. I was given much publicity when I won the position because I became the first black person in the world to hold a principal position in a major symphony orchestra. The timpani in a symphony orchestra is considered a principal position. As a matter of fact, the timpanist in most orchestras is among the highest paid—a fact which I suspect was a contributing factor in why I did not get tenure. I sued the San Francisco Symphony on grounds of racism but was not successful. Another factor which contributes to the evidence that we are not wholeheartedly accepted in the orchestral family is lip service given to our absence with a "rational" sounding explanation such as: "They really don't have enough experience to play amongst us."

I, along with my two black colleagues, Harry Smyles, oboist, and Arnold Brown, violist, initiated a campaign with the political encouragement and support of the Urban League in 1958 to investigate the reasons behind the absence of blacks in not just symphony orchestras, but in any musical aggregation other than blues and jazz bands. Black musicians did not "have a choice" as to what kind of music they could play. Everyone just assumed black musicians were alien to classical music and their preference for music was only jazz. If a player did express a desire to play the other music, he or she was discouraged as I was.

It didn't take long for us to get feedback from musicians all over the country of their desire to play classical music, and each expressed the desire to gain the necessary experience. It was as a result of this information that the Symphony of the New World came into existence. The first result of our working with the National Urban League was my being hired to play with the New York Philharmonic Symphony in 1958, making me the first black to ever play with that organization.

In the meantime, we took seriously what was said about the need for experience by black musicians in symphonic literature. Our next task was to do something about it and that's when we decided to form the Symphony of the New World. We had as our inaugural conductor a white man named Benjamin

Steinberg, and our first concertmaster was also a white man named Harold Glickman. We had several other white musicians as members making it an integrated orchestra. Many problems beset the orchestra, the major being financial. The sources of funding were denied us because we were considered racist, even with white members playing key positions in the organization. Clearly, the white elitists did not really want us to achieve that degree of much needed experience under any circumstance.

In those days, before one could get into the major symphonies, it was necessary to serve an apprenticeship in one of the secondary orchestras, most of which were in the south. When I was playing in the training orchestra called National Orchestral Association, there was a big joke among the players and me. They left the National Orchestral Association and went into the Dallas, New Orleans or Houston symphony orchestras, all in the South, which excluded blacks. They would go down to these orchestras and when they returned, I'd still be in the National Orchestral Association. However, I just happened to be in the right place at the right time by staying in New York, because that was to be the year that the New York Ballet Society became the New York City Ballet. The conductor was Leon Barzin who was also the conductor and director of the National Orchestral Association. He was very impressed with my work and offered me the job playing with the ballet in 1948. I was the only black person in the orchestra. To this day, I know of only two other blacks to play with the orchestra. I recently visited New York and the opera companies, and neither the Metropolitan Opera nor the New York City Opera have any black players as permanent contracted musicians.

It does anger me, however, that in 1985, hardly any progress has been made 27 years after we initiated the struggle for blacks to be employed in symphony orchestras. True, there are some orchestras with minorities. The last count of the 20 orchestras with two or more performances a week, or a schedule of 30 or more weeks has 28 black, 21 Hispanic and 52 Asian players.

It takes time I'm told by many of my adversaries. Black players have to have experience and training and "We all know black people don't support the symphony, and besides, they don't show up for auditions," they say. I wish to go on record and state once and for all that these are excuses given to preserve the elitist environment of the symphony family. We have *not* "come a long way baby."

Let's analyze first the subject of experience. Music is a very subjective profession. Just observe the various reviews of concerts and you get a perfect example of what I am referring to. Whenever we give a performance we like to get feedback from the audience and sometimes solicit their opinion. However, no two people ever have the same response. When you read the reviews of critics in the paper it is incredible. After reading two or more critics you wonder if they could have all attended the same performance at the same day and time. One critic will say the program was great and another will say the exact opposite. Now, when you apply that same critical evaluation to a player's performance, if he or she is not wanted, it is too easy to reject the player on grounds that the playing is not up to what is desired.

If baseball, football and basketball players were judged similarly to musicians I am sure there would not be as many black players in those sports. When an athlete hits a homerun, shoots a basket or scores a touchdown, there is no disputing the fact.

When a musician plays a phrase, if 10 people are judging, then it is quite possible to have one judge say the tuning is bad or the rhythm is not right or the tone is unacceptable. I can attest to that fact because that subjectivism is how in 1975, I was denied tenure with the San Francisco Symphony. I had received rave reviews from audiences and critics alike which of course was unusual. The players, however, said that I was not good enough to be part of their great orchestra. When I was bounced out of the orchestra did they hire someone with years of experience such as I had? Of course not! As a matter of fact, my predecessor's experience would be incomparable to what I had when I graduated Juilliard in 1949. Chances are that if the situation was reversed, I would not have gotten that job because I would have been told that I didn't have enough experience.

The stories of this nature are too numerous to go into. I sit in the back of the orchestra (in the percussion section) feeling like Madame Defarge observing and making notes of all that goes on. I disagree with the various programs which have been set up to give black musicians experience. If we pursue this tactic of saying that there must be special training for black musicians, then we fall into the trap of allowing apartheid mentality to reign in the profession and in other industries, whether in opera, chorus or classical dance. I therefore object to the program of special training for black musicians. That's just another way of trying to prove that we are inferior.

I know many European and European-american musicians who have been hired at the symphony or the opera with no experience, but solely on the concept that they "will learn." I remember having a conversation with a young player in the orchestra, after a rehearsal, of some standard work from the repertoire. He was complaining that we did not have enough rehearsal time to learn the work.

My comment was that by the time you get into a major symphony you should have had enough experience to know this music like the back of your hand. These rehearsals are not for us to learn the music, but for the conductor to put his personal musical stamp on it. You should learn in a training orchestra or in a community orchestra where not as much money has been invested in you for your education. Naturally he resented my criticism, but in the back of my mind was the thought that if he were black, then he would not have been considered qualified for the job.

The black community is known for its church-going music-loving parishioners. The choirs sing gospel as well as music of Bach, Beethoven and Handel at all the holiday festivals. So, to say blacks don't support classical music is another of the rhetoric used against us.

However, there are many in the symphony and opera orchestras whose parents are probably less involved in the music than any black family. I remember having a conversation with a young man in the orchestra whose parents had never attended a concert and knew nothing of classical music. "Where did you get your talent and inspiration from?" I inquired. He explained that his father was a successful contractor, and although at first did not take too eagerly that his son wanted to be a musician, eventually supported him in his effort by providing the necessary funds for his education.

Economics does play a critical role in our being able to avail ourselves of prestigious teachers. Racism affects us in the pocketbook and that is evident in where and with whom we study.

Part of my success was due to having studied with Saul Goodman, former timpanist with the New York Philharmonic. I was lucky to graduate The High School of Music & Art at the right time. The year I graduated, June 1945, was the year that Duke Ellington was offering scholarships to three outstanding graduating students, which would qualify them to attend Juilliard for three years. I was one of the winners, and as a result, I was able to attend the school that my parents never could afford.

My time spent at the school was extremely difficult because my colleagues did everything in their power to make life impossible. But I'm grateful for that because it helped me to develop the fortitude and strength to continue in a very hostile environment.

Every black youngster naturally is not outstanding enough to get a scholarship, but that doesn't negate the fact that there are many talented youth in our community. Those who have succeeded in breaking in generally have been recipients of scholarships making it possible to study with the prestigious teachers. Although they are talented, the job expectations are very low, which is interpreted that all the black players are extraordinarily talented, yet are still limited in their job expectations for job employment.

Most of my white colleagues were not scholarship students but their parents either had the income or contacts making it possible to send their offspring to the best and most prestigious teachers. Teachers have egos, and of course try to place their students on jobs which reflect their own image. Often these students are not outstanding but remain where they are on the teacher's reputation. Black players have difficulty in this area financially and socially. The average black family has neither the income nor access to these teachers.

I am well aware that if I had not won the scholarship to Juilliard and studied with Saul Goodman, I would never have been hired to play with the New York City Opera when I auditioned for them in 1949. They were reluctant to hire me to play timpani in a medium in which they believed only Italians, Germans and French musicians could interpret and play correctly. However, my teacher intervened, saying I was his best student. Being that he was the timpanist of the New York Philharmonic, they hired me on his recommendation. Studying with the right teacher these days was crucial.

It's no longer just a question of finding a good teacher to develop your craft; many children are being turned out from the conservatories with very few jobs available. Recently I attended a conference in New York City on stress and medical problems of the performing artist. One of the panelists stated that one of the contributing factors to stress is the statistic that less than 10 percent of graduates from a conservatory or a music school will find a job in their field. And those who are working are terrified of losing their position to a young aspiring candidate. With these kinds of statistics, it makes it 100 percent more untenable for the black student.

Even if you have been fortunate and win the opportunity to study with the right teacher, there is the next problem of purchasing an instrument. The professional string player is caught in this bind because decent instruments are outrageously expensive and can cost anywhere up to $10,000. Lending institutions have not been known to be generous in handing out loans to black people, so where can an aspiring black violinist raise the funds for a reputable instrument?

I think it is important to observe the number of white women who have suddenly become members of orchestras as compared to black musicians in the past ten years. Their presence confirms in my mind that it is only the manifestation of racism which deprives black youths of the opportunity to compete equally for the jobs in orchestras. Financially and socially, white women have many advantages over black men and women. In just the San Francisco Opera orchestra there are more women than the total number of blacks in all the orchestras in the world.

The women are not satisfied with the gains they have made and are demanding more representation. However, when I discuss the small numbers of non-whites employed, they tell me to wait, everything takes time. Why must we be patient and wait? For how long? Why should I be satisfied to see one or two black musicians in an orchestra when the white females are dissatisfied with their small representation? Their getting a job in an orchestra does nothing for the black community morally, socially or financially. If anything, their presence acts as a deterrent because they are classified as "minorities," therefore the minority quotas are satisfied when it comes to funding of equal opportunity employers. I see the pattern in many areas in which the power of money is necessary in order to reach one's goal.

I see no significant change in the pattern until we have enough money to finance our own orchestras and develop our own conservatories. I played with the New York City Ballet in the 1940s when there were no black dancers until Arthur Mitchell made his debut. Black women did not have a chance because as was told to me, black women's bodies were not suitable for ballet. Then Arthur was innovative enough to challenge their domination by forming his own dance company in a time period that boggles the mind. He has been able to defy the elitist tradition and have black youngsters with their body and foot configuration dance with as much form, vigor and sensitivity as any ballet company I have ever played with. And I have played in the orchestra for the American Ballet Theater, New York City Ballet, Bolshoi and the Sadler Wells, now known as the Royal Ballet. If it were not for Arthur Mitchell and Alvin Ailey, our black children would never have had the opportunity to dance professionally and make a career of classical dancing. Nothing made me any happier than to see beautiful young black bodies dance the ever popular *The Firebird* by Igor Stravinsky.

When I speak of apartheid mentality, I refer to the fact that because the white European origin people of America control the financial stronghold, through the job market, they are in the position to dictate what jobs we have and what our income will be.

If we wish to know what is going on in our community, then we have to have our own media. If we wish to act, we must form our own theaters and perhaps also our own film industry, and of course, if our youngsters wish to have a choice in which kind of music they would like to play, then it will be necessary to organize our own orchestras. The U.S. Supreme Court struck down the concept of separate but equal educational facilities as a form of discrimination. But it appears to me that if we want our children to be in a position to have freedom of choices, then we will have to pursue a course of establishing our own, which means separate but perhaps not so equal. At this rate, I foresee having two distinct worlds: One for blacks and one for whites, providing we can raise the funds.

Chapter 15

MARRIAGE, CAREER AND CHILDREN
Doing It All!

I was so happy when George and I married. I was happy with my job at the New York City Opera and George was happy as an internist at Queens General Hospital. We had a wonderful apartment in Sunnyside, Queens, New York.

All of George's friends were surprised when learning he was going to marry a "schwarza," a black person. The shock was even greater for his parents. They could not and would not accept the fact that their son was marrying a black gentile, after all they sacrificed to send him to medical school to attract a "nice Jewish girl." They were so upset that instead of returning the RSVP letter to our wedding, they sent a telegram announcing the death of their son, George Kaufman. They then sat Shiva, the ceremony of a death. George and I didn't know about the telegram because my mother intercepted it and wouldn't tell us about it until many months later.

All of George's friends from medical school, now young Jewish physicians, came to New York to celebrate our union. It was a joyous event! After the wedding, we went straight away to our honeymoon in upstate New York, putting off having to face a possible hostile agent at our new apartment.

No blacks lived in Sunnyside. Although it was illegal to discriminate against potential renters, it was always surreptitiously happening. An organization called SCAD, the State Commission Against Discrimination, was able to shine the light on discriminating practices in housing. When hearing of an available apartment in an all-white community, they sent a white couple and a black couple to apply for the same apartment. In every case, the black couple was denied access to the apartment for any reason, rational or not, that the management felt appropriate.

Unbeknownst to me, George had moved many of his things into our apartment. What could the management do then? They couldn't accuse us of false information because there was nothing in the contract about not renting to other than Caucasian people. We had out-foxed them!

Even though there were no visible signs of black people in the area, we had no difficulty with anyone—neighbors, store keepers or merchants. Sunnyside was considered a community of political action. Having those progressive people as friends comforted George, lessening his sense of loneliness after his family disowned him. With friends like those, our marriage started out on a blissful path with no negative attitudes directed toward us. Ironically, our marriage would have been declared illegal if it had taken place two years earlier.

We decided to have a house warming. In those days, it was typical to have fund raising parties for political causes. At that time, attention was on the beginning of the campaign of the Progressive Party presidential candidate, Vincent Hallinan. George and I were interested in his candidacy because there was the possibility that he would select Charlotta Bass, a black woman, as his running mate. That was a critical issue and we wanted to do everything possible to support them financially. If Charlotta became the vice president, it would be a first in American history.

Not only did we have politically focused parties, but in between, we met at the hootenanny, joyous folk music concerts. The music was written and played about the struggles of the blacks and the working-class people, and about ending fascism. Pete Seeger and the Weavers played at these events. George and I left those concerts feeling that we would win the battles by fighting for our beliefs.

George and I eventually decided to give a house warming party to encompass all our major political issues. Our apartment was not big; we had one bedroom and a large living room. That did not deter me. I used my address list from Crystal Lake Lodge and Camp Unity, where I had played in the band the year before, and invited everyone. With this party, I discovered that I loved to cook and entertain. I began to acquire a reputation not only as a musician, but as a cook and party hostess. I am not sure how, but word got around about Elayne the black musician and George the Jewish doctor, who we were and what we did, in the progressive Sunnyside district. We became local celebrities who were invited to every function, and we attended if we weren't working.

"First comes love, then comes marriage, then comes mother with a baby carriage," as the old saying went. I was thrilled when I discovered I was pregnant. There was no doubt in my mind because I had a menses which came like clockwork. The abortion I had at 19 didn't affect my menses rhythm or my health as many anti-abortionists liked to claim. This time, the discovery was ecstasy. When I told George, he was so happy. A simple thing like having a baby was one of monumental joy. George was doubly jubilant because he had completed his internship at the hospital. He was fully *Dr. George Kaufman* and he was going to be a father. At the hospital, he told everyone at the hospital within earshot.

I didn't tell my parents and opera colleagues until I had gotten so big that I couldn't wear my usual clothes. With pride, I walked into rehearsal and my parents' house, wearing a maternity dress. My parents and colleagues exclaimed, "You're pregnant!" All were excited for us.

In the meantime, I had to find an obstetrician. I asked all my progressive friends about a reliable physician. One name kept coming up, which surprised me—the name of a woman—Dr.

Clementina Paolone. No one I knew ever had a female doctor. On top of being a doctor, she was also running for city council on the American Labor Party ticket. With those credentials, there was no doubt that I would go to her. I had hoped she didn't have a long list of patients, but it did not matter. George and I called her and made an appointment for an interview, and went to her office in Greenwich Village. I immediately liked Dr. Paolone. She wasn't a typical doctor, yet she made me feel at ease that she would take good care of me—and she did!

My initial visit was not the usual medical exam; Dr. Paolone was interested in my life, because she was running for political office. She wanted to know what was important in our lives as citizens of the city. Visits to her were always long because she talked with all her patients. It was more like a political get-together.

My doctor put no restraints on me in the early days of my pregnancy. It was during this period that I embarked on a bus tour with the New York City Opera. Everyone worried about me except Dr. Paolone. When asked if I were going to continue playing in the orchestra, I said, "Of course, I'll play as long as possible and I'm feeling up to it."

My colleagues and my friends all asked: "But how can you play timpani when you're pregnant? Imagine a woman playing timpani while pregnant!"

Fortunately, I didn't have morning sickness so I never had to worry about missing morning rehearsals. I was sensitive to some odors, but not enough to make me sick. Many women said there was always something they craved. Later, I would realize that I too had a craving.

One night, coming home after a matinee opera performance, I had a craving I couldn't ignore. When George came home from the hospital, as usual he always wanted to know how I was feeling. I was fine, but I had a craving. When he questioned me, and learned what I wanted, he went right out to a butcher shop and brought back the thickest, most beautiful piece of filet mignon. It was tender and juicy; I was in heaven! I don't remember having any more cravings after that one.

The opera season always began in September. We went on tour at the end of November for a couple of weeks. "Elayna," Joe Fabbroni called me, "you know we a going on tour and I hear you are pregnant. My wife, she cannot go anywhere when she got pregnant. So, maybe you no can go with us. Maybe we send little Joe in your place?"

Well, I knew there was an old wives' tale that women should be very careful in the early months to avoid a miscarriage. I told Fabbroni that I'd speak with my obstetrician and hear her opinion. I called Dr. Paolone and told her the situation. I should have known she would give me free reign.

"Elayne," she said, "you are in good health and have a positive attitude. I wouldn't tell you what to do unless I thought you were endangering yourself. I know you're not doing anything foolish."

Being the manager, Fabbroni's fear, however, was to protect the job, which of course was his responsibility. He made sure everyone was on the job at down beat. I was sure he was thinking about what would happen if I got sick. Although my doctor and my physician husband had confidence in me, Joe was still apprehensive. Being an old-fashioned Italian man, that was his culture. So, I worried more about him and then I made up my mind he'd have no problem with me.

I traveled with the company on tour of one-night engagements by train and bus for three weeks. As my pregnancy progressed, I myself began to wonder how long I would be able to play.

The spring opera season schedule came out after the tour and promised to be demanding, followed then by the Light Opera season. I hardly had any time off. By then, my size had almost doubled, although Dr. Paolone was strict about how much weight I should gain. She gave me a limit of 25 pounds, requiring me to be careful with what I ate. This was all Dr. Paolone demanded of me. Other than that, the pregnancy didn't put any restrictions on me.

Everyone including me, wondered if my belly would eventually get in the way of reaching the drums or limit my movement going from one drum to the other. The growth was so gradual that I wasn't aware of any difficulty. However, as I got bigger, I was cause for much curiosity from the audience.

After I was hired to play with the New York City Opera at the New York City Center, the patrons came down to the pit when they heard I was there and stared at me. Then on top of that to be pregnant was a little more than they could take. At one point, I was tempted while playing there to put up a sign next to me saying, "Please, don't feed the animal."

The time was fast approaching when I'd be ready to deliver. Joe Fabbroni's main concern then was when would it happen. We were in the Light Opera summer season with a performance every night except Monday, we performed *Carousel*, the musical by Rogers and Hammerstein.

He asked me, "Elayna, when is your due date?" I couldn't say. All we know was the first child is like a crap-shoot. We never know if it will be early, late or on time, so we speculated.

Dr. Paolone examined me and said I would most likely deliver sometime around the middle of June. We all agreed I would play until Sunday, June 13. What a happy day! The entire cast and orchestra gave me a rousing sendoff with flowers, baby clothes and well wishes. I left that Sun evening with expectations of giving birth soon and not seeing anyone until after my delivery.

I saw Dr. Paolone on Tuesday, my usual visit, and she said, "You're ready to deliver any day now." George drove me home to wait.

The next morning, the phone rang and I answered. It was Joe

Fabbroni. "Hello, Elayna, how you a feel?"

"I'm fine, Joe, how's everything?"

"Elayna, you have your baby yet?"

"No, Joe. I'm, still waiting."

"Well," he said, pausing, "can you come in and play tonight?"

"What? Play tonight?" I said incredulously. I repeated, "Play tonight? Did I hear you right? What happened to my sub?"

"Davy Grupp, he break-a his foot."

"How?" I pressed. "Where? When?"

He explained, "Davy, he a break-a his foot tripping over the wires when he walk into the pit!"

I couldn't believe what I was hearing. Dave, a big strong man tripping over the wires in the pit after I had waddled in and out of the pit for nine months with no problems.

The pit is below the stage and in order to see our music, because it is dark, there are lights on every stand. These lights have cables which are attached to a central outlet. For every light, there is a cable going along the floor to the main switch. I never gave a thought to walking over those wires but for some strange reason, Dave tripped on them and badly twisted his foot. He managed to get through Tuesday night, but couldn't return for Wednesday's performance. So, Joe called me to come in and sub for my sub! What a big joke to the whole company to see me, a pregnant woman about to deliver, return to play for a big, healthy man.

I told George and called Dr. Paolone; they both thought I was crazy to go into work. But I went in and played Wednesday night and then Thursday night. George drove me to City Center and waited for me, just in case. I felt fine. I played not only timpani, but percussion and mallets. I played timpani and any other instrument called for, then sat during the dialogue on stage and got up to play again after the spoken dialogue. On Thursday, however, every time I stood up to play, I felt as though my back was still sitting on the chair and my energy was being drained out of me. I felt tired, which I never felt all nine months. At the end of the opera that night, I was extremely glad to see George waiting for me at the stage door.

"How ya feeling, honey?" he asked as soon as he saw me.

"Boy, am I tired!" was all I could say. Our drive home to Sunnyside didn't take long. We traveled just over the Fifty-Ninth Street Bridge and up to Forty-Fifth Avenue. I couldn't wait to get into the house to go to the bathroom, undress and lie down. Then I saw it. Fortunately, we musicians were required to wear black to perform in because, when I took off my black performance dress, there was a big red spot on my underclothes.

"George!" I yelled, "Look at this!"

He ran into the bathroom and I showed him. He looked at me and said with a knowing smile: "I don't think you'll be playing tomorrow night. You'd better call Joe and tell him you are in early labor."

"What? I'm in labor? How could that be?" I was in shock because I wasn't experiencing the pains I'd read about.

"Well, that'll come later," George explained. "We don't know when, but it could happen any time. In the meantime, call Joe Fabbroni. What you're having is a bloody show, meaning the baby has dropped and will begin the descent."

Nothing happened the next day and I felt that I could go back to work. George, being the knowledgeable doctor, would not hear of it. I called Fabbroni and said he would have to find a sub because I was in the beginning of labor.

"Ok," he said. "Good luck and let us know when it comes."

The waiting on Friday was the toughest, made even worse by the visit from Cleveland of George's best friend, Harvey with his wife, Ida. Harvey wanted to go down to the lower east side to the Katz's Delicatessen on Houston Street. It was known for having the best Kosher roast beef and hot pastrami sandwiches in the world. So off we went to Katz's. The smell of the food greets you when you are within a block of the place. We walked in, sat down and ordered. George and Harvey, who was also a physician, wouldn't let me order anything. In their infinite wisdom, they, said I shouldn't eat because labor was imminent and would be better on an empty stomach. How could I contradict these two experts? But the fact was I didn't feel like I was in labor. I was feeling great. So, I had to sit there, smell the delicious sandwiches and watch them eat with relish. That was the worst torture of my entire pregnancy!

After we went home, I began to feel little contractions around midnight, but not enough to say anything to George. Then, about five o'clock in the morning, I got my first real contraction. I laid and waited for others, but again nothing like what I had heard or read about. When I felt them consistently, I woke George and told him. He got up and told me to get prepared we were headed for the hospital. He called Dr. Paolone and alerted her.

We drove to Manhattan General Hospital and got there a little after eight o'clock, at which time I was admitted. I still wasn't feeling any discomfort. At around ten o'clock, Dr. Paolone came in and examined me. She said I was doing fine, as she thought I would. In those days, the expectant father was relegated to waiting with bated breath for the delivery. But because George was a physician, he was allowed to stay with me. Dr. Paolone seemed to arrive at the point when the contractions were coming more frequently. She and George stood next to my bed and engaged in a political discussion to a point that I was like an afterthought.

Every so often, Dr. Paolone turned to me and said, "Push dear, push." By then my feet were in stirrups and a nurse came and put something over my face and told me to breathe, relax and push. I was feeling euphoric.

The next thing I experienced was a great relief in hearing George say, "Honey, we have a son." At noon, Saturday, June

19, 1954, our son Stephen was born. Up until then I had been getting publicity about my musical achievements. I felt however, that what I wanted publicity for was being able to deliver a beautiful healthy son, even though many other women in the world were giving birth. To me, giving birth to Stephen surpassed anything I had ever accomplished.

I had read about the value of breast feeding over formulas. Yet, women were discouraged from breast feeding for all the wrong reasons. When the United States took control of Puerto Rico and the Philippines, they controlled the sugar from these countries; they had to do something with the sugar. The "great" medical minds decided that sugar was good for every baby's development so a campaign was launched to promote formulas for feeding babies in place of breast milk. Women were made to think that breast feeding wasn't necessary because the formulas were better. Fortunately, both George and Dr. Paolone were aware of this propaganda. When I said that I wanted to nurse my son, the nurses put him instead in the nursery to feed him. Dr. Paolone and George had to go to the nursery and fight the head nurse to release Stephen. To suckle successfully, the baby must not be given a bottle with the formula. So only with their insistence was I able to nurse Stephen. He was a good baby and immediately regulated himself to nursing like clockwork: every three hours.

On my third day in the hospital, I had a surprise. My best friend Milroy's husband, Danny Levitt, walked into my room. Milroy and I were friends before we married our husbands. We had met at Camp Unity, the left progressive resort in Wingdale, New York. I knew Danny because he was the best friend of a fellow named Alan Siegler who I dated briefly before meeting George. Alan and I were invited several times to Danny's house in Bensonhurst, Brooklyn. Danny was aspiring to become an actor and Alan, along with all Danny's friends, wrote for the progressive newspaper, *PM*. Danny invited us to his house because his parents were proud of their leftist ideologies. Jewish people who owned a candy store, they loved having us come to the house for political discussions. They always made a point of saying how they loved seeing black and white couples together. There were many black and white couples who met at Camp Unity and came to Mr. and Mrs. Levitt's house for political gatherings and discussions.

After the summer, there would always be Camp Unity reunion parties. At one of these parties, Danny met Milroy, who was an aspiring actress. She was very vivacious, bright and black. They became an item at first sight. Milroy became a part of our group and went along to the Levitt home. Their romance blossomed and after several months, Danny asked Milroy to marry him. They made a handsome couple; we were all happy for them. Everyone was excited about their impending marriage, except Mr. and Mrs. Levitt who were quite vocal in expressing their disapproval. They stopped having the discussions at their house and even stopped speaking to Danny. We all were dismayed at their behavior. How could they have been so open and positive about racial relationships and do such a complete 180-degree turnaround when it came to their son?

The answer surfaced when Danny's best friend and my friend, Alan Siegler, went to the house. He didn't beat around the bush and asked them directly why they had changed so drastically. Mrs. Levitt told us.

"Yes, we still think interracial relationships are good and it is fine for others. We're Jewish, however, and always looked forward to having a nice Jewish girl as a daughter-in-law. It never occurred to my husband and me that this would happen to us. It is okay for others, but not us."

Danny and Milroy proceeded with the wedding preparation in spite of the Levitts' actions. Danny's parents eventually relented and became friends with the couple. However, they never had any more discussions at their home.

I was delighted when Danny and his parents walked into my hospital room. Milroy had gotten pregnant the same time as I did, and we both had Dr. Paolone as our obstetrician. Milroy had a difficult pregnancy and was at risk of losing the baby until my husband gave her the infamous medication, Stilbestrol, to prevent miscarriage. Milroy had to stay in bed for almost the entire nine months and went with me to her appointments when she could. Because of this, there was no predicted date for her delivery.

When I asked about Milroy, Danny said she was rushed up to the operating room for a caesarian. We all waited anxiously for the results. After what seemed like an eternity, Dr. Paolone came down and announced everything was fine. Milroy had delivered a beautiful little girl. We were overjoyed and relieved. Mrs. Levitt was especially thrilled because she said how wonderful that Milroy had a girl and that I had a boy. She thought that if our children eventually married each other there'd be no problems.

After four days in the hospital, I happily came home with my beautiful bundle of joy. He continued nursing every three hours. With just a whimper, he indicated he was awake and ready for his special "milk container." The pregnancy and birth were so easy that there was no doubt in my mind that I would have the four children I always dreamed about. I couldn't think of anything that would stand in my way.

That summer was wonderful. It was the first since graduating from Juilliard that I wasn't involved in music. I was able to devote my time to George and my little son. In about the middle of August, however, I got a call from Joe Fabbroni at the New York City Opera.

"Hello Elayna, I'm a-calling to find out how you are a-feeling."

"I'm doing fine, Joe, and I feel great," I said.

"I'm glad to hear that. We're all wondering if you will be

coming back to work and when."

I knew I was going to return, but hadn't thought about it any further. His call brought me back to reality. I *had* to go back to work.

"Of course, Joe," I said, not batting an eye. "When does the season begin?"

"I will send you the schedule right away," he continued, telling me the date of the first rehearsal.

I hung up and had many concerns to ponder. I told George about the call and going back to work. Our first thought was care for Stephen. I didn't want to give up nursing, but how could I go to work and nurse? George said the only solution was to wean Stephen. I wasn't ready for that, but the alternative would be taking him with me, which would be a bit controversial. Most women weren't nursing their babies. So I didn't know anyone taking her baby to work while nursing. How could there be when the women in the chorus and ballet and the soloist were all either single or childless? It just wasn't the thing in that environment.

Once again, I faced having to do the unusual; this time, being a working woman with a baby playing the timpani in the orchestra. I don't know if I would have considered taking Stephen to work if he was a difficult baby. So, on the day of our first rehearsal, Stephen was in my arms as I walked into the hall. I was greeted with hugs from the musicians, mostly with disbelief that I was there. All the men were married with wives who stayed home with their babies.

George and I had found a wonderful carriage which could be broken down to fit in the car, and then could be taken apart and carried like a bassinet. I don't know if it was the sound of music, but at the rehearsal, Stephen slept until I had to awaken him for nursing time. All the men gathered around me to see my son. Most of them were accustomed to being awakened by crying, cranky babies. But Stephen was one who had to be awakened. The comments coming from the men were hilarious, most asking if I had put drugs in my milk. I was just as surprised, but delighted and proud. I would, however, have to consider weaning Stephen as the rehearsal period led closer to the opening performances.

As good as Stephen was, I couldn't take chances during a performance that he would wake up to be fed. I don't know which would be more difficult, weaning him or leaving him at home, but I had to face both at the same time.

So far, I had done well challenging all the old wives' tales about working and pregnancy. It was strange, though, seeing those women in history who having babies under every conceivable situation without fanfare. But, in my world, I was treated as doing something unusual. I had read about women in slavery who had no choice but to give birth to their babies in the field and keep on working.

From my perspective, however, the worst was yet to come. Caring for the baby with schedule demands of rehearsals and performances got me no sympathy because many of the men subjectively believed a woman's place was at home with her baby. They joked about it every chance they got. I felt pressured to be at every service, rehearsal and performance on time and ready to focus. I had to develop a kind of schizoid attitude totally separating my being a mother and wife at home, and then being a totally focused musician in the orchestra. This split would follow me throughout my career.

It may have seemed cruel, but if I was going to continue playing, I had to devise that way of dealing with home, children and my job. I was fortunate that my children's father was a physician, so I did not have to worry about making an appointment to take a sick child to the doctor, which could have conflicted with a rehearsal or a performance. I did, however, have a wonderful pediatrician, Dr. Jenkins.

My reputation preceded me wherever I went. When I called

him for an appointment, I mentioned I had limited time. He told me, "Just tell me when you can come and I'll try to arrange a time convenient to you." Because Stephen was born in June, and I didn't have to return to work until September, making the early doctor appointments easy to schedule.

The upcoming annual tour of the New York City Opera at the end of the season was fast approaching. Even though I was unnerved about leaving Stephen every day, I hated to think about being away from him for several weeks. No returning home after performance and waking up with Stephen in the morning. Could I handle such a separation?

My mother was the savior. She had stopped teaching piano and found she enjoyed caring for children. Teaching had become too inconsistent with students coming and leaving, and Mum needed the income. She discovered caring for the child of a working mother would be stable work and income. So, I took advantage of my mother's situation. At seven o'clock in the morning, I packed up Stephen and drove with him from Sunnyside, Queens to Harlem in Manhattan where my parents lived. I left him and my car at my mother's house, and then took the subway downtown to City Center. After rehearsal, I reversed the travel, picked up Stephen and drove home. If I had a performance, I made dinner for George and me, fed Stephen, put him in his father's arms and went off to play an opera. If there was a night with no performance, I made a great dinner. I had discovered that I loved to cook and all through my married life, I would always make interesting dinners. On those off-performance nights, I also had my pleasure of feeding, bathing and reading to Stephen, and putting him to bed, cuddling and kissing him. He slept through the night.

As the upcoming tour loomed before me, I hated the thought of leaving my baby, but it was my decision, so I had to live with it. We had a family discussion. How would Stephen be cared for in my absence? My mother made a proposal, which George and

I agreed to follow. We would take Stephen to Mum's house and she would take care of him until I returned. I had no misgivings whatsoever with this arrangement. I packed up Stephen and his belongings the day before we were scheduled to leave and sadly left him with my mother. In the years to follow, I would continue to tour while pregnant two more times, and get through with flying colors. However, I would always have the same concerns and sadness about leaving my children.

When George finished his residency at Queens General Hospital we moved to St. Albans. He was offered a position at the hospital and decided to accept it. Thinking it would be nice to have our own place, we had to decide where to live. We wanted to live in an area supportive of our interracial relationship. We investigated and spoke to everyone about the best community for us. Corona, Forest Hills, Flushing, Jamaica or St. Albans? Through reports and statistics, we decided on St. Albans and began looking for a house. We found a house that suited both our needs on the corner of 112th Avenue and Farmers Boulevard. It was perfect for a doctor to put up his shingle and big enough for him to make the bottom half into a waiting room, office and examination room. There was a full basement suitable for entertaining and a large kitchen which we would modernize.

Although St. Albans was farther away from Manhattan, the traveling was easy because the bus stopped in front of our house and connected with the subway, taking me right to City Center. Other times, I drove to the express subway stop, making the travel even faster. I continued playing, taking care of baby Stephen, and traveling back and forth to our new home. George set up his practice at our house. We were busy; I never took time off and I did not believe in taking naps.

The spring opera ended in late June. I didn't have work after that, so I took every call to play single concerts. By this time, Mum and Dad had followed us into Queens from Harlem by purchasing a home near us. It was so convenient for Mum to come to our house or for me to take Stephen to her house. We had everything to satisfy our needs and were very happy. The house was suitable for the arrival of our second child, which was imminent.

"How do you feel, honey?" George approached me one day, questioningly around the time I was scheduled to give birth.

"Well, I'm fine," I said. "I just saw Dr. Paolone and she said I'd probably deliver very soon. I just feel a little tired from driving home in the awful rush hour traffic."

George looked at me with concern. "Are you sure you're okay? I don't like the way you look."

"I'm just tired from the drive home," I defended.

"I think it's more than that, I think you're in labor."

"No way! I just left Dr., Paolone. I'm not having contractions."

"I don't care," George continued. "I'm canceling my office hours and taking you to the hospital and calling Dr. Paolone. Go get your stuff and let's go."

I stopped protesting, though I was skeptical, but did as he said and prepared to go to the hospital. I still didn't feel any discomfort and didn't even have the bloody show, and my water hadn't broken. George, however, was convinced I was in labor and we drove into crowded Manhattan. The traffic was slow, but I wasn't worried.

We finally arrived at Manhattan General Hospital where the admitting nurse took me directly to the admittance area. George called Dr. Paolone while I was being admitted. She was at home getting ready to go to a meeting. When George told her where we were, she couldn't believe it. She said she would come to the hospital immediately. In the meantime, I was taken up to the delivery room.

The nurses came to me and said, "You're ready to deliver, where is your doctor?"

Well, this was more than I could fathom. I was ready to deliver? I couldn't believe it and not only that, the nurses were telling me not to breathe or the baby will come before the doctor! This was most difficult, because with the baby ready to come, it was like trying to hold back the sun from rising. George was anxious, trying to console me and hoping that Dr. Paolone would arrive soon. He might have been worrying that he would have to deliver his own child. Gratitude washed over his face when seeing Dr. Paolone walk in, ready to go to work.

In what seemed like one second, I was placed in the stirrups and told to breathe. Those were two words of relief because it seemed like as soon as I breathed, Harriet was born. Everyone was shocked. How George knew she would come so soon was the mystery of the ages. The other mystery was how fast I delivered. I had to hold on for 20 minutes. Dr. Paolone further explained that I had been active. Playing the timpani took energy, and I was also playing tennis and taking ballet classes. She said most women were not so physical and active. If Dr. Paolone had not been a free spirit, I could not have continued the way I did; I'm sure any other doctor would have restricted my activities.

I now had two-year-old Stephen and baby Harriet to add to my duties as mother, wife and timpanist, a huge challenge which I had not counted on. I wanted children, but with that came uncompromising responsibilities. The babies' needs came first, but the orchestra schedule was a priority. Many other working women were teachers with regular hours.

The New York City Opera schedule didn't take into consideration anyone, especially not a woman, who was a wife and parent. Because most women were not yet of the mind to work full time, this was not a major problem to be considered by management. My situation was solely my responsibility, especially being the opposite of the norm. The orchestra rehearsed for three to five hours in the day. Those sessions were determined by the time needed by the opera conductor for its preparation, and then was followed by the eight o'clock evening performances.

Our day off was Monday, after a long weekend of rehearsals and performances. We performed on Friday, Saturday and Sunday, or six services in three days including matinees on Saturday and Sunday. There were days when it wasn't convenient to come home between matinee and evening performance. I appealed to George to come into the city with the babies, so I could spend some time with them. Other times, my mother took them to her house until after George's office hours, and then he picked them up, brought them home and put them to bed. His office hours were arranged to accommodate my schedule. His patients were considerate; some wrote about our uniqueness which made them sympathetic.

We weren't so happy with our staggering days off. George was off on Sunday, except for emergencies, and I on Monday. The months of the opera season put a strain on our relationship. We looked forward to the end of the opera season, after the tour, which was around the Christmas holiday. However, even though the opera season was over, I got engagements playing freelance concerts. There were many chorale organizations which gave major chorale performances of the *Messiah* every year. I played with the Paul Boepple Dessoff Choir, the David Randolph Masterwork Chorus and the Robert Shaw Chorale.

These performances weren't as arduous as the opera, but they required rehearsals and performances. It was tough on us in that no two days were alike. Although playing with these choral groups wasn't as demanding as the opera, the irregularity of rehearsals presented other problems. The children had a schedule and needs, which meant balancing the two, but I never turned down a gig.

How does one manage two babies, a physician husband, a big house and an unconventional career? My mother clearly saw that something had to change. She didn't mind taking care of two grandchildren, but she also had to care for other people's children. That limited anything else she could do for me. So, one day she came to me with advice.

"Laney, you should hire someone to come and clean the house. George's office needs cleaning and you can't expect his nurse to clean the office."

"Hire someone to clean the house?" I repeated. "I never thought about doing that."

First I thought it was bourgeois, because only my Caucasian friends had someone to clean. Second, this is what my mother did and she hated doing it. Third, I didn't think it was politically correct—me, a progressive, hiring a maid! But Mum persisted and did everything she could to make me realize the value of hiring help. So, I went around to my progressive Caucasian friends and asked about the procedure for hiring help.

My good friends said I just needed to go down to the USES office (United States Employment Service) where they have lists of unemployed people looking for work. I went there and put in an application. Something about the office and the entire procedure made it look to me more like a prison. The "convicts" were seated quietly, waiting to be called for their interview. It was all very depressing and I didn't wish to be there. I followed the directions posted on the wall telling me where to go and I went to the appropriate window.

After a short wait, I got to the interviewer, a humorless person, who seemed bored with her position. All day she had to ask the same questions: name, address, references, description of what you're looking for, hours to work and pay scale. After I answered all the questions, she told me that I would get a call when someone came in who fitted my profile. I didn't know how long I was supposed to wait, but I assumed it would be only a couple of days. But a couple of weeks went by and no call. I asked my friends how long it took for them to get someone.

"Generally, a couple of days," they said.

Why am I waiting? I wondered. I called the USES and inquired about getting household help. The person on the other end reassured me.

"Mrs. Kaufman, I'll see to it that you get someone immediately." A couple of days later, I got a call back from the office.

"Mrs. Kaufman, I have just the person for you. I have a young woman who is desperately looking for work and your hours suit her to a tee. She will come over tomorrow."

The next morning at about nine, our front door bell rang and I went to answer it.

"Yes," I said, "who's there?"

"I'm looking for Mrs. Kaufman," came the voice.

"Just a minute," I said as I opened the door.

There, standing at the entrance, was a Caucasian woman.

"May I speak to the lady of the house?" she said.

"Yes," I said.

She repeated, "I mean *the lady* of the house, Mrs. Kaufman."

"Well, you are speaking to her. I'm Mrs. Kaufman."

"*You're* Mrs. Kaufman?"

"Yes, I am."

"You can't be," she quivered, "you're a Negro."

"Yes, I am," I challenged, "so what!"

"I can't take this job, I can't work for a Negro," she said, turning and running away from the door.

I was deeply sad because there was a woman desperately needing a job, finding one which suited her, but then running away because of her prejudices. I called the office and reported her. I didn't want to do it, as I felt she needed compassion more than retribution. But because I had called, I got another woman in a couple of weeks. The woman I finally hired acted as an information machine; an interesting person with whom I got into conversations. It was during the course of those conversations that she revealed an intriguing fact. Somehow, most of the applicants knew I was black, due to the publicity my career had generated, except the woman who came to my house. It seems, according to her, that I didn't get anyone because none of the women wanted to work for a Negro woman. There was no status for those women, even though my husband was a doctor and Jewish, and I was a notable musician—being black erased all that.

Our new housekeeper, however, came every day in time to help Stephen and Harriet dress and eat their breakfast. I left them with her, because she seemed to be a responsible person, and George didn't object to her presence. She also had to clean his office before and after office hours. Because my mother did that same type of work, I was sympathetic to the lady.

I remember getting into a squabble with one of my Caucasian friends about housekeepers. They always liked to say how good they were to their "girl."

"How can you call a grown woman older than you, a girl?" I challenged. They had never given it any thought and even when I brought it to their attention, they didn't know what to say instead of "girl".

When the women's movement became a political movement, one of their demands was how they should be addressed. The expression "Miss" and "Mrs." went out in favor of "Ms." and the expression, girl, definitely was out. They were called women and ladies with reservations. I became sensitized and found myself using Ms. Jones instead of Mrs. Kaufman. Much later under unfortunate circumstances, I learned that George objected to my use of Ms. Jones.

From the beginning, I decided that because my workers called me Mrs. Kaufman, I would give them the same respect and call them by "Mrs." or "Miss." The women themselves had difficulty with this because they were acclimated to their role. They were supposed to call the lady of the house "Madam" or

"Mrs.," and the lady of the house called the housekeeper by their first name. The lady of the house couldn't give her hired help the same status. I thought differently. This person was in charge of my children and my home. That's a major responsibility and they deserved to know I respected their role in our home. It wasn't easy, because during the years of hiring housekeepers, some were so indoctrinated in their positions that they insisted I call them by their first name.

The first woman who worked for me told her friends where she was working and with whom. It brought back to me memories of hearing my mother and her friends talking about the families that employed them. That was how I learned that these black women had preferences for employers. It had nothing to do with pay because again, wanting to show I respected them, I paid a little more than the normal rate. In those days, it amounted to two dollars a day so I paid three dollars a day. But it didn't matter to them because they still preferred working for rich, white families, living in big houses in specific areas. I didn't fit into any of those categories, so there was no status working for me. I remember talking directly about this with my housekeeper.

"You mean they would prefer working for a rich white family who gives them no respect than for a black woman who goes out of her way to treat them as equals?"

"Yes," she answered.

That time was before the black power movement. George and I discussed at length the problems of attracting and retaining a daily housekeeper. We agreed it was time to consider getting a full-time, sleep-in housekeeper. We built an addition to our house with a room, bath and kitchen. It was a lovely little apartment, appropriate for a live-in housekeeper. The next challenge: finding the right person to hire.

My friends told me that the in-thing those days was to hire a foreign person. There were many young, college-aged girls coming to the United States to either further their education and/or get jobs. The best way to get into the country was to be hired by a family who would then act as their sponsors. Everyone was hiring young women from Sweden and Germany. I spoke to some of my friends who had hired these foreigners and asked where to go to get them.

With address and directions in hand, I went to a special employment agency in Great Neck, Long Island. When I walked into the agency office, the receptionist looked up at me.

"Can I help you?" she said.

"Yes. I'm here to inquire about hiring live-in household help."

Either not hearing what I said or assuming I was looking for work, she immediately responded. "I'm sorry, this agency is only for placing women coming from Europe for housekeeping jobs."

I let her finish then I said quietly, "I'm not here looking for work, I am looking to hire someone to come and work for me and I was told this is where I should come." She couldn't disguise her shock at having a black woman coming to look for household help.

"You're looking for someone to work for *you*?" she said incredulously.

The poor woman was dumbfounded. I wanted to sprinkle salt on her wound by toying with her, while at the same time, feeling sorry for her. People like her, and there were many, needed to be educated, not ridiculed. So, I changed my tactic and treated her like a child.

"This is the agency which brings in young European women to do domestic work?" I inquired.

"Well yes," she answered back with a questioning look.

"Aren't you looking for homes to place them in?"

"Yeah." Her expression hadn't changed.

"So why aren't you doing your job and taking my

application?" I challenged.

"It's just that..." She stumbled. "It's just that..."

I interrupted her and said, "I'm not doing such a good job."

"Oh no, that's not it," she protested.

"Then, why is it taking you so long for you to give me an application?" I pressed.

"You don't understand," she broke in. "We've never had Negroes at this end, looking to hire rather than be hired."

"Is it strange for you?" I countered. "You should be open to *anyone* who comes looking for household help."

"You're right, Madam, but you are the first to come to look for someone from Europe."

"Well, it shouldn't make any difference to you, just do your job."

"I'm very sorry Ma'am."

She proceeded to take my application with "oohs" and "ahhs" because I was a musician who played classical music and was married to a Jewish doctor. Suddenly, I became a different person in her eyes in the office, but if I were to meet her on the street, I would have still been a Negro with no credentials.

After the receptionist took my application, I asked her when I could expect to have someone available to work for me. Getting someone to sleep-in became critical when it was announced that the New York City Opera was going to Europe to play in the American Pavilion at the 1958

Brussels World's Fair. We would be away for six weeks. If I did get a person from the agency, I needed to have her with the family to be comfortable with Stephen and Harriet before I left.

"Well, it's inconsistent," she said, "but you can contact us and we'll let you know."

"I wish it could be more definite," I said. "I am going away and I must have someone to care for my children." She didn't offer any more information, so I left.

In the meantime, I spoke to a couple of my friends in Great

Neck. I was curious about availability of women coming from Europe. They said it was their understanding that girls came in almost every day. That was my first indication there was something not quite honest about the agency. I called a couple days later, only to be told: "We have no one yet."

Another couple more calls and I got the same answer. Feeling desperate, I went back to the agency only to find when I got there, three young women, waiting to be picked up by their prospected employers. I waited a bit to see who was coming. It just so happened that I recognized the first woman who came in. After going through the procedure to accept the young student, which took considerable time, I saw them leave together. As they left I went after her to ask her how long did she have to wait for her request.

"Did you make an application?"my friend asked me?.

"Yes," I said, "over a week ago."

"A week ago?" she gasped. "Everyone I know has gotten someone in days because there are more girls waiting to be hired than available homes to work in. Everyone I know has gotten someone almost immediately." This news disturbed me; I *had* to confront the receptionist.

My instinct was verified that I was dealing with racism. Although pretending to be impressed with my application, the receptionist had assumed that their young women would not want to work for me, a black woman. This was the kind of situation where you know racism existed, but proving it and being able to flush it out was almost impossible.

I was angry and frustrated, because none of the women who hired full-time sleep-in help worked. It was a status thing to have someone do the work and take care of the children, so they could enjoy their life of leisure. I couldn't let my anger consume me as I had to use my energy to find someone to take care of Stephen and Harriet.

A couple of nights later, George offered a suggestion.

"Honey, listen to this. I have a patient who came into the office today in despair. She had been working for a family, loved them, but they are moving away. She's been with them while their children were growing up. The children are grown up and moved out, leaving their parents in the big house forcing them to move to smaller quarters out of the city. She said they were good and respectful to her, making her scared when she heard about how domestic workers are treated today. She said she is unhappy at having to look for work. As I was listened to her, I thought to myself, perhaps she might be just the person we need."

I was overjoyed at the prospect of having someone dropped right into our laps. George and I called the woman, Daisy, and interviewed her. She came from Barbados, was in her fifties and had outstanding references from her former employer. We hired her immediately. It made my parents happy, too, especially because she was from Barbados. Daisy moved in and immediately related beautifully to Stephen and Harriet.

Now I could feel comfortable about going on the tour to Brussels. Of course, I wasn't happy to leave my babies, but again, that was the nature of having a career. Having a housekeeper that we all felt good about which also allowed George the freedom to leave his practice and join me in Brussels for a couple of wonderful weeks at the World's Fair.

It wasn't too long after my return that I discovered I was pregnant again. I had gotten pregnant three other times before at which time I had abortions; I was going to have this baby. Whenever I got pregnant, I counted the delivery date. If the delivery date was due during the concert or opera season, always between September and May, I would abort; all of my children were born during the off season. Stephen was born in June, Harriet in July and Cheryl in May. Having my children when I wanted them made me happy. I could have my children and career and not have to neglect either.

None of the wives of George's physician friends wives
worked. His friends, though they were progressive and still
members of AIMS (Association of Interns and Medical Students)
instead of AMA (American Medical Association), when it came
to their wives, they still had the traditional approach to the role
of the woman. I remember what George's best man said to us.

"I want my wife home to give my son her undivided
attention and have my dinner ready when I come home."

George's other colleagues weren't as vociferous, but
nonetheless, always managed to bring up the subject about my
working. My career was on the ascendancy, with frequent
mentions of my success in the press. Perhaps if I had been a
nurse or teacher, I would have stayed home because many
women who were nurses, teachers, and secretaries ended up
staying home. I was doing the unusual and it was the women
who had ambivalence to my dual role. Some would say to me
they miss the opportunity to go out and work. They were
married to physicians who were developing successful practices
so they couldn't say they needed to go out and work to
supplement the family finances, not at that time in history. They
simply had to rationalize that George and I were unique.

When I announced that I was pregnant with my third child,
our friends were unanimous in saying they couldn't understand
that with my schedule, why I needed another child. I didn't
know either. But all I knew was that as an only child, I always
dreamed of having four children.

I took advantage of having a full-time housekeeper, who at
that time I paid only fifty dollars a week!.

I also had my mother and father who lived about two miles
from us, and George who took care of the children when he was
free. This arrangement allowed me the opportunity to be the first
black person, male or female to play with the New York
Philharmonic when I was pregnant with Cheryl. What worried
me the most was people thinking I neglected my children. So,

when I wasn't working, I gave the children my undivided attention.

The months rolled by with performances, meetings and social outings. I missed nothing; this meant I got little sleep. I was living on a round-the-clock routine, because performances usually ended by eleven o'clock at night, be they opera, symphony or Broadway shows. It was almost midnight when I got home. Throughout my career, I never felt like going straight to bed after performances even though the children woke up early in the morning because I got them to bed early. Part of the evening routine was to feed them and George by six, play with the children and at seven, put them in bed. Then I left the apartment and went to work. Of course, I never thought about limiting my work as the pregnancy progressed. As I got bigger, so did the number of audience patrons coming down to the orchestra pit to "see" me.

The time was getting closer to my due date and I was feeling great. At the same time, an announcement went up on the opera bulletin board about a recording of the *Ballad of Baby Doe*. This was an opera featuring the famed Diva, Beverly Sills as Baby Doe. The recording took place all day Friday, May 8 and Saturday, May 9 at a recording studio on Broadway and Seventy-Third Street. It was exhausting, with the cast of singers, chorus and orchestra. This recording was so difficult with having so many people involved and the possibility of many things going wrong. Recordings have to be perfect, so if anyone sneezed or coughed, we had to stop and go over that section again. As people got tired, little things began to happen, putting everyone on edge. It was scary for me, because the timpani part of this opera was demanding with its many pitch changes. I didn't want to and knew I couldn't allow myself to make any mistakes. I would be too embarrassed if we had to repeat a section because of my error. Those two days were stressful for me.

A couple of days before the recording, I had my check-up visit with Dr. Paolone. Her husband was Italian and loved opera. I told her we were going to be recording *Ballad of Baby Doe*, knowing her husband would be interested. But she was concerned about me, so she surprised me by calling me the night of the first recording day.

"Hi, Elayne, how are you feeling?"

"Well, it was a demanding session, but I really feel quite good. We have all day tomorrow in which we will be recording until it is finished, regardless of how long it takes."

"Well, I've made a decision," said the doctor.

"A decision about what?" I interrupted.

"A decision about you. You're healthy and in wonderful shape. Your first child was an easy birth with you in labor for only four hours. Then Harriet came in 20 minutes, almost before I could get to the hospital. Now, another baby is due and, based on your history, this one should be even easier and faster. I'm going to do a radical thing."

"Oh, oh," I said. "What's that?"

She continued. "I want you to come to the hospital on Sunday at which time I will induce the birth of your baby."

"What?" I exclaimed. "I've never heard of such a thing."

"Oh, yeah. We don't do it often, only in very special cases when the mother is in good shape. I feel this delivery will be fast and the way you are, who knows where you might be, perhaps giving birth on the subway. I'm playing it safe and putting you in the hospital."

She then told George to bring me to the New Women's Hospital on Second Avenue and Sixteenth Street at three o'clock in the afternoon on Sunday.

"With Sunday being Mother's Day, this would be your Mother's Day gift," Dr. Paolone said. I could tell she was smiling.

All I could say was, "Wow!"

The next day, Saturday, I went to the studio to finish the

recording. It was interesting that the diva, Beverly Sills, was also pregnant. Her baby was due in August.

My intense feelings on Saturday were indescribable. I was filled with anxiety, wanting to play well and also sensing the tension from the whole company. At the same time, I was anxious and nervous about going to the hospital to have my third delivery.

We started the recording at ten o'clock in the morning and didn't finish until nine o'clock that evening. George picked me up and the baby delivery countdown began. It was a strange feeling of anticipation because I had no evidence of being in or going into labor. George had flowers for me, made breakfast, and took care of Stephen and Harriet because it was Mother's Day.

At three o'clock in the afternoon, we went to the hospital. When we got there, I was taken to a room and in no time, after I was admitted, I was put in a bed. They took my blood pressure with a complete check. At five o'clock I was injected with a needle that was attached to a big bottle. The liquid dripped slowly into my arm. I couldn't eat, so George was allowed to bring in food for himself. I began to think that Dr. Paolone made a big mistake because nothing was happening. I felt nothing except annoyance at being there. What a disappointment; I wanted to go home. The doctor wasn't even there. I thought she had abandoned me, but she finally arrived after eight o'clock at night and we all got into a political discussion. Then all of a sudden, an hour and a half later, I felt my first contraction. Not much to get excited about, but I told Dr. Paolone, that I felt a contraction. Only half an hour passed from the time that I felt the first big contraction to when Cheryl was born.

All I heard Dr. Paolone say was, "See, I told you so."

Even George couldn't believe how fast it happened. Cheryl was a beautiful nine-pound baby. With each delivery, my labor got shorter and the babies got bigger!

Everyone was convinced that the success I had during pregnancy and delivery was due to having the children when I wanted them and by working; I didn't have time to dwell on myself. My children reflected this as they were easy to take care of. They didn't cry and weren't cranky. It could be that having music all through their development made them peaceful. Cheryl was so peaceful that she caused me a major problem.

From the day that I brought her home from the hospital, Cheryl slept and slept. We joked that in the womb, she never got enough sleep, being kept awake by the drums, especially the cymbals when I was playing. I would go and look at her sleeping peacefully for one hour, two hours, three hours, four hours, up until almost six hours. In the meantime, I was in agony because I needed to have her nurse; my breasts were engorged with milk. I didn't know whether to wake her or let her sleep. But I was in so much pain that I had to wake her.

At every nursing, she always fell asleep before she completely emptied the breast, causing an interesting problem. Her nursing stimulated my breast to produce more milk. But she was taking less than I was producing. As a result, after a couple of months, the milk backed up, began to find a place to go and it went all through my system all the way down to my feet.

With so many friends around who were doctors and nurses, no one was able to come up with a solution. Nothing could keep Cheryl awake long enough to empty the breast and nothing could keep down my milk production. The doctors said it was due to my being almost flat chested, I produced more milk than large breasted women. Another old wives' tale—big breast equal more milk. It was just the opposite. My breast was all milk. At this point I could have nursed two babies. Instead, the milk began going through my system, all the way down to my feet. One of George's friends said I had developed elephantitis. Along with this came excruciating pain. I felt as though my body was one huge boil. Something had to be done. Cheryl was satisfied, but I was suffering. George and all of his friends got together to discuss this unusual situation. None of them had ever encountered this kind of problem, and they had to solve it fast because I had to feed Cheryl. The pain was too great and they worried that it could have an effect on Cheryl. George's friend Morty, a surgeon, came up with a solution which was unfavorable to me. I have to give up nursing and have surgery to relieve my engorgement. What, give up nursing? No way. But there wasn't an alternative. So, fighting, screaming and crying, I had to do what I hated; give up nursing and have surgery. I couldn't get over the thought that I had failed.

George's good friend, Morty, said, "If anything, you produced a baby who was too contented and didn't go by the rules."

I had my three children and wanted to have a fourth. But when I got pregnant with the fourth, I had an easy abortion. I realized, and so did George, that to have four children would be wonderful, but very impractical. When the children were babies, it was quite easy to feed them and put them to bed. They didn't require much hands-on time. But as they grew, they needed more of our attention.

When Stephen was three, I enrolled him at the UNIS International Nursery School for children of United Nations delegates. I remember his nursery school teacher, Prissy Pemberton, telling me that she could tell when I was away, because he became quiet and pensive.

I became sensitive about having to serve all these masters: my son, two little girls, my husband, my career and my home. It was demanding; there was no time to serve myself. Sleep was out of the question. I had to learn to function well with a minimum of sleep. All of the performances required rehearsal time, generally in the morning. To get to the orchestra on time meant getting the children up, dressed and fed before I left. Yes,

I had a housekeeper, but as long as I was home, I didn't deprive them of my attention.

I had a girlfriend Muriel who was married to a Jewish attorney and had two children the same ages as Stephen and Harriet. She came from a political family; her uncle was secretary of the Communist Party. They were involved in every political activity, which she never missed.

I also had a close friend, Milroy, who was married to a Jewish, want-to-be actor; we were a great group. We were all interracial couples with our children the same ages. Milroy and I had the same obstetrician and her daughter Ramona was born two days after Stephen and her son was close to Cheryl.

We were all compatible and interested in everything politically, socially and with our shared love and appreciation of the arts. This was our circle. It was nothing for them to pack up the babies and go to a demonstration, which they did often. They also went away on weekends to the progressive camps CHAITS for families and rented a bungalow for the weekend or for a week or two. If George had a weekend when he wasn't on call and I luckily had no commitments, we went with them. It was glorious, stimulating and entertaining. If I could go along and George was on call, I always managed to take my three children along. Because Stephen, Harriet and Cheryl were easy children, with a minimum of fussing, my friends didn't mind taking them along wherever we went.

My objective was that my children should never feel left out because their mother was performing. The wives of all of George's colleagues, as well as my friends, didn't work and those that did had hours more accommodating to the families. I, being in the entertainment profession, worked when all others were home. When I was free, everyone was working. George was busy, too. His days off when he wasn't on call were always a different day than mine. For people working in the theater, Monday was almost always our day off or the dark night. The toughest demand of my work with the opera was the weekend, beginning Friday night and going through to Sunday night. When we had matinees on Saturdays and Sundays at the opera, I invited George to come and meet me with the children; they loved coming in to be with me for dinner between shows.

On the weekends when our housekeeper was off, George often said, "Honey, I can leave the children with Mum and we could have dinner together."

"Oh no," I protested. "I want to spend time with the children."

George dutifully packed up the children, put them in the car, and drove to City Center in Manhattan where we had dinner together as a family. We generally went to Horn and Hardart on Fifty-Seventh Street, a novel restaurant more like a cafeteria. It was great if you had kids, because it was open, huge and unrestricted. We could be together, and together we were. My music, however, took first place in priorities of my time, making our togetherness revolve around the opera schedule or whatever job I got. I was getting more and more work, becoming the first black woman playing with the band in the pit for Broadway shows.

I began to hear from various sources that perhaps I should consider cutting down on the amount of work I was getting. The children were getting bigger and demanding more of my time.

What? I couldn't consider slowing down. I was traveling through roads never traversed either by blacks or women. I felt a responsibility to the struggle for integration and couldn't forego it. I had a two, a five and a seven-year old who also needed my time, which I gave them. I bent over backwards making sure I could continue catering to their needs.

George brought the whole controversy to a head one day. His practice had grown and I was getting more jobs beside the opera. We were both committed to our professions but were also committed to our political activities which revolved around integration in schools, jobs and housing. There were many meetings squeezed in between our respective professional obligations. Our lives were crammed full with being asked to support many organizations. The woman's movement was emerging as well as black power and the controversy around the Vietnam War. Everyone we knew—doctors, lawyers, teachers, mothers—were putting in time and demanding money for the benefit of one or all of their issues.

George was asked to go south to Selma, Alabama. The police there often manhandled and beat demonstrators participating in protests. A call was put out for doctors to come down and provide medical care for those protesters with serious injuries. Without hesitating, George answered the call. Of course, I had left him many times before, so I couldn't object to his taking on this commitment; he felt it was his duty.

I found myself being made aware of how difficult, though rewarding, it was to juggle not only work but all the extra activities. I loved what I was doing, and I loved my children. I could curtail the political issues, but they still needed support. For the first time, I was faced with the realization of having children and having a career that demanded working unorthodox hours. I couldn't wait for George to return home. We had to talk about the crossroads we had reached.

George returned home with a wealth of emotion in response to what he had experienced in the South. People fighting and dying for civil human rights that others took for granted. It strengthened George's resolve to be even more involved. He started out by becoming a member of Queens CORE (Congress of Racial Equality) and later the first white man to be its president, along with his two Jewish friends who were attorneys, Moe Tandler and Morty Friedman.

There was also a major event dealing with racism at the 1964 World's Fair in Flushing, New York. I was one of two African-Americans, hired to work in the World's Fair. I was playing in the show, *Billy Rose Aquacades*, a major attraction. George and his friends, as members of CORE had a general inquiry from the State Commission Against Discrimination. At the time of this meeting, it was discovered this international event had hired only two black workers, and I happened to be one of them.

George and CORE members found out about this, and immediately demanded that more blacks be hired. After management appeared to not cooperate, CORE made a call to have a demonstration against the management of the World's Fair. The story made the *New York Times*. This led to the World's Fair not opening on the originally scheduled day, and wouldn't open until more blacks were hired. Management finally met the demands. Had I not been married to George, I don't think this issue would have gotten any attention.

With all of these activities, we were busy around the clock. There were numerous fund-raising parties, which I rarely missed and went to after our opera or concert performance. I often went without George and came home after he was asleep. There was a feedback from our friends about the crazy life we led. But as far as I was concerned, the children were never neglected.

George must have felt something and wanted to talk about it. Over our years together, George realized I was a "drink and talk" person. Though I wasn't shy, I tended to be reserved in crowds, which harkened back to my fear of speaking in class at The High School of Music & Art. The social scenario was always basically the same; predominantly Jewish professionals at the parties and gatherings. But if I had a drink, I felt less self-conscious. George believed I was like that even with him. I can remember our wedding night. We went to a little private guest house in the woods in the Catskills Mountains. We got lost getting there and were exhausted once we arrived. This was our honeymoon but the hosts treated us as their long-lost children. They were gracious and bent over backwards to accommodate us. They were Jewish progressives who talked and talked at every opportunity possible. It really didn't bother me that we didn't have the privacy one would expect on a honeymoon.

I realized that I was afraid to open my mouth during those conversations. I sat and listened but wanted desperately to make a contribution. I always thought they'd laugh at me and wonder why this man had married me. My self-image took a back seat at this period. However, when I had a drink, I was transformed into another persona. Gone was all the fear and apprehension; my surroundings didn't hold me back. I never thought that I was an alcoholic. Drinking was just a way for me to be free and not feel inferior.

George learned that after a drink, not only would I speak, but I also expressed my deep-seated feelings. As an only child, I grew up talking to myself and not sharing my inner feelings which were basically hurt by friends. So, people knew me but really didn't know *me*.

George and I had been together, had three children, were both successful, respected professionals, but everything was getting more complicated. We had to assess where we were and our priorities, as we were going in too many directions.

One night, we were invited to a huge fund-raising party and we went together for a change. When we arrived, someone referred to us as "Dr. and Mrs. George Jones." That wasn't the first time, but that night, it hit a wrong chord with George. He turned to the unsuspecting person and stated firmly, "My name is Dr. George Kaufman."

I had never changed my name to Kaufman amongst professionals. People of course assumed that Jones was my married name; Since I was always getting publicity, I was always known as Elayne Jones, not Elayne Kaufman. I was reminded how angry George had gotten during my first tour after we married. He called the hotel where I stayed and asked to speak to his wife, Mrs. Kaufman.

"There's no Mrs. Kaufman on our roster, sir," the clerk said.

"What?" George exclaimed. "My wife is at the hotel and her name is Elayne Kaufman."

"Sorry sir, no one with that name."

George gathered his wits and ego about him, rethought and said. "Do you have Elayne Jones registered?"

"Oh, yes, sir. I will connect you."

George asked me to register as Elayne Jones Kaufman, which I did. However, there were many isolated incidents such as what happened that night, where people weren't aware of my married name. The incident fueled George's resolve to discuss our life with me. Unknown to me, he made sure I had several drinks to loosen my inner thoughts. I was happy and as far as I was concerned there was nothing wrong. I could ask for nothing more.

The party was wonderful. The people were lively and responsive to music and political conversation. It was getting late and the party was winding down. Somehow, I was always the last to leave a party and that night was no different, except George kept urging me to leave.

"Let's leave honey, let's leave."

"Okay," I finally said reluctantly.

When we left, George was quiet. We drove home with no conversation. When we arrived home, George didn't drive the car into our garage. Instead we just sat in the car in the driveway. After a couple of minutes in ominous silence, George spoke.

"Honey, I'm sure you are aware that we have something to talk about."

Well, I knew George was unusually quiet, but I wasn't aware that a talk was needed. By then I was feeling no pain having had a couple of drinks of Scotch.

"Well," George said, turning to me. "I think our lives are getting too complicated and I think the children aren't happy with the time we spend together. I don't think you liked it when

I went away down South. I don't really like it when you leave."

I sat there unable to respond. I didn't know what to say. I was happy the way things were going, so it was hard for me to see George as being unhappy. He was developing into a competent, respected physician in the community of mixed races and nationalities. And now he was being respected for his political activity. I couldn't understand why he was complaining when I was away. He was free to do whatever he wanted with no limitations and the children were cared for between my parents and the wonderful housekeeper we had living with us.

It seemed that I had developed a warped idea about men due to going on tour with the opera. The first year probably wasn't the best exposure to relationships and commitments for a young 21-year-old girl. That was a far cry from when I went up to play at the summer resorts. Over the summer, there were things going on between guests that I wasn't aware of because we didn't travel as a group, though we worked together. But going on tour was different. It was a large group made up of singers, dancers, musicians and stage hands. There were enough of us to require several cars on the sleeper train.

On the morning of our departure, we would all gathered together at Grand Central Station, in New York. We were about to take the train to our first city, Chicago. Many of the performers were married or in relationships. I watched how they embraced each other with hugs and kisses, crying over having to be separated for a couple of weeks, sometimes more depending on the cities we were scheduled to play in. How romantic, I thought, as we boarded the train. The whistle blew and the train pulled out for our long day's journey. When the train left Grand Central station, it traveled through a tunnel for about 15 minutes until it came into the open at the 125th Street station. I couldn't believe what I saw when we emerged. No sooner had the train pulled out of the station, I saw many of the spouses who had just left their sobbing partners, embracing someone else. I couldn't understand. Those scenes made an indelible impression on my mind. I witnessed the ultimate dishonesty on our return home after the tour. Each person greeted his or her spouse with ardor. Seeing that every time we went on tour, I developed the idea that is what happened to couples when they separated for any reason, for any time.

By the time I married George, I thought he would fool around with someone when I was away, as I had observed others do. I made the mistake of thinking that this behavior was typical of all men. Because I don't go around questioning people about their behavior when separated from their spouses, I had no way of thinking that the behavior of some artists on tour was the exception, not the rule. Consequently, I didn't take George seriously when he said how unhappy he was when I left. I thought that he surely was just saying the right thing.

I did agree with George that we were doing too much. I was playing with New York Opera and in between, I started playing with the Brooklyn Philharmonic with the conductor, Siegfried Landau. I loved that because I was playing on stage, rather than in the pit. This job required a lot of juggling. George suggested, much to my resistance, that I give up the opera to allow a little more time to spend with the children and him. It was a heart-breaking decision. From September 1949 to June 1960, I had been with the opera and I had loved it.

As reticent as the New York City Opera was to hire me initially, they were even more reticent at letting me go. I didn't want to give up the position, but I knew deep down inside that the needs of the family should take precedence. Management reluctantly accepted my resignation.

Without having to be out every night, I was able to give up having full-time help and was able to spend more time with the children. Stephen was nine, Harriet was seven and Cheryl was four. I wasn't working full time, so I almost completely took over caring for the children. I always had a deep-seated fear of being accused of child neglect because of my career. But in the process, I inadvertently shut George out of taking some responsibility for the children, which at the time, didn't seem strange. In those days, you rarely saw men taking care of the children. That was the woman's job, which is why in some societies, the woman's place was at home. That was the picture in the families of all George's doctor friends. The irony of that picture, however, was the fact that all the doctors' wives had maids, and the maids were always black. Clearly, black women didn't have the same rules because if they were caring for the children of these women, who was caring for *their* children? That was double standard. I was the only wife who had a full-time nontraditional career and the only physician's wife who was black.

I was happy to be at home, being mother and wife in a way that I had never been since marriage and the birth of my children. But there was a hole in my life, small, but present, which made me miss the stress of playing full time with the opera. All was not lost. Although I was no longer with the opera, Joe Fabbroni never forgot me. Although he never put it in words, his actions made me believe that he liked my work.. He had a couple of side jobs which he always called on me to play. Many of these jobs were recording with well-known conductors like Pierre Monteux and Leopold Stokowski.

Stokowski conducted the New York City Opera in the year the oratorio, *Carmina Burana* was staged. This was an exciting composition written for chorus and orchestra, which actually featured the percussion. Stokowski made history when conducting this oratorio. It had never been staged but always performed as a concert piece. He rehearsed the orchestra. The chorus, stage and dancers rehearsed separately until it was all put together at dress rehearsal.

Everything seemed to be going well, when suddenly Stokowski stopped conducting and everything came to a grinding halt. The stage manager ran out from behind the stage.

"Maestro, what happened?" he called out. "Why did you stop?"

"Why is dancer wearing clothes?" said Stokowski.

"What, wearing clothes?" said the stage manager incredulously. "I don't understand."

"Why is she wearing clothes?" he repeated.

"Maestro, she has to have clothes on."

Actually she, was Carmen de Lavallade, a beautiful African-American dancer who was wearing a leotard the typical dancer's costume. She was one of the first black women ballet dancers.

"You don't understand," continued Stokowski. "*Carmina Burana* is an oratorio about monks and their lives in seclusion." He continued. "They were celibate but they still dreamed about women. Any man, even a monk, when dreaming about women, visualizes them nude. The dancers here represent the women being visualized by monks and she should be nude."

"That's not possible Maestro," pleaded the stage manager.

"I say she must represent the nude vision," Stokowski demanded.

"Well, we'll have to discuss it Maestro," the stage manager said. "So, let's finish the rehearsal for now." We continued and finished the rehearsal. A couple of nights later, we would perform *Carmina Burana* with Carmen de Lavallade apparently satisfying Stokowski's demand.

After rehearsal, all heads were put together to discuss the nudity demand. They experimented with everything and eventually designed what today is known as a body suit. It was designed with flesh color so that when the dancer wore it on stage, the lighting made it appear as though she was nude. Stokowski was responsible for the apparent nudity and he was happy with the results. He was also happy with the woman playing the timpani—me! *Carmina Burana* has an important part for the percussion, using five players plus the timpani, which is almost like a solo part. A demanding part, rhythmically and technically, it was scored for five timpani which also required a bit of athleticism.

The oratorio was a timpanist's dream. I savored playing the composition as well as listening to the music composed by Carl Orff. We gave five performances and received high acclaim and cheers of approval from the audience. Carmen de Lavallade and Stokowski made front page news: "Nudity on Stage" and "*Carmina Burana* emerged as a stellar addition to the orchestral repertoire." I also benefited from that performance.

A couple of weeks after we finished the five performances of *Carmina Burana*, Joe Fabbroni called me.

"Elayna?" he said. "I hope you are feeling fine and the children are well."

"Yes, Joe. The children and I are all well. And you?"

"I'm fine. You know I have been hiring musicians to play recordings with Maestro Stokowski. I have a recording session coming up and he says he wants you to play the timpani in the orchestra."

"What did you say?" I said, wanting to make sure I heard him correctly.

"I say, Maestro Stokowski, he a-want you to play timpani."

"He wants me?" I couldn't believe what I was hearing.

"Yes, he say he like-a your playing in *Carmina* and would like to hire you for the recording."

That news made me extremely happy. I couldn't believe it. Playing timpani in the orchestra for the Stoki recording. What a thrill!

"Are you available?" Fabbroni continued.

"Wow, of course, I would love to play. When will this take place?" He gave me the date; the time was at midnight after the opera performance. "At midnight?" I questioned.

"Yes," he affirmed. "That's because it is the best time to get all the musicians he prefers."

Stoki was specific about what musicians he wanted for his

recordings, and even the engineers and producers he chose. I felt privileged to be asked to play. I accepted the engagement without even asking George. I was so happy to be hired for the recording. It never occurred to me, however, George would be upset because I would be coming home around three o'clock in the morning. George didn't approve, but he never said anything. Not then. I was playing with the top musicians in the city from the New York Philharmonic, the Metropolitan Opera Orchestra and freelance musicians from the radio stations. This job led to me playing on many of Stoki's recordings. But there would be a fly in the ointment, not George, but my teacher, Saul Goodman.

Playing the recording with Stokowski opened many other freelance jobs for me. Some of the musicians playing the recording were also contractors who hired me for many other little jobs in and around town. I got my first crack at subbing in a Broadway show. This was a whole new world, which put more strain on my family obligations. I never knew when I'd be called to sub for someone always in an emergency, which meant at the last minute, and drop whatever I was doing.

So, how do you juggle a husband, three children, getting dinner, putting the children to bed and getting a baby sitter? It was a challenge which I felt obliged to meet head on. "Hurry up!" was the name of the game. Fortunately, my children weren't defiant when it came to eating or going to bed. They could have made life difficult for me, but they were resilient. My children were the way they were because they felt my rhythm while they were in the womb.

I was also fortunate in that my children never seemed to come down with colds, which was common among my friends' children. If they did have the sniffles, my husband was there to give them baby aspirin. Friends said my career was successful because I had unfair advantages of a doctor in the home. I didn't have time to dwell on the negative. Because I loved and enjoyed every minute of what I was doing, it definitely had to have a positive effect on my children.

Chapter 16

FIRST BLACK IN THE NEW YORK PHILHARMONIC
Playing with the Best

I was living in New York, had gone to The High School of Music & Art and then Juilliard, played at Tanglewood and then with the New York City Ballet and New York City Opera. I had amassed significant orchestral experience. I played with the National Orchestra Association Training Orchestra. Yet, I was to experience seeing many of my white male colleagues getting into orchestras throughout the country. But my chances were still limited getting into a major symphony orchestra. We knew there was a problem because almost no blacks were in any professional orchestra; even big bands were racially divided.

In September 1958, I was playing with the New York City Opera and pregnant with my third child, Cheryl. As was the schedule, the opera always went on tour following the fall season. That year, our tour took us to Chicago, Detroit, East Lansing, University of Wisconsin, Milwaukee and ended in Cleveland. Before I left for the tour George made a proposal to me.

"This tour is hard, especially with you being three months pregnant, Honey," he said. "I see on the schedule that it ends in Cleveland where my best friend Harvey and his wife live. So, I will drive to Cleveland, meet you there and we can drive home together." Harvey was George's best friend all through Chicago Medical School, and best man at our wedding.

We hadn't seen Harvey and his wife, Ida since Stephen was born. This would be a wonderful opportunity to see them. We made plans for George to meet me in Cleveland. We would visit with Harvey and Ida and their children, and then drive home together.

Harvey had an ironic gratitude to George for his happy marriage and family. Both Harvey and George were Jewish boys who were devoted to their respective families and culture. Yet with their experiences and needs of their patients, they came in touch with and opened their eyes to the world around them. George's were opened first when he met, fell in love with, and married Elayne and was opened to a challenging world. It contributed to his endearing relationships with his patients.

But we knew that his family objected to the marriage and disowned him. In the meantime, Harvey experienced a similar reaction when he met and fell in love with his wife, Ida. However, the ending took a different path. She, like George's choice, was also not a "nice Jewish girl," but was more acceptable to his family because as they said, "At least she was not a 'Schwartz' … a Black girl."

I alerted my orchestra manager that I wouldn't be going back to New York on the train with the company. Joe Fabbroni, our personnel manager, didn't have a problem with my plans. He would never have agreed if we had another stop. With Cleveland being our final stop, however, I could be on my own. George and I left Harvey and Ida at five o'clock in the morning. As we drove off, we were greeted with a huge snow storm and narrowly avoided a catastrophic accident on the Ohio Turnpike. After a harrowing journey, we arrived home in the evening. I was so happy to see my two children, Stephen and Harriet. How could I ever stand to leave them again?

Although it was late, many urgent messages were waiting for me from the manager of the New York Philharmonic, the Symphony of the New World and the union: "Call the New York Philharmonic first thing in the morning." There was no indication of the nature of the urgency. My curiosity kept me awake all night even though I was exhausted. Why were they looking for me? I couldn't even speculate what it could be.

Slowly the time passed, and I got a call first thing in the morning from Joe Fabbroni. "Elayna, where were you? Everyone has been a-looking for you."

"Well, you know Joe, I drove back with my husband and we actually left a day later than the company. But tell me, why all the urgency?"

"You do not know Saul Goodman, he is a-sick and the New York Philharmonic wants you to come in as a sub."

"WHAT!" I exclaimed. "They want *me* to come in as a sub for Goodman?" I stood there in disbelief.

"Yes, they ask-a for you," Fabbroni affirmed. "They-a call everyone to find you when you did not return with the company."

I couldn't believe what I was hearing. The Philharmonic wanted me to play for Goodman. I assumed that I would be playing timpani. It was a frightening as well as an exhilarating feeling all at the same time. I was also wondering what had happened to Goodman. He had never missed a performance during the years with the orchestra, or a class as my teacher at Juilliard. My thoughts went back to the many experiences I had with him and the boys in the percussion section.

Fabbroni gave me the phone number for the New York Philharmonic manager, James Chambers. I knew that their rehearsals always began at ten o'clock in the morning. Deep down in my soul, I dreamed of being in the orchestra and I knew everything about the scheduling of its activities. They rehearsed 40 minutes then took a 20-minute break. That was the general procedure. Any deviation was subject to the approval of the orchestra manager because the schedule was a contracted requirement. Any changes generally came about by the needs of the conductors, being a question of their ego and their experience. I decided to call just after rehearsal started when things were settled. Nervously, I dialed the number.

"Good morning, this is the New York Philharmonic backstage, Jimmy Chambers speaking." I took a quick breath.

"Hello, Mr. Chambers, this is Elayne Jones." I didn't go any further when he interrupted me. "Oh, I am glad you called. I was just about to call someone else."

"What happened?" I asked?.

"Oh, while you were away Saully had a bad case of bronchitis and was ordered to bed by his physician against his protestation. This happened last week and it did not present a major problem because the instrumentation of the music we were playing required only timpani and no percussion. Arnold Lang moved over from his position as cymbal player and played timpani. Next week, however, we have percussion in the repertoire and need someone to play Arnie's position. Are you free to play?"

"Oh, yes," I said without a second thought. He then went on to give me the rehearsal and performance schedule. I noted it in my datebook and hung up.

"Wow!" I yelled to George. "I'm going to play with the New York Philharmonic." I said it over and over as if to be sure it was for real. My glee came down a notch, though, when it finally hit me that I wouldn't be playing timpani, but cymbals. The next thought was why I was hired to play cymbals when there were all these guys who were available? I had already been designated as a timpanist, which is what I wanted. I had always played timpani in every orchestra and every job for which I was hired. I was puzzled, but it wouldn't be too long before I found out the reason behind this unprecedented action.

After I hung up, I called my friend Harry Smyles and told him my news. He already knew. He said that the Philharmonic had called the Symphony of the New World and spoke to the conductor, Ben Steinberg. They said that in keeping with the concerns of racism, they were ready to hire a black musician if the opportunity presented itself. That opportunity had come because Saully was ordered to bed, leaving an opening. They were thinking of hiring me as a sub.

Ben told them that I was a fine musician and very competent and that they wouldn't go wrong to hire me. So, of course, Ben told Harry, who told Al, who told everyone. Elayne is going to play with the New York Philharmonic and word got around to everyone in the business. Evidently, the efforts and struggles of Douglass Pugh and the Urban League had put pressure on the Philharmonic which would make me the first black to play with them. Was this the management's way of making amends after two previous black musicians hadn't made it in the audition?

Playing as sub in the orchestra isn't the same as becoming a contracted player. As a sub, you earned the minimum union designated wage. With the Philharmonic, however, that minimum was better than the standard wages for other orchestras, except the Metropolitan Opera Orchestra, where wages were competitive with the Philharmonic. These were the two major orchestras with a higher than usual minimum wage. Anticipating being the first black to play with the New York Philharmonic stirred up hurtful memories about another once famed orchestra.

Prominent among the major orchestras was the famed NBC, National Broadcasting Company Symphony created and conducted by the great Arturo Toscanini. Those musicians had quite a reputation based on the claim that Toscanini himself picked each player. Heard all over the world, the NBC Symphony was special, playing every Saturday night from a ninth-floor studio in Rockefeller Center. Out of that orchestra came the famed WQXR String Quartet. Of course, no black musician ever came close to being a member of that NBC Symphony, because the survival of the NBC Symphony depended on Arturo Toscanini, who everyone thought was immortal.

When Toscanini passed away, however, the future of the orchestra was in doubt. It was an outstanding orchestra and everyone made a major effort to keep it alive. With determination, support and money, it remained intact. But NBC was only interested in the Toscanini name for its sponsorship and bought the name, not allowing anyone to use it. A committee was formed that came up with the name for the "Toscanini-less" orchestra, "Symphony of the Air". As a result, they were able to attract notable, reputable conductors as well as financial support.

The man who was voted to be the manager of the Symphony of the Air was a gentle sweetheart of a man, a bass player, named Philip Sklar. He was progressive and had worked with our New World Symphony to help train the black bass players. When he wasn't available, another bass player from the NBC named David Walter also contributed his expertise.

As scheduled, there was an upcoming concert of the Symphony of the Air, but two of their players had already gone and committed themselves to play a commercial recording. The two musicians were a flutist and the timpanist. Philip Sklar went to the New World Symphony conductor, Ben Steinberg for recommendations.

I understand the conversation went something like this. "I have to hire a couple of players for our next concert," said Philip. "I'm considering asking Antoinette Handy."

Antoinette was a talented young woman who came up from the South to get the advantage of what we had to offer in the North. She was conscientious and musical, and everyone liked her.

"I have no doubt in my mind," said Ben, "that Antoinette would play superbly on the flute so by all means, hire her."

"Thank you, Benny," said Philip. "I want to say I am also thinking about putting Elayne on the timpani."

"Fine," said Ben, "you cannot go wrong with those two."

Philip called me and offered me the job playing with the Symphony of the Air. I was delighted and no stranger to the musicians. Antoinette came in, a little shy because she wasn't from New York, and didn't know the musicians. We rehearsed and had no problems. Antoinette had a beautiful sound and played professionally. The concert went well, but then the furor began.

It seemed there were contributing members from the board who registered complaints about the "two Negroes" in the orchestra. They approached Philip and voiced their disapproval to him. He defended his position and his right to hire the best possible musicians.

"Everyone was pleased with the concert, so what are your objections?" he challenged them.

"Can't you see?" he was told. "You've hired two black women. Toscanini had no black musicians and no women in his NBC orchestra!"

"That does not matter, Toscanini is not here anymore," defended Philip.

"Yes," they argued, "Toscanini is not here but the orchestra is and what we are selling and raising funds for is the continuation of *his* orchestra."

"I understand what you are saying," Philip went on, "but I hired other musicians who did not play with Toscanini in the NBC. But who would know the difference? They could not say that is not the NBC." His opponents countered with. "But when they see those two, the people donating their money will be suspicious and say that is not Toscanini's orchestra. The orchestra cannot exist without financial funding and if these contributors withhold their funding, the orchestra will cease to exist."

Philip was furious. He argued with them to no avail. Then he made the argument that if any person could play with the orchestra who was not formerly an NBC member, then they were not quite honest in saying they wanted to support Toscanini's orchestra. What they were saying was simply that they did not want black women to play.

Right away, Philip went to public relations at NBC and to Ben Steinberg and Douglass Pugh. He told them of his conversation and his conclusion. The story made the front page of the *New York Times* with accusations of racism. This publicity did not fare well for the orchestra, which eventually led to its demise. Antoinette and I were not allowed to play with the orchestra and the next concert was canceled.

I was looking forward to playing with the New York Philharmonic even though I was only playing cymbals. The fact that I would be the first black to play with the orchestra became my primary concern. The path I had chosen led me into unchartered waters, from high school to that day. Each step brought an unexpected twist in the road which I had to deal with along the way.

Although I played and toured with the New York City Opera and played with the New York City Ballet, the Philharmonic was considered the top of the line. I felt a different kind of excitement and expectation. I was like a babe in a candy store.

I arrived at rehearsal early, because I didn't know what cymbals I would be playing. Jimmy said I should just show up, they have everything. I walked in through the musicians entrance and the doorman stopped me.

"What can I do for you, Miss?"

"I'm a musician playing with the orchestra."

"What is your name?"

I told him and he looked at a list. "I don't see your name."

Fortunately, at that moment a player came in and rescued me.

"Hey, you're the timpanist, aren't you?"

"Yes, I am."

In a joking manner he said, "You're here to play with us, ha ha."

"Yes, I am."

"Really?" he answered, disbelief in his voice.

"Well, Goodman is sick and they sent for me."

"You're gonna play timpani?" he said with even more disbelief.

"Well, not quite, but I wish I was. Arnie is playing timpani and I'm playing in Arnie's position."

"Hey, that's exciting! Another girl in the orchestra and in the percussion section! Come on in!" The other girl was Orin O'Brien, bass player and the first contracted woman to play with the Philharmonic.

My new colleague led me in past the startled doorman and up the stairs of the stage entrance. I thanked him, not knowing who he was or what instrument he played as he carried nothing. Most of the men left their instruments in their locker except the conscientious players or those with solos who needed to practice after the rehearsal.

The men started streaming in, and among them was Jimmy, the manager who gave me a warm greeting. "Happy to see you and that you decided to join us. Let me take you over to where the percussion boys hang out."

Jimmy led me across the stage where the chairs, stands and music were set up ready to begin the rehearsal. The percussion and timpani took up the entire rear of the stage. He then went to a set of doors off the stage, knocked and entered. All the percussion players were there, having arrived earlier than most of the other sections.

"Hey, Jonesy, you're here!" I looked and it was as if I was back in Juilliard. There were the guys I played with in school—Arnie Lang, Buster Bailey and Walter Rosenberger. They had all gotten into the Philharmonic after graduating. "Hey, great to see you, just like good old school days!" they said.

"Yeah, sure is," I answered. But somehow there was a

difference being here in the Philharmonic.

I had to analyze what made that difference. All through Music & Art and Juilliard the talk and focus were always on achieving access to this world-renowned orchestra. To get there meant, you were good. There I was with my classmates who had achieved, and I was with them. There was also a kind of professional order, which may have been in my mind, but I felt special.

Walter was the first to come over and hug me and say, "Glad to see ya." He was a phenomenal mallet player who walked with a limp, the result of a near fatal auto accident.

Buster Bailey came over. He was an incredible snare drummer and always had a smile on his round pudgy baby face. He was older as a result of having served years in the army. And lastly, Arnie, who was a year after me at Juilliard. We all had studied with Goodman.

Walter was the principal percussionist responsible for ensuring that all the music conformed to the conductor's wishes. Sometimes the orchestra parts were different from the conductor's score. The orchestra parts often belonged to the orchestra library and may have been purchased from one music publisher like Boosey and Hawkes. The conductor's score, however, may have come from a European publishing house. The music might be the same, but elements like dynamics, phrasing, fingering even instrumentation would be different. The principal of each section has to check out the differences. Then he has to check the instrumentation and the number of players needed. The early music of Mozart, Beethoven and Hayden required none to one or two percussion instruments, and then you get to later composers like Stravinsky who wrote for multiple percussion instruments with many players. My first day with the Philharmonic, Prokofiev's Fifth Symphony was the composition on the program. It was scored for more instruments than normal. With Goodman out, an extra player was needed, and that's where I filled in.

Anticipating my question, Walter said, "I know you are the timpanist with the New York City Opera. This is the first time that Saully is out. Arnie plays cymbal when Saully is here. But Arnie is also contracted as the assistant timpanist in the program notes. Therefore, although we would love to have you play timpani, Arnie has to play and you play Arnie's position. See, he would have been playing cymbals and wood block; which is what you will be playing, okay?"

"Okay," I said. I was a little disappointed, but accepted Walter's explanation.

At the sound of a bell, we all walked out to the stage. The cymbals in their stand were already out, Walter having put out all the necessary instruments earlier. Then there was a table with the wood blocks, large and small, a triangle and several size triangle beaters.

Just before the rehearsal began, I tried out the various size wood blocks on the table. I had to hear the sounds because all wood blocks don't sound the same and then they sound different with different mallets. All this you have to be aware of because conductors generally like to stop and say, "Let me hear the sound of that instrument you're playing." Then if they see you picking up a mallet to hit the wood block, they will try to be "knowledgeable" and say, "Play with this mallet, now let me hear the next. Well, I think you should try the second."

Some guys would be "smart alecks" by putting down one mallet and picking it up again pretending it is a different mallet. Musicians played these tricks on conductors, especially if they thought the conductor was trying to show off how much they knew about the instrument.

I went over and checked out the cymbals. Being a timpani player, I never had to play cymbals in the orchestra. I certainly played them at Juilliard in the percussion ensemble classes. All the other sections in the orchestra had ensemble class. That was when the strings divided into small groups. The main objective was to learn how to play and listen to one another which was a prerequisite for playing with any group, be it duets, trios, quartets and so on. Ensembles included string, woodwind, brass but no drum or percussion.

Saul Goodman, being an innovative person, as seen in the way he played the timpani, got a bright idea one day. He presented this idea to us for learning ensemble skills. He summoned all the percussion students to the huge orchestra rehearsal room.

"It's important for us to have ensemble skills like the other sections, so I have an idea for percussion ensemble," he said.

We all chuckled because there was no music written for percussion ensemble. But Goodman came up with a new plan. The class had worked on Rimsky-Korsakov's Scheherazade and Berlioz's Roman Carnival Overture, symphonic pieces calling for a large percussion section. Saul took these two works and created a chamber ensemble with them. Each one of us had to take turns playing all the parts which included the bass drum, cymbals, triangle, tambourine, snare drum and timpani. It was strange listening to this ensemble without the music, but doing so achieved the desired effect. We played as an ensemble learning how to play together by listening and paying attention to who was playing and not playing too loud to drown out the next instrument. It was a valuable exercise. Goodman had created something that would eventually become a course in every school for every percussion player. Out of this came an entirely new area of composition for the composition students: "Music for Percussion Ensemble."

I had my turn playing cymbals, bass drum and snare drums. It was during those days at Juilliard that the guys made fun of me by saying I would never be strong enough to *really* play with power on cymbals or the timpani.

Well, there I was about to play cymbals with the New York

Philharmonic. After setting up the wood blocks I went over and picked up the cymbals. They were the huge, heavy, beautiful, top of the line, Zildjian cymbals. I picked them up and crashed them together. What a sound erupted from them! The cymbals in all the other orchestras I played in didn't have instruments like those. They were the kind of instruments that made the Philharmonic special. Having only the best and most expensive instruments which gave the orchestra its top sound. The wood blocks I was playing were made of the best wood and they made a pure beautiful sound. The cymbals were specially made for the Philharmonic of the finest and most expensive metal from Zildjian. I loved striking them. The vibrations seemed to go on endlessly, until I stopped them by bringing them against my body. Stopping the vibration was something I had to think about carefully because I was four months pregnant with my third child.

The men could dampen the vibrations by placing the cymbals against their chest. I couldn't dampen them against my chest because being four months pregnant, my breasts were a bit inflated and tender. I had to think of another way to dampen the cymbals. I certainly couldn't ask the guys because they didn't know that I was pregnant. I had to figure that out before the rehearsal began. In looking through the music I had noticed there were a few ff-fortissimo attacks. So, what could I do? I aimed at a little spot just above my belly and between my rib cage where it was beginning to swell. It worked like a charm.

After the rehearsal as I was leaving, Jimmy, the orchestra manager, met me and said "Nice job, Elayne, now don't forget to look at the posted schedule on the bulletin board."

I went back in to check the schedule. Even that was different from other orchestras. All the timings were for rehearsals and for every composition to be played at this program series. There were four days of rehearsals, Monday, Tuesday, Wednesday with Thursday noted as a dress rehearsal. This program would be played Thursday and Friday nights, and Saturday and Sunday afternoons. The series consisted of an overture, a piano concerto and lastly the Prokofiev's Fifth Symphony. Because I played only in the Prokofiev, I didn't have to come back until the Thursday dress rehearsal, and even though I played just the Prokofiev, I was paid for the entire series.

By now, I couldn't wait to make my on-stage debut with the Philharmonic. Up until now, I was playing with the New York City Opera down in a pit, and seen only by some discerning opera lovers sitting up in the balcony which gave me quite a following of the balcony patrons.

At the end of the rehearsal the musicians came up and congratulated me as if I were a novice. I wasn't a novice at playing; I was the first ever black musician to play with the New York Philharmonic! I was exhilarated to be playing with this group of musicians. Why? I loved feeling that I was among the best. I wasn't playing timpani; I was hired only for this engagement while Goodman was ill, but playing with the best was definitely in my mind.

Another thing stood out for me—the way those musicians were treated. It seemed as though everything was done for them up to actually playing the instrument. That alone could make you feel special because there was so much respect for you as a musician.

Until this time, because of the way we were seated, I saw mostly the string players. But after the rehearsal when I was leaving with the guys, I soon recognized most of them as the guys I played with at Music & Art, Juilliard and then National Orchestra Association, Tangelwood or the New York City Opera. All older than me, they greeted me like a long-lost baby sister. Those young men had continued their music career often after having spent two to four years in the army. So generally, I was mostly four years younger than them.

"Hey Jonesy, happy to see you here," said Gil Cohen,

trombone player, who got into the New York Philharmonic from the New York City Opera. "This is where you belong. You think you're too good for us?" he went on jokingly.

"Well," I answered, you know I'm only here because Goodman is ill and because of the Urban League exposé about racism.

By then most of the trombone, trumpet and French horn players were passing by and also giving me a, "Hi Jonesy." I had never experienced any of the antagonisms from those guys that I got from some other players at Juilliard and Tangelwood. They were true professionals. Being members of the prestigious New York Philharmonic, they were more secure in themselves. As they left, most said, "See ya tomorrow."

I left Lincoln Center feeling really good about myself. I couldn't forget, however, that my being there wasn't only due to my ability but to the struggles that called for an end to racism in the orchestra. There was still much work to be done because with one or two exceptions, none of the other orchestras in the country, none of the other orchestras in the pit of Broadway musicals or the radio stations had any black musicians. The door had been opened just a crack for me. How far could I get beyond that door?

It was the night of our first performance and there we would be in full view of the audience except for several rows in the orchestra. The concert started with the overture, then the piano concerto and then intermission. I arrived at the hall early to listen to the program and check on my set up. Listening to the Philharmonic was nothing new to me because I had heard them from my high school days when they played at Lewisohn Stadium and then at Carnegie Hall where I was able to sneak in and hear all the orchestras which came to play on tour. Listening to them that night was nothing, yet it was *everything*.

The first half of the program ended and it was time for me to join the orchestra on stage. I walked out on the stage to make sure my wood blocks, mallets and cymbals were in order. Walter came and double checked, and the other guys, Buster and Arnie, were all attentive and ready. Pretty soon the entire orchestra came out, then the concertmaster, and lastly the conductor made his appearance to an appropriate applause. Yes, I was nervous. You would not think I had been playing for at least 10 years, yet I felt as though I was making a statement, no, I was making history.

I reviewed the music with Arnie looking back from his position at the timpani as if saying, "This is basically straight ahead so you should have no trouble reading it." The concertmaster came out, turned to the oboe player and motioned to him to play an "A." When he stood up and played the note, a cacophony of sound erupted from the orchestra. The musicians tuned up like any other orchestra.

The concertmaster sat down satisfied. The orchestra was in tune, at which point the conductor strode out. He took his position on the podium and gave the down beat, and Prokofiev's Fifth Symphony began. I had never played this symphony before so I had to listen intensely, concentrate and count like mad. Turned out that it was half as difficult and challenging as when I had to play *Der Rosenkavalier* by Strauss with the New York City Opera without having played in a rehearsal. I got through the Prokofiev with no problems. All I had to do was read the music and play the rhythms.

The occasion didn't go unnoticed. After the concert, several people were waiting to greet me at the stage door other than my husband and my two sleeping children. Everyone enthusiastically told me how wonderful it was to see a black face on stage, and a woman in the percussion section.

I made an interesting observation that night that symphony patrons were not generally opera patrons. As a result, seeing me perform was a historic event for many of them. For me, that was only the beginning. I had a taste of that fine eminent orchestra;

that was exactly why I wanted to be—a member of a major symphony orchestra! Almost like the impossible dream, but visualized in my mind. What would be the next important ingredient to make my dream a reality?

Chapter 17

AMERICAN SYMPHONY ORCHESTRA
A First in History

In 1961, one year after I left the New York City Opera, an announcement was made that Leopold Stokowski, the world renown conductor, was forming a major symphony and would soon be holding auditions. This had the entire music community up in arms. With Stokowski as the conductor, this orchestra would play a vital role in the community. Even more significantly, he announced there would be an emphasis on youth, ethnicity and gender; obviously, a first in the history of the symphony orchestra. The music community was even more anxious about the possibility of auditioning. Who would get into the orchestra? Everyone began preparing for the audition.

One day, Joe Fabbroni called me. "Hello, Elayna? Are you-a okay?" He then went on with his usual greetings, but that time, also said, "Elayna, Maestro Stokowski wants-a you to come up-a to his apartment."

"What?" I exclaimed. "To his apartment? What for?"

"He wants to talk-a to you."

"He wants to talk to *me*?"

That was frightening to me for me to hear, as I thought only of the worst. Did I do something wrong at the last recording? But, even if I did, why would I have to go to Maestro Stokowski's apartment? Fabbroni could offer no clue except to tell me get to his house on Fifth Avenue by seven o'clock on Tuesday night.

I didn't know if the circumstances warranted me to tell everyone, so I kept it to myself. I didn't even tell George. On the appointed day, I just said I was going to a union meeting. I got the babysitter and left. When I arrived at Stoki's building on Fifth Avenue, I was taken up to the penthouse. The elevator opened up directly into his apartment. It was like entering a museum and library simultaneously. There were books, music, artwork and instruments wherever my eyes landed. It was overwhelming. As the doors opened, Stoki strolled over toward me dressed in a maroon smoking gown. With his white mane of hair, he was quite an imposing figure.

"Come in, come in," he beckoned.

I walked in gingerly.

"Come, come have a seat," he insisted. I hardly wanted to sit because even the chairs looked like treasures. "Sit down, he said again. "The others will be here shortly. You're the first to arrive. Would you like a glass of wine while waiting?"

"Yes, Maestro," I said quietly. Who else was coming and why? I wondered. I still had, of course, no idea what the meeting was all about. As the butler came in and gave me a glass of wine, I heard the door open.

"Hello Mr. Nagel, Miss Jones is already here." I heard Stoki say.

Nagel? I thought to myself. Then it hit me the moment he entered the room. Robert Nagel, trumpet player! His name was synonymous with beautiful trumpet playing. Why was he here? Why was *I* here? Bob walked in and as we were about to greet each other, we heard Stoki addressing another visitor. We both stopped in our tracks waiting for the next person. In walks Stoki with Stuart Stanky following him. Stuart had a reputation for being an outstanding contra bass player. He was on first call for most recording dates. So here he was, joining us. He walked into the room and we all greeted each other with handshakes. Stoki asked Bob and Stuart if they wanted wine, to which they both said yes. Stoki disappeared. The three of us, looking perplexed, questioned each other about the cause of the meeting.

"I haven't a clue," said Bob, a clean-cut, baby-faced young man.

He didn't look like the typical self-assured and cocky trumpet player when they knew they were good. Bob was a refreshing face among us. Before we could do anymore speculating, the butler came in with wine for Stuart, with Stoki close behind. The butler disappeared and left us alone. Stoki joined us.

"Good evening gentlemen and lady. I'm glad you could join us."

"Thank you," we said in unison spontaneously.

"No doubt you're wondering why I invited you here this evening."

"Yes," we answered.

"Well, to get to the point," Stoki continued. "You know that I am organizing a symphony orchestra."

"Yes," we affirmed.

"I want this orchestra to be the best it can be. It will be called the American Symphony Orchestra, made up of the finest musicians of all ages. I have requested musicians from all over the country to come and audition."

"That sounds wonderful and inspiring, but where do we fit in?" said Stuart, the most aggressive of the three of us.

"Well, I want to have a great orchestra and I want to start with whom I consider the most talented musicians who want to create and build a great orchestra," said Stoki.

I couldn't help but think how unusual the picture was before us. There was the great Leopold Stokowski actually talking to *us*. He generally had an affected way of speaking, in short sentences, when he did speak. But that night, he spoke to us as human beings. What an extraordinary experience!

Again, Stuart broke in. "What can we do to help build the great orchestra? Where do we fit in?"

Stokowski didn't bat an eye and answered him directly. "I

want you three to be the nucleus of this orchestra. I'm inviting you as permanent members."

I was stunned. Did I hear that right? We would be permanent members without an audition? Was I dreaming? Would I wake up and find I wasn't there?

Stoki went on. "I hope you agree to be members of the American Symphony Orchestra."

We were all shocked. Even the aggressive Stuart was silenced.

With none of us saying anything, Stokowski said, "Do you want to think this over? Let me know."

Bob spoke up first. "Do I understand, Maestro, that you want us to play in the orchestra without auditioning?"

"Yes, you heard right," responded Stoki. "Think it over and call me if you have questions. I must go now. I have work to do. I will hear from you in a couple of days."

With this, he escorted us to the door. Down the elevator went with three dazed musicians. We looked at each other.

"Can you believe what just happened?" said Bob.

"You can never predict or completely understand the inner workings of people," I said.

"Yeah, everyone always says how cold and impersonal he is," said Stuart. "Yet he invites us to his pad and makes an unorthodox proposal."

"Well, I know that conductors have been known to choose their concertmasters privately," said Bob, "but I never heard of side men being chosen with a private meeting at the conductor's home. Stokowski is such a prominent figure, that even if this is unorthodox, no one will challenge him."

"Will you accept and join the orchestra?" Stuart asked both of us.

"I'm flattered at being considered," Bob answered thoughtfully. "I do have many commitments and teachings. I'll have to consider the advantage of the commitment with my present responsibilities. It will be a major decision."

"How about you, Elayne?" Stuart said.

"Well, I'm flabbergasted. I can't believe I was so honored by Maestro Stokowski. And to have the job without an audition. That's unbelievable. It will take a while for me to digest this. I have another concern though. I just left the New York City Opera. The scheduling was so heavy that it made problems with my family. I have three young children and my physician husband. I will have to figure this into whether or not I can do it without neglecting my family. It's a real big decision and I'll have to discuss it with George."

We talked for a bit longer while standing in front of the apartment building and then departed for our other respective engagements. I went home with my head spinning. I still couldn't believe that I had been in Stokowski's home with two outstanding musicians and was offered a job without auditioning. Wow! I took the subway home and picked up my car at the last stop of the F train. I smiled all the way, wanting to tell everyone on the train what had just happened. While driving home, however, my joy turned to concern for my family. I didn't think it would be a major problem, because the schedule for symphony orchestra was not as full as that of the opera. We didn't discuss anything about contract, pay or schedule. Actually, we discussed nothing. All I knew was that Stoki invited us to play with the orchestra with no details. This hit me as I got closer to my house. Stokowski just took it for granted that we would be so grateful to be asked by him and that we were dismissed before we were given any details whatsoever. I felt this was his ego.

When I reached home, George was out on a call and the children were sleeping. I had time to assess the offer. I still felt good about Stoki's opinion of my playing, but beyond that, I knew nothing. I was deep in thought when George returned from his house call.

"Hi, honey" he said, giving me a little greeting kiss. "How are you today?"

"Oh. I'm fine. I have to tell you something interesting."

"Yeah, what's up?"

"Well, when I went out today, I said I was going to a union meeting, but it wasn't that. I was invited to a meeting with Leopold Stokowski."

"You did what?"

"I was invited to Stokowski's home." I told George I was invited to Stoki's house and what had happened. After talking more with George and thinking further myself, I said yes to Leopold Stokowski's proposal.

The American Symphony Orchestra was a fine orchestra made up of young talented musicians. Stoki believed in having youth around him and exposing them to the professional music experience. At the same time, he also believed music should go to those who couldn't come to the music. So, he initiated bringing the orchestra into the schools and the hospitals.

Like Dean Dixon, Stokowski, being an innovator, had a need to develop his own audiences. He went one step further by dividing the orchestra into little groups, like a chamber orchestra, which played in accessible school auditoriums. Our repertoire included Prokofiev's Peter and the Wolf; Tripp's and Kleinsinger's "Tubby the Tuba"; and Benjamin Britten's Young People's Guide to the Orchestra.

At the beginning of each concert, Stokowski encouraged the kids to write their impressions of anything they heard. At one of our big concerts for youth at Carnegie Hall, we performed Tchaikovsky's 1812 Overture. One group of kids was serious and asked Stokowski how Tchaikovsky knew about the Quaker Oats commercial. The music to that commercial happened to be taken from Tchaikovsky's 812 Overture, but the students obviously didn't know which came first. That question became a valuable history lesson for them.

It was clear from their questions that the children were interested in learning about the trombones, flutes, bassoons, oboes and especially the black lady playing the timpani. To accommodate the questions, Stokowski told us he would find music to feature these instruments.

He said to me one day, "We must find a way to feature you because they all ask about you."

Well, I thought, there wasn't much music for timpani in the repertoire at that time, so I had to find something to present. Then it hit me. Why don't I do or try doing what I did when I was working at Camp Unity?

Chapter 18

WOMEN VS. WOMEN
Can I Afford to Support the Women's Movement?

In 1995, I stepped back and took a closer look at the role of racism among women and men in all levels of American society. I revisited its impact on my own life and career as a professional, a woman and a person. I needed to express my opinions and feelings about the intentions, action and inaction of what I saw as the "white women's movement." Here is what I wrote at that time.

The woman, poor and deprived as she may have thought she was, could dream of becoming a princess by marrying the right person. That was the Cinderella story whether it happened or not. One could dream, and having dreams is what life's all about. But, what dreams did we blacks have in Harlem, New York in the United States?

Every successful person was white, every rich person was white. All the so-called beautiful people were white. Everything and anything of worth was white. Those images and edicts permeated our lives to such a degree that we were only accepted if we looked nearly white, either with straight hair (or what we called in my neighborhood "fly hair"), or fair skin, or a straight nose. I can remember hearing, If you're white you're right, if you're brown stick around, if you're black step back. I didn't fit any of those images, so I had nothing. Did that mean that I couldn't have any dreams? How could one feel good about oneself under those circumstances? You had no self-esteem and knew you would amount to nothing because your teachers told you so. How well I remember my female white teachers telling us that we would amount to nothing but maids or porters anyhow so why bother teaching us or trying to make us behave.In our schools in Harlem.

I was luckier than most black young girls, because I managed to escape from this stigma having learned the piano, which my mother taught me, and resulted in getting me out of Harlem. I passed the entrance exam through my piano and academics and got into The High School of Music & Art.

In backtracking to my young years, I am pained by the memory of what had happened to Marian Anderson, the talented and powerful singer. This great woman was denied the opportunity of singing at Constitution Hall by the Daughters of the American Revolution.

I wonder now, can I, a black woman, afford to support the white women's movement? I remember as a youngster envying white women because their image only went to denigrate me. No way in those days could you have convinced me that they had any problems. I participated in the struggle for eliminating the "white chauvinist pig" because this was far more imperative in the life of all black people throughout the world whether they be poor from Appalachia or very wealthy. Let me give you an example.

In the face of total resistance from my white colleagues, I did everything I could to be successful as a musician and at the same time try to be a good wife and mother. My husband was a Jewish physician with irregular hours and my hours were even more chaotic. Therefore, I had to have someone take care of my children on a full-time basis. The problem I had would not have been acute if I had a nine-to-five job. Because musicians work at odd hours, I needed someone to sleep in. I placed ads in the newspapers and frequented employment agencies. I was in contact with poor working people who desperately needed work, but they would not accept working for me simply because I was black! It didn't even matter that my money was available and as green as anyone's. They just didn't think there was any status in working for a black woman. The fact that I was married to a Jewish man didn't make any impact whatsoever on their reaction to me. Those same people were willing to work for and accept any indignity from any person as long as she was the white mistress.

All of my mother's friends were domestic workers and when I was a child, I sat and heard the abuse they had to take from the women for whom they worked. They were obliged to clean homes and children so that the lady of the house could be free to go shopping. When I was 13, I had a summer job of taking care of a young boy for a family on Long Island. I wasn't allowed to be seen on the beach until after six o'clock in the evening. How many white women were subjected to this kind of indignity? How could you tell if the white woman was the nanny or the mother?

Speaking of indignities. From 1949 to 1960, I had played with the New York City Opera. Every fall we traveled around the country to cities like Detroit and Chicago. We gave a performance in St. Louis, and Camilla Williams, a beautiful black soprano was to sing *Madama Butterfly*. I was playing timpani with the orchestra in the pit. But, at that time, blacks were not to be seen or heard on stage. Consequently, Camilla did not sing, and a substitute took her place. A sub couldn't be found for me. The "solution" was lowering the pit so I wouldn't be seen by the audience! On all these tours, I always went through other traumatic experiences of not being able to stay in hotels and eat in restaurants with my colleagues. More often than not, I had to face extraordinary difficulties. As a musician, there are enough pressures worrying about playing. Not having a place to eat or sleep only intensified the pressure. Sure, white women have problems, but I can't emphasize enough that all of the humiliating situations I encountered didn't affect my white female colleagues in any way. In spite of my status and reputation as an intelligent musician, I still suffer a degree of trauma whenever I go anywhere—like a tennis club for the first time.

Have you ever considered how important images are? Probably not. I, however, sit in the orchestra and I feel as though I don't belong. Everything is white, European male and female. Have you ever considered how difficult it is for me to rise above this and feel that I am capable? Yes, the white woman wants to compete equally with men, but her father, brother, husband or lover is part of the establishment, so in a social sense, once she gets the job, she is one of them. I remain an outsider. No matter what my abilities, I am still not equal. What would change that? To have as many other black men and women pursuing equally financially, socially in every area of our lives, and not just token numbers!

I find it almost impossible to align myself with white women when seeing pictures of them in Boston jeering at the black children on their way to integrate the schools in order to get a decent education. I have some friends who are understanding and not all whites are racists, but I believe the majority are racist.

I recall a conversation I had with several of the male members in the tennis club where I'm the only black. They were complaining about their daughters getting into law school, medical school and so on. I argued that every time a white female gets a job as a minority she displaces a black man. Have I heard the white woman's movement fight for the right of black men and women to get equal education and better job opportunities so their families could enjoy the better things of life like belonging to a tennis club if they so desired? Or just being able to provide basic food, clothing and shelter for their families? No! I have statistics that show many more white, single women than black women are on welfare. However, even with welfare, the rents in the black community are often much higher, with worse conditions than those of the white ghetto.

I couldn't help but think that the occupations white women have access to have been denied many hard-working black families. Think about it. The only professions that blacks have "made it" are what they could manage in the streets—baseball, basketball and football. When I was growing up, boxing was the main source of pride in the black community.

When you read stories of amazing performers like Billie Holiday, you learn they always had to go through the back door. It's only in the last two decades that this practice is being eradicated. I had to go through the back door when I was teaching in apartment houses in white communities. I would be told by the doormen when I went to teach students on Central Park or West End Avenue apartments, "Go through the service entrance." I have a dear friend, Antoinette Handy, a flutist, who one time went for an audition on Park Avenue to where the conductor was staying. She failed the audition because she became so upset when the doorman insisted that she use the service entrance. The white persons going for the same audition weren't subjected to that humiliation.

Have I heard any protests from the white women's movement about such racist policies and practices? No. If anything, I observe that they have divided us from our men. I don't say the men are perfect, but neither are we and we cannot stand in this racist world alone. My analysis of the "white women's movement" is to challenge the white European male dominance over the world by taking it over for themselves. They want power and they will get it most likely at the expense of the black people's struggle for equality.

I would like to take a survey of white women who have never worked. I'm sure I'd find that the percentage of women who have never worked, and who complain about being unequal or whatever their problems, have had better quality lives. They probably do not live in sub-standard homes and do not eat inferior food. They probably can send their children to the best schools and they can afford designer clothes. They have all this and more while black families who have toiled all their lives, still struggle just to survive. Not only that, they've toiled at jobs which give no meaningful income or pride.

Just think, when you go to the theater, dance, opera, drama, it is only since the late sixties that blacks have been portrayed or performed in anything other than situations depicting them as servants. Not only does one not have a self-image, but what is conveyed to our audiences reinforces that blacks can only be maids or porters in fantasy or reality. Have I heard protests from women registering disapproval of those images? Not nearly audible enough if at all.

Why my focus on the women? I was the first black person to play with the New York City Opera as a principal player. I was the first black person to play with the New York Philharmonic Symphony. Those were historic happenings; yet, no publisher or other professional ever came to me and asked, "Would you write a story on how you survived in these environments?" Wherever I go, however many other people ask me, "How come there is no book about your experiences?" The only answer I believe is that because I'm not a white woman.

Getting the job was one thing but staying there is still a problem, even to this day. I have had to spend altogether too much time defending my right to be where I am. Most significant is the fact that I often said I was not a liberated woman. I was just ahead of my time. What has happened over the years? Women have succeeded in greater numbers than have blacks. As a result, all the jobs I've had in the past where I was the only woman or black, have more than doubled the number of women. I remain either the only black or an increase of maybe one person less than one percent. Give up? No way!

Back in 1971 when the suit against the New York Philharmonic was initiated on grounds of racism, we thought the women would have rallied with us. Instead, they came up with the same nonsense statement used by others: Blacks are not qualified. Support, no, but perpetuation of the superiority syndrome. What I hear is that white women are capable of being racist just like their white male counterparts. If they are raised by the same parents and go to the same schools, how can they break away from the racist ideology and environment? Let's face it people, when blacks in the South were fighting to get into the halls of wisdom and fighting for the right to vote, the white woman already had access to these institutions. True, Susan B. Anthony fought for the right of women to vote, but blacks were not included in that battle.

I think by now you have some idea of the direction I'm going in. My dear friends, the struggle isn't women's rights, but the *inhumanity* of one to the other. The chauvinism of one group against another—we find religions against each other—nations fighting for superiority and dominance over each other through economic strangulation.

My experience as a musician these 45 years have convinced me that the problem I must address myself to is the supposed inherent superiority and power of the European tradition over the cultures of those of African descent, Asians and Latinos. I have had to remain extremely strong and then be called people of the Third World. Why are we Third World? That keeps us always behind and not "equal" to those of the "first world." I don't subscribe to the fact that there should be no differences made—the world and what it has to offer belongs to all of us equally regardless of race, sex or color.

Fighting this fight led me into the presence of Joseph McCarthy's Un-American Activities Committee because it was assumed that my political activities made me a communist. Yes, I was political because I realized I had to fight and break down doors to get where I wanted. I hear women speak today of the glass ceiling, which means you have already gotten on the other side of the door. We, however, are still pursuing getting our feet *through* the door!

There were days I went from school to orchestra rehearsals to political meetings. I was always way ahead of my time and peers when you see what I've done and where I've gone. It isn't much easier today. Even though I have a prestigious job with the San Francisco Opera, every step I make takes constant emotional strength. A colleague once asked me if I could function without having to do battle. I wonder if the day will ever come for me to be able to answer that question.

Chapter 19

TRANSPORTING MUSIC FROM AFRICA TO THE CONCERT HALLS
Yes, It's True

I was swept up into the raging struggle of the women's movement which consumed our merging self-esteem, fueled by books like Simone de Beauvoir's *The Second Sex*. At the same time, I was teaching at the Mercy Catholic High School, Westchester Conservatory and had private students at home. I got each of these teaching positions through progressive male musicians I worked with, who were impressed with my energy and commitment to the arts. I never discussed my life with them; they didn't discuss their lives with me. So, I was surprised when out of the blue I got a phone call from one of those colleagues.

"Hi, Elayne. How are you doing?"

"I'm fine, just busy," I said. And busy I was.

"Yeah, I know," he interrupted. "I had a conversation with Valerie Capers recently who said she heard your lecture demonstration recently at the school in Freeport. She was very impressed with your musical knowledge, obvious love of what you did, and your way with the students."

"Thank you," I said appreciatively.

"Well, because of this I'm calling you." He paused and then continued. "You see, I am on the staff at the Bronx Community College. The college is on a campaign to grow and expand. The Bronx is going through a transition, and we wish to be a part of the transition in the community."

I was aware of this transition. The Bronx Community College was in a section of the Bronx which was previously Jewish. Over the years, Jews were abandoning the area, leaving for more upscale middle class housing. Hispanic and black families were replacing them where they left. This transition was not accomplished without problems, which were basically cultural clashes. I remember walking through the streets passing groups of boys on the stoops playing a rhythm and blues number. Not far away, a Latino group in a circle playing bongos and drums was competing for the same air space. Each culture had a need to express and therefore, maintain its identity and culture. Who would reign supreme?

At the same time, there was the rising voice for black studies, along with women's studies, in all the educational establishments. The young African-American boys began expressing themselves not only with their R&B music, but through graffiti, which was emerging as a demonstration of freedom and frustration. They spread their message on the walls of buildings and throughout the subways many times, almost obliterating the windows of the subway cars. A friend of mine was visiting from Barbados and wanted to see me in Queens. She never got to my house. Having a hard time deciphering the graffiti-covered subway directions, she got onto the subway train going in the opposite direction from my neighborhood and wound up at the other end of the city.

New Yorkers, as well as tourists, suffered with this artistic intrusion. Eventually, the city government got involved and made the first law banning anyone under the age of 18 from using spray paint cans. This edict didn't do much to curtail the artistic protestations. Subway cars then were treated with a material that prevented spray paint from adhering to the train surface.

It was in this environment that I was asked and subsequently hired to teach at Bronx Community College. I started on September 22, 1971. I taught piano and a non-western music history class, which was new at the college. Up until my being introduced to the Bronx Community College, I was never aware of the value of a community college. I only knew about four-year colleges such as City College, Hunter College and Brooklyn College. Yes, I knew of Harvard, Yale, Princeton and the other Ivy League schools, but not community colleges. I learned about that system as if a swimmer thrown into unfamiliar deep water. The Bronx Community College was set up for students who wanted to go to college, but their grades were just under the requirements to enter the traditional four-year school.

After I was hired, I met with the heads of departments and learned about the historical role that community college played in the lives of its students. They told me that I would find a variety of attitudes among the students. Some students really wanted to move on to the traditional college and would work hard. Others who might be unsure of themselves and influenced by parents and peers, could have less clarity about what they really wanted. Such distinctions were important in how I prepared for students.

The course I was asked to teach resulted from the demands of the black youth. Originally titled "Non-European Music," it was to cover the music of Africa, Asia and the American Indian. I wasn't given an outline or books on the subject because there were none; I had to set up the entire program. I visited all the libraries, wrote to various sources, and did research in order to have something to teach. It became apparent to me that to use the term western music excluded or ignored the music of the Indians from North America and South America, and of course, the Africans. After a few months, I changed the title of the course to "Non-Western Music."

Could I share the valuable experience I had? I thought. I had gone into schools throughout the boroughs, playing for the students with Leopold Stokowski and chamber groups from the symphony. However, I had no idea how these students reacted to or absorbed what we played for them. I did have several subtle expressions passed on to me from the black students, indicating that we were playing "white man's music." I had my feet in both cultures: the symphony of Europeans and the jazz or swing of the black community. I loved the fact that I could listen and play Brahms, Bach and Beethoven, then turn around and listen as well as play the music of Duke Ellington, Count Basie and Tommy Dorsey.

How I would convey my experience was another hurdle with some students. Not only did they challenge me with "white music," they challenged anything white. I heard them accosting each other with the fact that not only did they object to music, but they were also opposed to "speaking white." I was already responsible for creating the Symphony of the New World to give black musicians the opportunity to learn to play classical music! So, the next step was to elevate the students' thinking about *who* could play the music of all the various cultures. I believed music could be enjoyed by all, once exposed to the music. Inasmuch as I was a drummer, although by now I primarily played the timpani, I was keenly aware that drums originated from Africa.

How often people approached me about being a woman who played drums in the symphony! I joked that I was bringing Africa to Europe. At the time, little did I realize this "joke" would expand into history. I began doing research about the various drums in libraries at Juilliard and at Patelson's Music Store. I had no idea this research would reveal more than just drums emerging from Africa. I literally stumbled on the history of all the instruments to such a point that I eventually created a program, "Africa in the Symphony." This knowledge gave me the ammunition I needed to construct the new course at the Bronx Community College. It was at this point I renamed the course, Non-Western Music.

I was apprehensive, worrying about how the department heads would react to my suggestion. When I was asked to defend my course title, I explained to them the reaction I got from the students whenever I played classical music: "How come you play European or white man's music?" From my heart, I knew it was possible to enjoy any music like anything else if you know about it. I convinced the board, and they allowed me free reign to design the course.

I put together the piano course for beginners, including theory and ear training for all my students. Valerie Capers, who had mentioned me to my colleague, was a beautiful black pianist and was also visually impaired. She was my major support. She, too, had studied and played classical music, as well as jazz. So, Valerie was happy to have me support her own efforts to embrace total music knowledge. In addition, she was the chairman of the music department.

The next path was getting the students to sign up for my class. As we suspected, they questioned what this course had to offer and what credits would they get towards going to college. At that point in time from 1969 to 1970, music was an appendage part of the arts and an integral rung in the ladder going up for a person's education. Music credits were important towards moving ahead. There were still, however, students who rejected the course to do their own thing, which rebelled into what we know today as Rap and Hip Hop.

I strongly believed my job was to educate and encourage students to grow, enjoy and learn everything the world has to offer, musically. In my class, I first introduced them to all the instruments. The majority of students in that community knew little or nothing about stringed instruments other than the bass. They had never heard or seen a symphony orchestra, nor had they traveled outside their neighborhood or "the hood," as it was called. I needed a way to bridge this divide.

At the time, I was also playing with the American Symphony Orchestra under Leopold Stokowski's baton. He had a reputation of being a taskmaster, causing symphony musicians to quiver at the thought of working with him. In the presence of children, however, he was like butter. He even encouraged everyone to attend his rehearsals, which were always open to visitors. I then realized this was perfect for my class.

Like me, until I went to The High School of Music & Art, students in my Non-Western Music class had never experienced people, life and cultures outside their community. From the year that I entered Music & Art in 1942, then graduated with a scholarship to Juilliard School of Music, then on to being accepted to spend an extraordinary musical summer at Tanglewood with the Boston Symphony Orchestra and finally in being hired to play with the New York City Opera, I had a musical education and exposure to the culture that went with it. Many people, black or white, had scant knowledge and access to such experiences. At Bronx Community College, I thought that through music, I could educate students by opening their world and their senses so they could impartially judge what exists in other communities. I designed my course with that objective in mind.

To alter students' prejudice about black music and white music, my assignment for the semester was to attend three classical concerts, three jazz-swing or R&B concerts, then three concerts of their choice. They were required to write their impression of the music, negative or positive. I wasn't prepared for the protestations from the black students, especially when they read the assignment.

"Go to a symphony concert? Downtown? In Manhattan? Ms. Jones, can't we just go here in the Bronx?" Those were their comments, with their fears about traveling out of the comfort of their community. I tried to explain that they were in school to be educated, and getting educated is going beyond the periphery of where you are and what you have been doing.

To counter their reactions, I played a trump card, or so I thought, to challenge them. "I can offer you a unique experience," I tried to tempt them.

I explained to them that I played with an orchestra at

Carnegie Hall in Manhattan, which they could attend free. Of course, the "free" part appealed to them. I was able to give them directions to come and see me play. I had to first prepare them for such a new experience, the nucleus of my course. I had already introduced them to the large variety of instruments from the strings, woodwinds, brass and percussion. Then they had to compare them with the instruments that they saw or didn't see in other groups at clubs or wherever they went to hear other required music.

An unexpected reaction surprised me when reading the reports of the students. In each report, students gave a personal reaction to how they had to behave while listening to a symphony, and what separated it from being at a jazz concert. "You had to sit and be quiet. You could not express your emotions." This was a surprising issue to which I had to give considerable thought.

Leopold Stokowski was the only conductor I knew of who allowed and sometimes even encouraged the audience to applaud after a movement of a symphony and not save it for the end. He got no support, since tradition said you must be reserved and restrain your emotions until the end of any classical performance. To this day, I believe this attitude has kept many people, regardless of culture or race, out of the classical concert halls.

My Non-Western Music course was so successful that years later I would be offered an opportunity to produce a TV show on PBS called, "Africa in the Symphony." I was happy to be able to show that all the instruments in the orchestra had their origin in Africa, all except the trombone and the organ. That information somewhat neutralized student resistance to classical music. I didn't insist that students should love classical music, only that they not demonize it.

Many years later, I would have wonderful feedback about the positive impact that my music history class at Bronx

Community College had on students. I was living in San
Francisco and played timpani with the San Francisco Symphony.
Whenever I could, I returned to New York to visit my parents
and friends. I was treated like a hero there, being taken to
restaurants for a festive lunch or dinner. One day I was sitting
with friends enjoying the occasion when three young women
approached me.

"Ms. Jones," they hesitantly inquired.

"Yes?" I said.

They took turns speaking to me. "Did you teach at the Bronx
Community College in 1969?"

"Yes," I said.

"Well, we were in your music history class. We never thought
we'd ever see you. You gave us an education unlike any other.
Unlike our friends in our community, we could enjoy and
appreciate all music." At that point, the three of them embraced
me with warm and loving hugs. It was better than any award I
could have received!

Many people who saw me perform told me how much they
loved to watch me play. I brought to this medium my
background of expressing visibly what I heard in Harlem, what
I sang in the church choir, what I danced to at our parties, the
music I played when I worked at the resorts in upstate New
York, and the kind of music I heard when I went to Barbados. I
brought these cultures of music, which were imbedded in my
musical understanding and appreciation. I didn't see one venue
of music as better than the other, because I was happy I could fit
into and play easily into any style of music. I brought all of this
along with me, and I was aware that even my colleagues in the
orchestra were not privileged to my broad musical involvement.
After all, my musical history was paramount in my ability to
embrace music of all cultures.

When I was playing in the San Francisco Opera orchestra,
my colleagues joked about what I did during our intermission

or between acts. Every Thursday evening, the radio station, KALW 91.8 FM played music not heard on the major media stations. I loved listening to a program hosted by Henri Qubaca. He played the music from Africa, Latin America and the Caribbean. I couldn't miss listening to music, which to my way of thinking, represented nearly all of the world. So that's what I listened to, during our INTERMISSIONS. It didn't matter to me that we might have been playing music of Wagner, Verdi or Puccini beforehand. None of my colleagues could comprehend how it was possible to listen to one period style of music while playing another. I love music and feel it in my soul regardless of its origin, rhythm or melodies.

Chapter 20

WORLD SYMPHONY
Being Treated Like a Star

A rthur Aaron was a successful orchestra contractor. At one time, he was hiring for every major job in New York, so I was overjoyed to be high on his list of musicians to hire. He called me one day and I didn't think anything was strange about that even though he was calling early in the morning. Arthur liked to tie us down for the next gig on his list. He gave us the schedule of upcoming rehearsals and concerts.

"Hi, Arthur, what's up?" I said.

"Sorry, to call you so early, Elayne, but something has come up which should excite you which is why I'm calling now rather than later." He piqued my curiosity and I couldn't wait to hear what he had to tell me. He went on. "Remember when we played those pop concerts with Arthur Fiedler?"

"Yes, I remember. Fiedler was quite a character."

"Yes, that's his reputation," Arthur agreed. "Anyway, you made an impression on him. I met with him last night, and he is planning to put together a unique orchestra for a special engagement."

"Oh, what could that be?" I said, anticipation rising in me.

"He wants an orchestra made up of the best players from each orchestra around the world."

"I never heard of such a thing."

"Neither had I," Arthur concurred. "In the meantime, he had sent out inquiries to all the orchestra managers. I got the one sent to Stoki. What was interesting was that in the inquiry to the

American Symphony Orchestra, he said he wanted specifically the young lady playing the timpani to be part of his orchestra."

"What?" I exclaimed. "Did he mean me?"

"That's right and when I met with him last night that was his request. He was evidently very impressed with you during those pop concerts we played at Madison Square Garden."

"Wow, this is unbelievable! I never thought he even noticed me."

"Well, he did, and he would like you to play. Now we have to get down to specifics like can you, do it? It would mean being away for about 10 days. The temporary schedule is to rehearse at Carnegie Hall, then fly down to Orlando, Florida, to play for the opening of Disneyworld, then fly to Washington D.C. to play for the opening of the Kennedy Center, and then return home. As of now, that's the schedule."

I was speechless. It was more than I could manage. Too many details to think about all at once.

"Okay, Elayne, I know it's a lot to swallow, so I'll let you think whether you can do it, then I'll get more specific details."

How could I turn down an opportunity to play in an orchestra made up of musicians from every country in the world, and as Arthur said, the best instrumentalists? Imagine, I thought, being asked for by Arthur Fiedler! I didn't know all the details yet, but I knew I would have a lot of maneuvering to do with my children, mother, private students and the WCM Westchester Conservatory of Music, Bronx Community College, Marti High School and the American Symphony Orchestra.

Arthur called a couple of days later with the specific details. "You don't have to worry, Elayne, I have had a nice relationship with Fiedler when he conducted in New York, away from the Boston Pops. He was aware of our American Symphony Orchestra schedule so this engagement is tucked in between our rehearsal and concert series."

When he finished, I said, "Gee I'm glad it worked out with the American Symphony Orchestra schedule. That was one of my worries."

I breathed a sigh of relief. The first hurdle was overcome. As usual, although a gig was a week or a month or just one day, I had to think about my children.

Arthur called back the next day with the schedule. It wasn't too bad. I only had to worry about the three days I wouldn't be home. We would fly down to Florida for the gala opening of Disneyworld in Orlando on October 23, then up to Washington, D.C. for the opening of the Kennedy Center on October 25, and return to La Guardia the next day. Yes, only three days away from home and my children. Luckily, my Aunt Violet was visiting from Barbados. When we mentioned to her that I had an opportunity for a job and would be going away, she volunteered before I even asked her to stay at my house the few days that I'd be away. There was no more need for me to worry.

Those three days of performing with the World Symphony would be a memory to last forever. At the first gathering of this unusual orchestra for the rehearsal, I was apprehensive and curious. Who would these musicians be? When Arthur Fiedler greeted us, he emphasized that his orchestra was made up of symphony players from every orchestra in the world. He made us at ease by saying that music is an international language and although the person sitting next to you may not speak your language, when we play, the notes are the same in any language.

"Now turn to the member next to you in your section and say something welcoming," Fiedler directed.

I turned to my three percussion colleagues. I smiled and said, "Hello, I am from New York." They couldn't hide their surprise at having a woman, who was black, playing the timpani. Most likely, they hadn't experienced a woman in *any* orchestra. I sensed that underlying their shock would be the thought, but can she play? Since I was used to that, I would simply do what

I love—play music.

"Now, the best thing to do after greeting each other is to play music together," said Fiedler. "For starters, we'll read through Aaron Copeland's *Fanfare to the Common Man.*

I had played this magnificent overture for the first time when I was a student at Tanglewood in the Berkshires when Serge Koussevitzky conducted student musicians from around the United States. With Fiedler, I was playing the overture with professional musicians from around the world. Did this make a difference? Basically, no. Until they spoke they could have been from around the corner, from Brooklyn or from the Congo.

At Arthur Fiedler's downbeat, we played through the entire composition. Being that we all were from major symphonies, we would have already played this overture at least once. But for some reason, playing with those musicians gave me goose bumps. The overture, under any circumstance, is stirring on its own. It starts with the trumpets, timpani and bass drum—a commanding solo forte opening. It can't help but bring the audience to attention, and with the timpani so dominant, everyone noticed me, especially the men in the orchestra. When it ended, they all turned around and acknowledged my presence. Fiedler had a look on his face as if he had won approval for making a monumental decision to include me in the orchestra.

After the rehearsal, I was treated like a star, with all the players, especially from my section, asking me questions. Where did I come from? What orchestra did I play with? In the past when I've been approached this way, it always made me nervous. They would be focused on me, making me feel all eyes were on me, so I *had* to be perfect. It could have been my imagination, but I couldn't dismiss that idea from my mind. Could I have risen to the top and gotten respect if I didn't put myself in that frame of mind? It's not easy always being under such stress. Maybe all people go through this whenever they are competing for a position or are a soloist.

I was treated like a star for the days of that wonderful job. We played our first concert in Carnegie Hall to rave reviews. Whether it was Fiedler's relaxed attitude or the quality of each member of this unique group of musicians, we blended together as though we had played together for years, not days. Touring together generally tends to make musicians either closer or hating each other by the end of the tour. For us, it was the former. If only music were the vehicle for all of us to learn to live in harmony with each other.

Chapter 21

A BITTER DISAPPOINTMENT
Smitten with the Challenge

My son Stephen was attending The High School of Music & Art and playing violin in the senior orchestra. He could appreciate what I had accomplished in my career. He also knew the story and challenges behind my efforts. One day, he came home from school with disturbing news.

"Mom, I just heard that Roland Kohloff was hired to be the timpanist of the New York Philharmonic."

"You gotta be kidding," I said with disbelief. "How could he get the job when he didn't audition with us in September?"

"I dunno," said Stephen, "but that's what David said." David Lang was the son of Morris Arnie Lang, the percussionist with the New York Philharmonic. Arnie and I had auditioned for the position of timpanist being vacated by Saul Goodman who was retiring. We auditioned with Pierre Boulez the conductor overseeing the auditions. After going through the preliminary and on to the finals we were tied for the job.

Boulez said to us that because we tied for the finals he would have us re-audition in the spring. We both figured we'd have a re-audition and planned on that happening. There was no further talk about any other audition being held. In the meantime, Arnie continued on playing cymbals which is the position he held and had auditioned to move up; I continued playing timpani with the American Symphony Orchestra.

It just so happened that Arnie's son, David, was in the same class at Music & Art as Stephen. Somehow, unbeknownst to us,

Roland Kohloff had come in from San Francisco where he was the timpanist, auditioned for the New York Philharmonic and was hired.

Arnie was upset about this unorthodox event and told his son. His son came to school and told Stephen. Hearing the news was very painful for me. I was already dreaming how great it would be to be the timpanist at the New York Philharmonic, then all of a sudden, my dream was smashed. Even more devastating was the fact that I had many friends in the Philharmonic. Each one of them said to me they had no idea when or how Roland got the job. It was another blow similar to the one I had previously from the Philadelphia Symphony Orchestra.

Much later, I was to find out that the New York Philharmonic board had been alerted to the results of audition for Arnie and me. They hastily got together to discuss the inevitability that a woman who is black could conceivably win the prestigious job of timpanist for the great New York Philharmonic. Would this be a positive image for the orchestra? Would the patrons see the orchestra as less than first class?

This was the same scenario that happened when another black woman, Antoinette Handy, who played the flute, and I were hired to play with the Symphony of the Air. Known originally as the NBC Symphony during the leadership of the great Arturo Toscanini, the symphony was a world class orchestra. When Toscanini retired, the orchestra members decided not to disband that great organization. NBC management didn't object to continuing the orchestra but said they could not use the name NBC Symphony because it was originally created for Arturo Toscanini. After many discussions and ideas marketing the orchestra, they finally agreed to Symphony of the Air.

The orchestra voted Philip Sklar, the outstanding bass player, to be personnel manager. He was chosen because of his exceptional musical ability, as well as his personal and professional integrity. Philip was also a progressive human being. He was able to maintain the high quality of the orchestra to earn positive reviews from the critics. Then he did the unconscionable thing. He hired two black women to substitute with the orchestra when the two musicians hired to play were unavailable for only one particular concert. It seemed that a board member happened to be at the first rehearsal. By the time that we finished, the three-hour rehearsal, word had gotten around: There are two black women in the orchestra. Traditionally, there was no problem getting a usually slow board to an emergency meeting.

Before the next meeting, the board members had gotten together and made a decision. They called Philip and told him that he had to find two male players to replace the women, putting him in a quite unenviable position. He was doing an admirable thing, hiring two black women, not even men, but he was being coerced to go against his best principles. Why? He was confronted with their rationale.

The Symphony of the Air was being promoted as Arturo Toscanini's NBC Symphony and that was the basis for getting funding. The board reasoned there were no women or blacks in Toscanini's symphony. How then could they get critical financial support if it was not Toscanini's symphony? What a dilemma Philip faced. He called Antoinette and me to alert us to the events. Of course, the board members didn't see their directive as being racist or sexist. By the next day, however, the story hit the front pages of the *New York Times* and spread like a wild fire: "Symphony Denies Black Women Jobs." This incident was eventually responsible for the demise of the Symphony of the Air. We often wondered how this story would have ended if Antoinette and I had played without the board making an issue of our presence, or if we were white women.

This incidence had loomed in my mind when I heard that the

New York Philharmonic was going to get involved with the results of the audition Arnie and I played which ended in a tie. I couldn't get the thought out of my mind that perhaps I played an audition good enough to be chosen for the job. It turned out that they couldn't let me have the job and decided that we had tied for the finals. A tie gave them the chance to put off having to make a decision at that time.

Regardless of the motive, the Philharmonic committee made the decision and Arnie and I had no choice but to accept it. We were told Maestro Boulez had decided for us to re-audition in the spring. So, we focused our sights on auditioning again for the last time in the spring. As far as we knew, there would be no other audition until then. Just imagine our shock when we heard Roland Kohloff had gotten the job. I really cried because I was so close to achieving my goal. It wasn't as traumatic for Arnie, because he was already a member of the orchestra. But he was disappointed in not being able to move up to principal position of timpanist.

Fortunately, the upcoming holiday season filled with performances would keep me from dwelling on feeling that perhaps I wasn't good enough to play with a major symphony. I don't know why I was so obsessed with playing in a symphony. I was doing well and I had to say to myself, Elayne, just think of the marvelous experience you just had.

There is an old saying: "If you don't want me I don't want you." Having been privy to playing opera, symphony and with Broadway shows, I got to hear preferences or prejudices of musicians expressed by each type of music—more often than not an expression that the symphony is elitist or who wants to play the same music day in and day out. The symphony did have a status, from the way they dressed, appearances, to the salary and security it offered. Those musicians who weren't lucky to get this position put it down.

Although I had faced all the obstacles to pursuing a career in music I realized in spite of that I played every style of music. I didn't know where my path would take me; I just took whatever job came my way and went in whatever direction it took me therefore giving me a wealth of invaluable experience. The disappointment with the New York Philharmonic led me to say, "If they don't want me, I don't want them!"

Yet, I wasn't satisfied. I was smitten with the challenge. Most musicians would have been happy to achieve what I had, but the challenge was still there for me to be a member of a major symphony orchestra.

Chapter 22

LEAVING NEW YORK
Making a New Home in San Francisco

At first when I arrived in San Francisco I wasn't sure I wanted to get the job with the San Francisco Symphony. However, I was anxious to play well at the audition. During my stay, I made a friend, Bob LeSoine. He had also auditioned for timpanist but didn't make it past the preliminaries. I did. Bob came back to the auditions every day and invited me to stay at his house. While at Bob's home, we got to know each other. I told him about my experiences. He became so impressed that he wrote an article about me, "The Groovy Timpanist," for a local newspaper.

When the symphony auditions ended around three o'clock in the afternoon, Bob picked me up and took me around San Francisco. We went from the Golden Gate Bridge to the Embarcadero, the Fillmore, Broadway and then we drove through Golden Gate Park. I was taken with the smell of the eucalyptus trees. Reminding me of my childhood and my mother rubbing me down with eucalyptus oil when I had a cold, the pungent scent made me feel at home. Then there was the gorgeous weather.

The January day that I had flown out of Kennedy Airport was a typical cold, grey, cloudy winter day in New York. The trees were bare of leaves and nothing was green. When we landed at San Francisco Airport, I arrived in a different world. It was warmer than New York, the sun was shining and the day seemed longer than in my home state. Here there is no winter! On the cab ride into the city we drove through many districts where the houses weren't drab and big, but were painted in many colors and styles. I couldn't believe my eyes.

It wasn't until Bob took me around San Francisco, though, that I found myself thinking what a wonderful place to live. As much as I wasn't sure I wanted the job with this Symphony when I first arrived, I wanted it more after experiencing the city. I always hated New York in the winter and here would be a place to live without winter. Yes, I could love this city. With my new-found realization, it became more urgent for me to do well in the audition. I did do well and when Bob was driving me back to the airport, I had a contract in my hands. Although I could not remember what I played when I won the Juilliard Scholarship, I would never forget what I played for this audition.The tympani part to "Le Sacre du Printemps".

As high as the plane flew, my spirits were higher. The flight had an unexpected joy. My elated spirits spilled over to smiling and joking with the flight attendant. Early in the flight, she came to me and whispered into my ear.

"We have a celebrity on this flight."

"Really, who?" I said.

"Shirley Chisholm," she confided.

Wow, I was impressed because Shirley Chisholm had just entered the campaign to be the President of the United States! A first.

"Would you like to meet her?" the flight attendant offered.

"I certainly would."

"Come with me quietly," she instructed. I followed her out of cabin class and into first class seating. We stopped beside Shirley Chisolm's seat who seemed to be resting and in deep thought

The flight attendant was quite astute. I had said to her earlier in my jovial state that I had just won the job with the San Francisco Symphony — a first for a black woman. So, she put this together and introduced Shirley and me to each other as two women making history. The congresswoman and I embraced and exchanged warm well wishes for continued success. I left her to continue her much needed quietude and I returned to my seat. What exaltation I felt. I thought that day represented the positive results of all the years of struggle for black women.

When we landed at Kennedy Airport in New York, a large entourage greeted Shirley with signs proclaiming her as the next President of the United States.

Nobody but my children knew that I had flown alone to San Francisco to audition for the job with the San Francisco Symphony. So, my son, Stephen, was the only one waiting for me at the arrival gate. He was overjoyed to see me, and I was overjoyed in telling him about my experience and success.

Chapter 23

TENURE
Heartbreak and Resolve

On May 14, 1974, I was on the threshold of being the happiest woman in the world. Just one more step to accomplish my goal in life of being a tenured member of a major symphony orchestra, but the door to success was slammed in my face. In 1994, I reflected back on that heartbreaking experience and the role that racism played. Here is what I wrote back then.

Getting the job in San Francisco would be so gratifying because I knew I didn't want to live where I had to confront racism and realized I wouldn't be happy in any other city. I had read about and learned from several sources that San Francisco was a liberal city. I thought it would be perhaps the least racist city in America and as cosmopolitan as New York. So, after the position of timpanist became available with Roland Kholoff leaving San Francisco Symphony and getting the position of tympanist with the N.Y. Philharmonic, somehow I got the courage and initiative to call San Francisco and inquired as to if and when auditions would be held to fill the tympani opening. Luckily, I spoke directly to Vern Sellin, the orchestra manager. I was so surprised when he answered and to my inquiry, said, "Ms Jones, we'd be happy to have you come out and audition. We'll send you all the details."

So without telling any one except my son, I secretly made reservations and flew out to audition for the San Francisco Symphony.

I auditioned for the job along 40 other hopefuls and was hired.

A little over two years later, I was buying champagne in anticipation of having a big celebration of being on my way towards being a role model for black youth. Sadly, instead of a celebration, I found myself in a state of shock and disbelief trying to maintain my composure. The orchestra committee of the San Francisco Symphony denied my tenure.

That action caused an international reaction because during the two year period of my "probation," I had gone on tour to Europe and the Soviet Union with the San Francisco Symphony and everywhere we went, I received critical praise for my playing. How could I be denied tenure?

A young Japanese bassoonist who had won his job when I did, was also singled out by all the critics for outstanding playing; he also didn't get tenure. The other six players who were hired with us, however, were accepted into the orchestra. They were white.

Something just didn't seem right to me or anyone I spoke to about the committee's decision. After reviewing the events of the previous two years I played with the orchestra, I made the decision with the encouragement of my many supporters, to sue on the grounds of racism.

I lost my case.

The decision was extremely traumatic and for a time I entertained the idea of giving up music altogether. However, my love for music and performing was an all too powerful force to allow me to give up. After all, I had been playing music professionally since 1948 and had given it every ounce of my energy. I had sacrificed everything to reach this point. Although I didn't get tenure with the San Francisco Symphony, I was awarded tenure with the San Francisco Opera and remained in the city.

One might say, why give up with apparently only one set back. Many other musicians have been denied tenure and moved on to other cities to get on with their lives. The year before, the principal trombone player was denied tenure and immediately left the city as did the Japanese bassoonist. These people were considerably younger than me; I was already 44 when I got the job. Even though playing with the Opera, I questioned my wisdom in remaining in San Francisco rather than returning to New York.

When I accepted the position with the San Francisco Symphony, I was confident of my ability and believed I would get tenure and remain with the orchestra until I retired. I made a total investment with that in mind. I moved my three children out with me and went through all the optimistic rituals such as purchasing a home, enrolling the children in the appropriate schools and severing all my connections with New York. Granted I probably should have turned around and returned to New York, but something deep inside me made me stay and fight the decision. I had seriously underestimated the depth of the racism even in "liberal" San Francisco.

While my case was pending, musicians and conductors from all over the world sent reassuring messages to me. They read about the case and felt obliged to contact me.

Leopold Stokowski was in London and sent a telegram saying if there was anything he could to for me to please contact him. In 1971, just before moving to San Francisco, the late Arthur Fiedler invited me to play with his World Symphony, a special orchestra of outstanding musicians from all the major orchestras in the world. Every musician with that group sent me a message of hope because they knew I was an outstanding musician. Surprising to me were the hundreds of positive letters from concert patrons in cities where I had performed. They said my playing was outstanding and memorable. Without exception, all the Bay Area symphony and opera patrons expressed that I was a positive addition to the musical quality of the orchestra. With all these endorsements, I knew I would win my case. Without my asking, many voluntarily contributed money to cover the expenses of the lawsuit. I was pleased when people on the streets urged me, "Do not give up, you have too much to offer."

After the negative decision by the judge, I received even more letters from the patrons voicing their disappointment; they said they hoped I wouldn't leave the Bay Area. At the time, I was flattered to have such sentiments expressed with more encouragement to remain.

All through the early years of my professional life I had to weather the storm of resistance to my presence. I was playing an instrument traditionally played by European-males and in an organization, that was and still is dominated by people of European-American origin. I had grown accustomed to not being wanted—that is until I could prove I was conscientious, responsible, dependable, capable and musically, outstanding.

After doing all the right things, it was truly painful to be denied that which I am confident I deserved. I was the best candidate when I auditioned and I knew my experience made me equally as good as anyone in the orchestra. If they were all above reproach, why would there be criticisms of their intonation during performances, their rhythm, and also their tone by the critical community? It was as though they were making me the scapegoat for all that was wrong with *them*!

The journal that I kept showed conclusively that there was never a rehearsal in which the conductor didn't make some criticism of their playing and in some instances, weren't happy with their performances. There have been several conductors who have since said to me that perhaps the problem was not my playing, but the orchestra's playing. Musicians tend to be extremely subjective when it comes to judging the ability of performing peers or colleagues. The only time that musicians agree on ability is generally when they are close friends. Therefore, when they are in the position of making a determination of another player, it is impossible for them to be objective unless the player is a friend. However, when racism is in the picture, all objective reasoning goes out the window.

When confronted with the charge of being subjective and racist, they protested vehemently by stating that they have black friends or live near blacks. They didn't realize what racism is. The European,European-americans, are in a position of power. All the values and morality of our society must have their stamp of approval. They sit in judgment and, their judgment is based entirely on their level of insecurity. It has nothing to do with whether or not they like us. It's only that most European, European Americans subconsciously believe in the inherent inferiority of blacks or believe that whatever they do is correct or more valid when compared to blacks. They believe that their role is to educate us. They can't cope with the fact that we might be not only as good as they, but better. This was perfectly demonstrated in the tenure decision by the San Francisco Symphony.

Remember, I was a principal player, the person who is the head of a section and always paid above the rest of the section, first ever for an African American. I was experienced, and I was competent; conductors and audiences acknowledged that fact. Above all, I wasn't and couldn't be subservient to any of the members of the orchestra. This situation was compounded by the fact that the orchestra had a conductor and another principal player, who like me, were not of European origin. Having these three non-Europeans in the orchestra in leading positions was a little more than their egos could handle. So, they managed to get rid of all three of us under the aegis of "democracy." When I joined the orchestra, antagonism was brewing toward Seiji Ozawa, the music director because he had "demoted" a couple of "principal" players. The result was, they thought the orchestra, rather than the conductor, should decide who gets tenure and makes artistic decisions.

Because of my own political convictions, I went along at first because I believed in democracy. Little did I realize at that time,

I would have been the victim of the "democratic" action. Players are very sensitive about the position or the "chair" they sit in since the position is supposed to reflect the quality of the player. There are always those players in secondary positions who believe they are better than the person occupying a principal position so they harbor some inner resentment. This attitude was bound to be operable in my case. They wouldn't mind having an African American in the orchestra as long as the position was equal to theirs or below, but certainly not above. All the people on the committee which denied us tenure were second chair players.

If only we could have convinced the judge of the racism, but he focused on sexism primarily, before racism. There were women in the orchestra so having sexism as part of my charge severally weakened the case. Because the judge, like most people, could not or would not believe racism could exist in the San Francisco Symphony, my case was thrown out before having it heard before a jury of my peers. I am convinced I would have won my case if that had occurred, and I would have stayed in the orchestra to become the world's finest timpanist. Leopold Stokowski already had stated that he thought I was one of the finest in the world.

I could never figure out why people have always regarded musicians as being free of prejudice. My experience has been just the opposite, because I know that the majority of musicians are not political! Most of their time is spent practicing. I can remember when it was difficult to get them involved in making demands to better their own wages. Today, musicians are a little bit more aware in that sense, but they do reflect the same degree of racism, no better no worse than society.

Years have passed since that fateful day. How many blacks have become members of the symphony orchestras since that time? Perhaps less than two percent. The usual disclaimer is that there are no blacks interested in or capable of taking a key position in a major symphony. In a way that might be true, but only due to the fact that there just haven't been enough role models. But I believe more than that, it is due to the economics of the black community. My musical career was totally financed by scholarships. My parents could never have afforded to finance my education and my experiences. The fact that statistics show wages in the African-American community trail significantly behind those of the European-American families, translates into making it difficult for them to pay for lessons from the "right" teachers and pay for the best instruments.

I had hoped my presence in the orchestra would have done much to inspire and help young African Americans by generating scholarship programs to provide them with financial opportunities similar to mine. I had been giving lecture-demonstration concerts in schools in the Bay Area from Monterey up to Novato. I was doing everything to make myself visible to not only youngsters but adults. African-American adults entertain the antiquated belief that symphonic music is for European people, but I knew I had the ability to convince them to attend concerts and learn to appreciate every kind of music. The letters I received from the black community after the tenure denial reflected and confirmed their belief that symphonies were racist.

What does a situation such as being denied tenure when you know you deserve the job, do to the psyche? In spite of the conductors and patrons support, it creates tremendous doubt in your ability. You go through inner questions—is it racism or perhaps I'm not as qualified as I believe.

I have been playing with the San Francisco Opera for 24 years and never felt better in all my 69 years. However, I'm considering retiring and returning to New York so I can use the wealth of my experience to further the aspirations of African-American musicians. I won't be happy until I see as many African-American men and women as European-American men and women in all positions to earn a living at music of their choice whether it be with a symphony, opera, ballet or jazz. .

What this generation is reacting to, what it is saying,
is that they realize that you, the white (European) people,
white (European)-Americans have always
attempted to murder them. Not merely by burning them or
castrating them, or hanging them from trees, but
murdering them in the mind, and in the heart!
James Baldwin

About the Author

Elayne Jone was born in New York City, January 30, 1928. With a musical talent and personal drive that enabled her to transcend racial and gender barriers, she became the first African American woman in the New York Philharmonic Symphony Orchestra. A world renown tympanist, Elayne Jones is a graduate of the High Scool of Music and Art in New York. She then attended Julliard, being among the first winners of the Ellington Julliard Scholarship. Jones' professional career began in 1949 with the New York City Opera. Over the course of five decades, Elayne Jones played with the American Ballet Theatre, Arthur Fiedler and the World Symphony Orchestra, Leopold Stokowski and the American Symphony Orchestra, Seiji Ozawa and the San Francisco Symphony, and the San Francisco Opera. In 1965 she won the La-Guardia Memorial Award in recognition of her outstanding achievements in music. She has presented over 375 solo lecture demonstrations nationally and internationally of percussion instruments in schools and colleges, and in 1975, National Educational Television produced and aired a TV special on PBS featuring Jones entitled, "A Day in the Life of a Musician." Countless performances by Jones include television, recordings, musicals, and ballets. Elayne Jones is universally recognized as one the most prominent African Americans of the 20th Century. Alongside music, Jones was also an accomplished amateur tennis player for some 43 years, until an injury forced her to give up the game. Some of the high points in playing included tennis matches with tenor Luciano Pavarotti and conductor Seiji Ozawa.

Jones retired from her career in music in 1998. A mother of three, she currently resides in the San Francisco East Bay Area, in Walnut Creek, California.

ABOOKS

ALIVE Book Publishing and ALIVE Publishing Group
are imprints of Advanced Publishing LLC,
3200 A Danville Blvd., Suite 204, Alamo, California 94507

Telephone: 925.837.7303
www.alivebookpublishing.com

CPSIA information can be obtained
at www.ICGtesting.com
Printed in the USA
LVHW040057301222
736158LV00001B/127